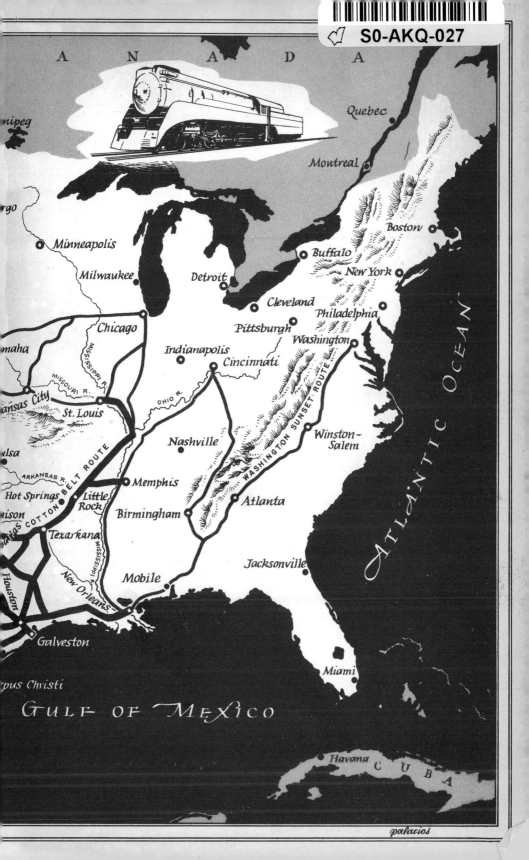

Southern Pacific

SOUTHERN PACIFIC

The Roaring Story of a
Fighting Railroad

NEILL C. WILSON

FRANK J. TAYLOR

McGraw-Hill Book Company, Inc.

NEW YORK   LONDON   TORONTO

SOUTHERN PACIFIC

Library of Congress Catalog Card Number: 51-12666

Published by the McGraw-Hill Book Company, Inc.
Printed in the United States of America

PREFACE

THIS IS the story of a railroad. The Southern Pacific, like many other American railroads, was built by tough-willed men. Probably they were the only type that could have flung the line over the mountains and deserts and through the special obstacles peculiar to their time. Out of bold initiative and enterprise they drew rewards. They reared gaudy mansions, rode in ornate private cars, wore silk hats, founded banks and seats of learning. They were admired, honored, emulated, envied, execrated. Then they stepped from the scene. What's important to this narrative is the thing they left behind—a going railroad. It had become a thing of life, with the power to give life. It tossed out sidings and there sprouted towns. It slashed across wastelands and there sprang ranches, farms, reservoirs, factories, cities. Other men took hold. Call boy or president, they tackled their problems and served their hour. They were hired, fired, promoted, pensioned. The railroad keeps on. Its restless growth has created homes, businesses, well-being for millions of people, and transportations for whole states.

The story of this railroad is a page of the national saga.

NEILL C. WILSON
FRANK J. TAYLOR

CONTENTS

	Preface	v
1.	Webster Didn't Approve	1
2.	Crazy Judah	6
3.	Hand Shovels and Horse Carts	11
4.	The White Demon	22
5.	Life in a Silver Palace Car	32
6.	Playing Rough	40
7.	Double-heading the System	47
8.	The Fearful Price of Riches	53
9.	The Railroad Throws a Party	59
10.	Bayou and Prairie	67
11.	Highballing for Texas	74
12.	Here Come the Zulu Trains	83
13.	High Iron past Shasta	89
14.	Huntington Again—Close View	93
15.	The Old Kings Step Down	100
16.	And Then There Was Harriman	107
17.	Kicked Out of Politics	116
18.	South of the Border	123
19.	Down the Radiant Shore Line	126
20.	Gandy Dancers and Bridge Monkeys	129
21.	Getting Out the Big Hooks	132
22.	Grabbing the Wild Mustang's Tail	139
23.	Snow—Still Fighting It	148
24.	Boom, Bust, and Bang	155

25. Softer Riding—and Faster   161
26. But Freight's the Thing   167
27. Certain Gents in Masks   178
28. Ferryboat Days   191
29. The New Whistle in the Canyons   201
30. The Day's Work   206
     Appendix A: Relax—You're Safe   211
     Appendix B: More about Steam   217
     Appendix C: Under Smoky Roofs   226
     Mileposts   233
     Bibliography   247
     Index   249

LIST OF ILLUSTRATIONS

Theodore D. Judah and Collis P. Huntington   6

Leland Stanford, Charles Crocker, and Mark Hopkins *following page*   6

Locomotives "C. P. Huntington," No. 149, and "El Gobernador"   38

CP meets UP at Promontory, 1869; passenger coach of same year   38

Driving of last spike on Sunset Route, 1883   70

Early freight at Painted Cave; first high bridge over Pecos River   70

Mansions of Crocker and Stanford   102

Huntington, Hopkins and Company hardware store; and Mrs. Mark
Hopkins's dream-house   102

Bill Hood's loop on the Tehachapi grade; construction gangs in 1875   102

Diesel meets steam on Tehachapi grade   102

First train into Santa Barbara, 1887   134

Coast Daylight alongside the Pacific   134

Erecting snowshed in Sierras in the sixties; filling in Secrettown
trestle in 1877   150

Snowplows of 1867 and 1890   150

"Goat," a yard engine of 1884; Shasta Daylight, 1951   182

The "C. P. Huntington" compared with a 2-10-2 and a Daylight locomotive   182

1

Webster Didn't Approve

IT WAS TIME to call a halt. The plump-waisted man in brass-buttoned cutaway and choker rose to address the Senate. Familiar faces were before him in the little semicircular chamber with its sixty chairs. Clay, always ready to offer a compromise between North and South. Calhoun, ready to tear up the Union rather than let slave states be outweighed by free. And Benton, the Missourian, interested less in North or South than in the wide, raw West.

This chatter of a railroad to the Pacific! Daniel Webster's eyes filled with scorn. "What do we want with . . . this region of savages and wild beasts, of deserts of shifting sands and whirlwinds of dust, of cactus and prairie dogs? To what use could we ever put those endless mountain ranges? What could we do with the Western Coast of three thousand miles, rockbound, cheerless, and uninviting?"

His listeners nodded. What, after all, was a railroad, that day in 1840? The country had a few of them, just enough to scare the horses. But did it not have rivers, lakes? Did it not have canals, including the fine new ditch from Albany to Buffalo, that took travelers 363 miles in five days at a cent and a half a mile?

". . . Improve communications with the West? No, gentlemen—I, for one, will not vote one penny for such an enterprise—the whole Western country is not worth it."

But time plays tricks.

Events soon moved far beyond the powers of a Senate to stay them. Frémont, and a scout named Kit Carson, brought home descriptions of the land beyond the Rockies that thrilled the nation even as the reports of Lewis and Clark had done years before; as the tales of fur trappers and sea voyagers had been doing for decades. Pioneers, in the 1840s, moved onward into Oregon by hundreds. A war was fought with Mexico, and territories acquired by bayonet and checkbook. And then, in 1848, gold was discovered in a California river. By 1850, California wanted to be a state. Territories with outlandish names lying between the coastal fringe and the Mississippi might want to become states, too. The unquenchable issue of slave lands versus free was up for debate again. Yet, explosive as the situation was, an Illinois congressman, Stephen A. Douglas, was storming, "I do not care whether slavery is voted up or voted down." What Douglas demanded was Federal aid for railroads into the Middle and Far West.

Railroads, again! Always railroads!

Seventy-two-year-old Henry Clay, weak and tired, rose in the Senate and offered his compromise of 1850. Let California come in as a free state as her proposed new constitution demanded, and the other territories of the new raw West could later decide the slavery matter for themselves.

Webster, realist that he was, made amends for his withering remarks of a decade before. Recognizing or believing that he foresaw the rise of an independent Pacific republic, with San Francisco as its capital, if statehood for the upstart Western territory were not immediately granted, he pronounced to the attentive Senate:

"In my opinion, sir, it is highly expedient to admit California now. . . . The case is urgent and pressing. No new state has ever appeared asking for admission into the Union under circumstances so extraordinary and so striking. . . . There is in the history of mankind, within my knowledge, no instance of such an extraordinary rush of people for private enterprise to one point on the earth's surface."

Before the tired Kentuckian, Clay, and the dying but defiant South Carolinian, Calhoun, Webster continued:

"It would seem that on this very day there are fifty or sixty thousand persons traversing the great plains between the Missouri and the Rocky Mountains, all bound to California. Other thousands are passing around Cape Horn: other thousands again crowd, press, fill up, and more than fill up, every conveyance that will take them to and from the Isthmus."

Statehood was granted. California became the thirty-first star. Sixteen free states to fifteen slave, and the other new territories to decide for themselves. In eleven more years there would be war, bloody and hideous. But meanwhile the West, juvenile, obstreperous and ebullient, wanted a railroad. Insistently, a railroad!

Actually, a railroad eventually to reach to the Coast was even then being launched, though before completion it would more nearly resemble a train of roads than a single road, and much of its motive power would come chugging from west to east to meet the locomotives slogging east to west. And before San Francisco and New Orleans were tied by rail,

another overland road, the Central Pacific–Union Pacific, would span
prairie and mountain 600 miles northward. But the as yet unnamed Sunset Route of the future Southern Pacific was being projected. Down in
New Orleans some men were hatching a railroad that would run from
the Mississippi westward. And in Houston another group were plotting
a line that would carry from Buffalo Bayou to—who knew?—perhaps to
the Pacific.

New Orleans being what it was and is, the meeting in that town
probably took place around a breakfast, luncheon, or dinner table. The
idea talked up by Col. James E. Gibbs was stimulating. True, Louisiana
had two small railroads already. They were the New Orleans, Jackson
and Great Northern, which ran to Kentucky, and the Ponchartrain, which
had been operating since 1830 and had 5½ miles of track, one car, and a
turntable.

"And we have the steamboats! New Orleans has been made great by
her steamboats," someone may have pointed out.

"That's true, gentlemen," Col. Jim Gibbs may be pictured as conceding.
But he had had engineering training and was set in his views. "The
Mississippi River will always be our life artery. But the steamboats run
no'th and south. I'm thinking about east and west. There's country off
westward that's calling for transportation, and that means rails! If we
don't act, the uppity men from up no'th will."

"Where will this railroad run to?"

"To Texas, suh! To the Sabine River. And, gentlemen, we'll cross the
Sabine. We'll go across Texas itself!"

"Across Texas? That's a big state. Where to, across Texas?"

Cried G. W. B. Bayley, who had been doing a lot of thinking, "Why, to
Mexico! To Mexico, and the Pacific Ocean!"

Why not! More sazerac cocktails, and the New Orleans, Opelousas and
Great Western Railroad—the "Opelousas"—began to take form on the
tablecloth. Over the next few months, it developed into something definite.
It obtained a charter from the Louisiana legislature, authorized capital
stock $3,000,000. Colonel Gibbs was its chief engineer and Bayley his
assistant. The subscription books were opened in April, 1852, and the
response was a rousing $2,994,235. That was near enough to three mil-
lion. Work began at once on the other side of the Mississippi, at a place
called Algiers. How long would the railroad actually become? Nobody
knew yet, but Colonel Jim would tell you how wide it would be. Its gauge
would be 5 feet 6 inches, laid on ties 11 feet long. Where did he get that
figure? It was simply his idea of how wide a railroad ought to be. And
the grading started for the Atchafalaya River, 80 miles away.

The year 1850 saw also the chartering of a scheme of some Texas men, the Buffalo Bayou, Brazos and Colorado. They had come into possession of the right-of-way and partial grading work of the Harrisburg Railroad and Trading Company, which had been incorporated on January 9, 1841, and done some grading at or near Harrisburg and purchased ties for construction of a railroad. But in 1850, Texas did not have a mile of rail. The BBB&C incorporators were full of purpose and raring to go. Gen. Sidney Sherman was at the throttle, and up beside him, heaving on coal, was Bill Rice, who later endowed Rice Institute with $10,000,000.

Early in 1851 a surveyor, John A. Williams, arrived from Boston to lay out the route. He chose Harrisburg (now a part of Houston, then its bitter rival) for the starting point and set the gauge of the road at 4 feet 8½ inches. A quarter of a century later this became standard gauge all over the United States, for no particular reason except that a standard had to be found somewhere—railroads were trying out everything, even up to 6 feet. The first locomotive arrived via Galveston in 1852 and was immediately buckled up by a Galveston storm. It weighed 10 or 12 tons and was called the "Texan." It would pull on a straight track but failed to follow curves, and ended up as the power plant for a sawmill. Eighty men finished 22 miles of grading and rail laying by early 1853, and there was a big barbecue. The line by then owned 2 locomotives, 5 passenger cars that once had been horsecars, and 24 freight cars. The cars would hold 20 passengers or 16 bales of cotton.

Whatever the ambitions were of the Opelousas, the Buffalo Bayou, Brazos and Colorado was ahead of it in actually operating west of the Mississippi. It started laying rails from Harrisburg at the head of the bayou, and by 1855 it had reached the Brazos 30 miles away.

The year 1850, which saw the launching of the Opelousas and BBB&C, repeal of the Missouri Compromise, and statehood for California, also saw a victory perch on the banner of Stephen A. Douglas in the matter of an encouraging Federal policy regarding railroads. Congress authorized the awarding of public lands, with which the nation was surfeited, to groups of private enterprisers who would lay rails in certain prairie regions and beyond. The Illinois Central sprang to accept. Other roads came into being. The government eventually turned over about 155,000,000 acres to the railroad builders. As the lands were tenanted chiefly by Indians and buffaloes, and the increment to the nation in transportation facilities was of history-making proportions, it was perhaps one of the best business bargains the government ever drove.

Federal lands went to no railroads in Texas. That vigorously independent state handled its own land arrangements:

The principal office must be on the line of the railroad.

No dividends if insolvent.
Trains must run on schedule and schedules must be publicly displayed.
Every train must have a brake and brakeman on the hindmost car.
Signs shall be at all crossroads to "Look out for the cars."
A bell of at least 60 pounds, or a steam whistle, shall be on each engine.
Intoxication of trainmen shall be a misdemeanor.
Conductor is authorized to eject any passenger refusing to pay fare.

Texas was in the railroad business, seriously and permanently!

The further doings of railroad builders in Louisiana and Texas are at the very core of the SP story. But to continue tracing that story, we will have to turn from the BBB&C, the Opelousas, and others, climb back into our prairie schooners, and go once more to California, where the hullabaloo was not quieting down, but getting worse.

2

Crazy Judah

THE SOUTHERN PACIFIC of today is a many-pronged railroad. Its Overland Route from San Francisco to Ogden is successor to the Central Pacific, which was built across California, Nevada, and half of Utah in 1863–1869. Its Sunset Route, Los Angeles to New Orleans, is in part the creation of the men who built the Central Pacific, and in part it is the Opelousas and the BBB&C just mentioned and several other enterprises down bayou and mesa way.

As soon as those hundred-thousand California-bound adventurers reached that not always golden shore, because of the months and months they had spent getting there, they wanted a railroad. They had wanted it for travel westward. And now that they had made a fortune, or lost it, they wanted it for travel homeward again. The trip outward, by wagon or ship, had been performed with a certain gaiety. There was nothing gay about the thought of journeying back the same way. And as long as they were stuck in the West, they wanted rails for local travel, too. They agitated for both long hauls and short.

The first line to be incorporated came in 1852. It was called the Sacramento, Auburn and Nevada. It surveyed 68 miles from Sacramento up through Auburn to Nevada City, and it ran its instrument lines onward over Henness Pass at the top of the Sierra—just in case. But the estimate for building the first 68 miles, $2,000,000, frightened off the promoters. A better start was made also in 1852 by a group who called their outfit the Sacramento Valley Rail Road Company. They incorporated for $1,500,000 and set out to build from Sacramento northeast to Negro Bar on the American River and certain points beyond, although not too far beyond. "Future extensions," announced Col. Charles L. Wilson, the president—he had built a plank wagon road from San Francisco's waterfront to the Mission Dolores, and operated small steamboats on the

THE SEER AND THE DOER

Top. Theodore D. Judah, who conceived the western portion of the first transcontinental railroad, made the survey, and interested the Big Four

Bottom. Collis P. Huntington, whose resistless energy drove the Central Pacific through, and built the Southern Pacific

THE OTHER THREE OF
THE BIG FOUR

Top. Leland Stanford
Middle. Charles Crocker
Bottom. Mark Hopkins

Sacramento River—"will be to Tehama on the north and San Francisco on the west."

What is important about the Sacramento Valley Rail Road is not the limit to its ambitions or the fact that it actually laid rails, built cars, and imported a locomotive, but the identity of the man it engaged to be its chief engineer. For he, more than any other single individual except Collis P. Huntington, became responsible for the bursting of the mountain barrier and establishment of an overland railroad. Because of Theodore Dehone Judah, within a decade and a half people were able to travel from New York to San Francisco not in three to six months, but in seven days.

Colonel Wilson, with a mandate from the people of Sacramento in his pocket, went east late in 1853 to find an engineer who could build his line from the heart of the state to Mountain City, Grider's Ranch, and Lincoln, not to mention San Francisco and Tehama. (The ultimate dream was trackage, on the valley level, of about 250 miles.) To the colonel came recommendations that he look up a young fellow who had just built a railroad bridge across Niagara gorge. The man was Judah.

A little man in clothes that looked too big for him, Judah arrived in Sacramento as soon as he could get there. He found it a rough place— the jump-off point for the mines by stagecoach, ox wagon, pack mule, and "Foot and Walker." The town had grown up almost overnight around the baronial fort of John Sutter, a benevolent settler who had befriended many a stray newcomer before his lands were overwhelmed by the gold rush. Fires, river floods, and cholera had swept and reswept the tent and shack community, which occupied low ground in the elbow of the Sacramento and American rivers. Saloons did a rushing business, and so did the stores, housed in brick buildings with fire-resistant iron shutters, including those of Huntington and Hopkins, who dealt in hardware, Crocker, who sold cloth goods, and Stanford, who supplied provisions.

Judah built the Sacramento Valley Rail Road. It snaked upriver toward Folsom and it did not go very far, but a railroad it sure enough was. The time came when it was gathered into the Southern Pacific system, and the line continues to run freight trains to Placerville, the old Hangtown, to this day. So perhaps it, along with the Opelousas and the Buffalo Bayou lines, should be accorded honor as a first sprout of the present SP system. At all events, in June, 1855, a locomotive arrived after a trip around the Horn, and the local newspaper, the *Union*, reported, "Workmen are engaged in erecting buildings for the reception of locomotives and cars, adjoining the town pump." On February 22, 1856, Californians had their first train ride within the boundaries of their state.

Judah had bigger schemes. There were persons at Placerville who hoped that the Sacramento Valley line would go on and on, up over the Sierra rampart and beyond, putting their gulch town squarely on a transcontinental whose other end would rest at the Mississippi or Missouri. Judah kindled to the general idea but he changed it to suit. He did not consider the crags behind Placerville as the place for a railroad. He made some twenty trips into the Sierra, searching for a better route.

In the course of these trips he met Daniel W. Strong, a druggist of the mining town of Dutch Flat. Strong wanted a wagon road brought up through Dutch Flat and onward for the Virginia City mines in Nevada. Wagon road or railroad, either one suited Strong, so he grub-staked Judah, and in August, 1860, Judah announced that he had found a place via Dutch Flat where a railroad could be built over the 7,000-foot hump with a maximum grade of 100 feet to the mile. It was a long hog-back, winding and rugged, but a natural ramp.

Judah prepared incorporation articles for the "California Central Railroad," and picked up promises from citizens of Dutch Flat and other camps for one-third of the $115,000 he needed to qualify his project under state law. Then he hurried to San Francisco to raise the rest.

San Francisco showed little interest. It wanted a railroad, all right, but it was a seaport city. It did not want to hurt its shipping business. More to the point, its moneyed men wanted to build that overland railroad themselves if they ever got around to it. They put Judah down as a crank, called him "Crazy Judah," his project "Judah's Wisp."

The subject of a Pacific railroad had become one of increasing national interest, not only because it represented transportation, but because it involved the ultimate extension or nonextension of slavery into new territory. Where the railroad went, new states would arise, each with its senators and representatives. The South wanted its share of them. While army engineers made surveys westward over the barriers along several possible avenues, stagecoach lines were organized to pin down and establish the routes of travel. The South succeeded in swinging these, by their mail contracts, through San Antonio to San Diego and—in the case of the great Butterfield line—from Memphis and St. Louis through Arkansas and Texas via El Paso and Yuma. To prove that the central or Salt Lake route was shorter, speedier, and open the year around in spite of snows, the heroic Pony Express was established as a rival.

All these were phases of the Pacific railroad controversy. The real issue was not geographical but political. Meanwhile Judah had solved the location for the Pacific railroad, to his own satisfaction, by planting it firmly on the Sacramento–Salt Lake parallel. And he was determined to bring it into being.

In another age Theodore Judah would have been a crusader, leading hosts against the Saracens. He was a dedicated man. A Pacific railroad, along the lines he conceived it, had become for him not a business, but a religion. He was also a down-to-earth realist who actually had solved the problem of finding a way across the mountains for the diamond-stack wood-burners of his time. The route he had discovered is the route up the Sierra wall, the "Sacramento Hill" of railroaders, that is in use today. But like most persons who are seized by a single idea, he could be a bore. People ducked and dodged. He returned to Sacramento, not discouraged, but mystified. If the big capitalists at the seaport would not listen, maybe Sacramento's merchants would. He called a meeting. One of the men who dropped around was Collis P. Huntington. The hardware dealer said nothing, but listened. The meeting failed to raise money. But Huntington went back to his store and discussed the subject with his partner, Mark Hopkins. They talked, quietly and between themselves. Then they took action.

Years later, testifying before the Pacific Railroad Commission, Huntington told how the associates were brought together.

"In a general way," he said, "I believe that every member of the company came in at my personal solicitation. I spent many evenings until a late hour, after going through my regular business, in going to see men. I went to see only those who were thrifty, and those I believed to be safe businessmen." He said he wanted Leland Stanford, the local grocer, in "because he was a good businessman and a clean man in all respects." Of Charles Crocker, the dry-goods merchant, "He was doing a thrifty business and I counted him one of the best businessmen in California."

That is one version. Another is that James W. Bailey, a Sacramento jeweler, introduced Judah to Leland Stanford, and Stanford called a meeting at his home. To this meeting Huntington and Hopkins came, and Charles Crocker.

At all events, in a meeting on the second floor over Huntington and Hopkins's store, or in Stanford's home, Huntington remarked, "I'll pay my share to have a proper survey made, if the rest of you will do likewise." Mark Hopkins fingered a scraggly beard and nodded. The others nodded, too. No one was bound to go ahead with the proposition until the results of the preliminary survey were in.

The survey found Judah's route feasible. The enterprise was launched. The Sacramento merchants may not have contemplated building all the way to the Missouri, but anyway they would build across the Sierra, and annex the valuable freight trade with the Virginia City mines. The rest of the dream they left to another day. But it would be useful as a means of talking Congress into giving aid.

The engineer hurried to Washington—by ship—to see what he could accomplish. He had been there before, without luck, but this time circumstances were different.

Judah reached Washington three months after Bull Run. Huntington also came on. The project of a Pacific railroad was at once put before Congress. This time it was not a political but a war measure. No longer was there a Southern faction to deny Federal assistance to a line that would follow the short central route. By the summer of 1862 the Pacific Railroad Bill had passed both houses. It called for construction of the road by two companies, one building westward from the Missouri, one building eastward from the Pacific Ocean. On July 1 it was signed by President Lincoln.

Huntington notified his associates: "We have drawn the elephant. Now let us see if we can harness him up."

3

Hand Shovels and Horse Carts

LET US GET ACQUAINTED with these men. Time's passage has named them the "Big Four." They were not big when Judah drew them into his project. What is important is that they had the capacity to grow. The Four increased in stature with each new demand and challenge. Without technical knowledge, without experience in large affairs, without important means or influence, without even a clear initial concept of what they were undertaking, they bulled their railroad through.

Charles Crocker, who took charge of the physical job of jamming grade and rails up over those mountains, was thirty-eight. Born in New York State, made muscular as a farm hand, sawmill helper, and blacksmith, he had headed for California in 1849 and teamed freight to the mines. It took a good chair to hold him—he weighed 250 pounds. A beard shaped like an oriole's nest swung tidily from his chin.

Mark Hopkins, another upstate New Yorker, was forty-seven. He was thin and scrawny, his whiskers were long and spare, and he had little to say, possibly because he lisped. His manner was mild. His job was to listen and watch. He was a frugal blower-out of lamps—a saver of small expenses. His honesty and sagacity were appreciated by the other three. When they warred, a word from him drew them together.

Collis Potter Huntington, the drive wheel of the bunch, was thirty-nine. At thirteen he had been doing a grown man's job on a Connecticut farm for seven dollars a month, which he had saved and probably still clung to. He had peddled jewelry and butter, made for California in the general rush, and brought several kegs of whisky along, which he had sold at a fancy mark-up. His 220 pounds were solid and healthy. His eyes were the shrewd, hard eyes of a born trader. His beard was clipped and aggressive.

Leland Stanford, a son of an Albany-Troy post-road innkeeper, was thirty-six. In his teens he had chopped wood for Albany cookstoves, though later, when the day came for driving the golden spike that finished the railroad, his swinging muscles were out of practice and he missed the stroke. He had tried the law and, though he became a storekeeper when he got to California, his legal smattering made him popular as an informal justice of the peace. He took to politics. He had been to Chicago in 1860 as a Republican delegate to the convention that nominated Lincoln. He had lately run for state treasurer and been defeated, but was soon to run for governor and make it. He had the money resources of the four. In the fifties he had become interested in a mine at Sutter Creek and sold out for $400,000. Huntington picked him to occupy the center of the stage.

Crocker, the outdoor man, the ex–mule driver, handled the workers. Hopkins, the indoor man, handled the books. Huntington raised the Eastern money and did the strategic thinking. Stanford raised the Western money and waved to the crowd from the back platform.

There were others, but they were minor figures. These were the men who counted. During the construction days of the railroad they clung and rolled together like the four wheels of a car truck. For getting things done there never has been a quartet to beat them.

The Central Pacific Railroad Company of California was incorporated on June 28, 1861. Stanford was named president, Huntington vice-president, James Bailey secretary, Hopkins treasurer, and Judah chief engineer.

The capital stock was set at 85,000 shares of $100 par. Judge E. B. Crocker, Charlie's brother, came in. Each put himself down for 150 shares. Subscription books were opened in San Francisco, and the incorporators waited for the rush. The sum of $8,500,000 was wanted to carry the rails to the state line, and Judah figured that $3,221,496 was going to be needed to build the trackage the first few miles that would qualify for government aid. But men of money in San Francisco sniffed at the Sacramento storekeepers as railroad builders. Someone subscribed $20, someone else $500. All in all, only about $15,000 was raised.

This was where the enterprise should have bogged down. But it did not. The associates rose to the challenge and even their enemies, of whom they later had plenty, had to acknowledge their nerve. They decided to build the line themselves, out of their own private resources and personal credit, until they could win public assistance.

Since the Pacific Railroad Act, signed by President Lincoln on July 1, 1862, called for construction of the railroad by two companies, one building westward from the Missouri as well as one building eastward from the Pacific, the Union Pacific was organized at Chicago the following year. The date was September 2, 1862, the organizers, Henry Farnum and T. C. Durant.

The Pacific Railroad Act gave each company a 400-foot right-of-way across all government lands, and such areas as were needed for stations, switch yards, shops, and quarries. It also gave the companies alternate square-mile sections of public lands on both sides of the tracks, and provided for loans of United States bonds to bolster the credit of the builders. These bonds required an interest payment of 6 per cent by the two railroad companies, but Huntington saw to it that a provision in the act delayed payment of interest until the bonds matured.

The Central Pacific was given the right to build, specifically, only from the navigable waters of the Pacific to the California line; but Huntington later got this provision changed to place the junction 150 miles eastward in Nevada. Still later, in 1866, it was changed again—to wherever the eastward- and westward-pushing lines should collide head-on. That made it a race between the two, toward each other and against space and time.

The Central Pacific was given two years in which to build its first 50 miles of railroad, after which the builders were required to complete 50 miles per year. The whole task had to be finished by July 1, 1876.

By a two-year margin, the Central Pacific was first to start actual building.

In the fall of 1862 Judah's men completed their working survey. Crocker gathered men, carts, draft animals, wheelbarrows. Huntington was in the East, buying the railroad's first hardware. When he went East, he took along unlimited powers of attorney from his associates. At one time, when he found the road's credit poor but the personal credit of the merchants quite respectable, he telegraphed for a sheaf of notes endorsed by the others in blank—in effect, a set of blank checks on their personal resources, to be used by him as needed. He got the notes and put them behind the Central Pacific bonds he was offering for sale. The personal notes guaranteed the railroad's bonds for the next ten years.

The day arrived for the ground breaking. It was January 8, 1863, and the nearby American River had overflowed its banks. Leland Stanford, governor of the state by that date as well as president of the Central Pacific Railroad Company, turned the soil with a spade of silver. The silver was borrowed, but silver it had to be; a good show was needed. Bales of hay had been thrown on the mud to give him footing. There were cheers and speeches.

Huntington was not there. He had told his associates, "If you want to jubilee in laying the first spike here, go ahead and do it. I don't. These mountains look too ugly and I see too much work ahead. We may fail, and I want to have as few people know it as we can."

He might have added, "We're tackling earth and granite—mountains of it—with nothing but picks and shovels, and one-horse carts. We're tackling remote forests with nothing but axes. We're taking on an untried job, one for which there's no precedent. And I have to meet the payroll."

Construction had started at the western end, the end farther from the source of supplies. The mountains provided earth, timber, and stone. All else—rails, rolling stock, black powder, picks and shovels, carts and wheelbarrows—had to come from the opposite seaboard. Most of it had to be shipped around the Horn.

The country between California's valley and the Rockies was known for its hardships to emigrant wagon and overland mail coach. It was still an almost untouched wilderness. The Sierra Nevada, the grand obstacle which was in sight of Sacramento on clear days, was an abrupt escarpment gashed by granite gorges, and so steep in its passes that wagons sometimes had been lowered down certain of the jump-offs by ropes and chains.

Hostility arose in many quarters. Congress, in the Pacific Railroad Act, had required a telegraph line to be built along the route. That aroused the enmity of the existing telegraph company. The little Sacramento Valley Rail Road, running off a few miles eastward from Sacramento, had no love for a rival, and its owners set themselves to knock off the new contender. The Sacramento Valley line's owners were San Franciscans, controllers of many industries, men used to being kowtowed to; they remained actively opposed to the Sacramento group for years. And there were other foes. The Pacific Mail Steamship Company saw its monopoly of freight from the East threatened. The Sitka Ice Company, which brought ice down from Alaska and sold it to San Francisco's bars, lobbied actively against the outfit that would soon be bringing ice from the Sierra. The stagecoach lines, which were big and flourishing, leaped into the fight.

The enterprise was denounced as a humbug. The Big Four obtained from Placer, San Joaquin, and Sacramento counties a favorable vote for a $750,000 subsidy. Objectors threw the bond proposition into court and kept it there until 1865. But "Stanford and Company" plugged on. If the struggle was going to be rough, they could be rough, too. They fought injunctions with injunctions; they picked up all the tricks of legal and political maneuver, and they began to invent a few. It was that kind of fight.

From the state of California they procured a valuable bit of help—

a guarantee of payment of interest on the company's bonds up to $150,000 per annum for twenty years.

The Central Pacific's first locomotive was the "Governor Stanford." Brought around the Horn to San Francisco in the windjammer *Herald of the Morning* in August, 1863, it was unloaded at the Sacramento levee from the schooner *Artful Dodger* on October 7 of that year. It almost fell into the river while being unloaded, but was saved for a more heroic career and a distinguished end as a museum piece at Stanford University, where it rests today.

Next upon Central Pacific rails went the "Pacific"; and No. 3 was the "C. P. Huntington," later to be numbered Southern Pacific No. 1. It was 29½ feet long, weighed 43,500 pounds, was said to be able to haul four cars weighing 22 tons each at 35 miles an hour up a grade of 26 feet to the mile. Fifteen miles per hour was probably nearer the fact. The old "Huntington" is still in existence—it stands in a place of honor in front of the Sacramento depot—and at times has been fired up and used for ceremonial purposes. It was followed by No. 4, the "T. D. Judah." And that, by the way, is about all the honor Judah ever got.

The first headquarters building erected for the railroad was a shed, put up in two days at a cost of $150. When that was turned into a paint shop, headquarters moved to 54 K Street, over Huntington and Hopkins's store.

The American River was crossed and 18 miles of track laid to Grider's Ranch, now Roseville. Central Pacific's first train rolled in November, 1863. It was a work train and did not get any ceremonies and speeches. But by the spring of 1864, when rails had reached Newcastle, the time had come to operate a passenger train and sell tickets.

Crocker was the chief contractor, but in the beginning he was not the only one. There were several. They bid aggressively against each other for labor and ran the price up. The result was shortage of hands for all and failure to complete agreements.

Huntington stayed in New York for the most part, making the purchases. As the railroad company would have no revenues until it had some track and rolling stock, its treasury soon went empty. There was one period of three weeks when there was not a cent in the till. This was the corporation which, less than six years later, was to constitute the largest aggregation of capital and securities in the United States.

The Pacific Railroad Act had many features that were tough on the promoters. One was a provision that the rails must be made in the United States. With mills all engaged on war materials, the price of rails shot up to almost double.

Confederate cruisers were on the prowl. In spite of them, rails and locomotives had to round the Horn. Insurance rates rose, and so did freight rates. The first locomotive shipped by Huntington had a freight bill of $2,282. Later the freight bill on such an engine became $8,100. The variation in the value of paper and gold money was also a constant, throbbing headache.

When Huntington got back to California on one of his trips, he found Bailey weakening about paying his one-seventh share of the cost of construction of the first 40 miles of road. Judah, too, was mutinous. He did not like the way part of the money for building the line was being sucked back through a construction company managed by Charlie Crocker and owned chiefly by the Big Four.

"Either you have to pay in your assessment with the rest, or sell out your interest, or buy me out, or the work stops," Huntington huffed.

He took a horse and rode out along the line and ordered each of the nine contractors on the job to stop work. Judah and Bailey rushed to San Francisco and tried to find someone who would buy Huntington and Hopkins out. The pair had given them two weeks to do it. One capitalist, McLaughlin, almost made the grade. But the option expired, as crafty Huntington had probably expected. Bailey and Judah returned to Sacramento, knowing they were out of the railroad. They received back the money they had paid in.

Judah wrote to a friend, "I have a feeling of relief . . . that the responsibilities of events, so far as regards the Pacific Railroad, do not rest on my shoulders." He is said to have received $100,000 for his agreement to step aside. He went east by a steamer, contracted yellow fever at Panama, and died soon after. He had laid out, in detail, the western end of the Pacific railroad. He had battled it through Congress and pretty much written the act that sponsored it.

In the rush of events, Judah's part in the all-important preliminaries was soon forgotten. In the naming even of stations and sidings he went ignored. Years after, a new generation of railroaders got around to honoring him. When W. H. Kirkbride became chief engineer of the Southern Pacific system five or six decades later, he decided to pass the hat for a Judah monument. The SP rank and file cheerfully came in, and the monument is there today, in front of the Sacramento station. Kirkbride also saluted his predecessor engineer across the years by naming the summit of the Sierra, where the highest tunnel pierces it, "Judah Ridge." While the name did not stick, it is respectfully referred to the mapmakers as a deserving honor.

Too many contractors being a nuisance, Charlie Crocker contracted with his partners to build the first 18 miles. They were finished February

29, 1864. When this stretch was in operation, the company let its next contract. This was for 13 more miles. Eight months after the laying of the first rail and seven after the first locomotive went on the tracks, 31 miles of railroad had been built and passenger and freight services were offered as far as Newcastle. The Central Pacific was an operating reality, over those few valley miles at least.

Then things stuck. The funds of the builders were exhausted. Only 9 more miles and they would have the "elephant" not merely by the tail, but around the ankle on a good stout chain. Where would the money come from for the next 9 miles?

By the terms of the Federal Act, aid to the tune of $16,000 per mile in the valley was to become $32,000 per mile in the foothills. While Crocker's workmen made fills and cuts and laid rails and ties, Huntington—again in the East—fought hard to have the interpretation of a "foothill" liberalized. Before the line reached the actual footings of the mountains the public learned with hilarity that the line was already scaling "hills." In reality all was flatness covered with wheat, mustard, and wild poppies. A laughing press congratulated the promoters who had "removed the base of the Sierra Nevada to within 7 miles of the city of Sacramento."

Charlie Crocker charged up and down the line, exhorting the construction crews to faster labors. What they were up against, and how they handled it, will be told in a later chapter.

Huntington borrowed, hocked, and huckstered in the East. Throughout the period that he was buying locomotives, rails, and spikes by the hundreds of tons for the Central Pacific, he also continued buying horseshoes, shingle nails, barbed wire, and axes for Huntington and Hopkins, hardware dealers of Sacramento. The man who came to deal in tens of millions kept equal track of dealings in a few hundreds; he had always been a merchant and a trader, and remained one.

It was Huntington, working like ten beavers, who lifted the Central Pacific toward California's eastern line by the power of his will. For months he went on a schedule of four nights a week of train riding. "I rode through the hot weather," he recalled later. "I used to go over to Washington, stay in New York through the day, and take the night train for Boston; worked there through the day, took the next day in New York, and the next in Washington. . . . I even put off being sick until Sundays. I would keep going all week, then Sundays I often had to spend in bed."

He sat about Treasury offices in Washington until, by persistence, he wore out the officials and got what he wanted. He worked upon congressmen, and got an important easing of the provisions of the Pacific Railroad Act of 1862. As signed by President Lincoln on July 2, 1864, the amendment doubled the amount of land grants, increased Federal aid in the mountain regions, and made the government bonds a second mortgage on the railroads instead of a first mortgage. That doubled the money-raising possibilities and made success financially assured.

The big problem, aside from money, was labor. White men in California, if they had to swing a pick and shovel, still preferred to do it in the mines. The sensational new camps of Nevada sucked away Crocker's laborers as fast as he could fill the ranks. Many a toiler took the job simply because it was on the route to the Comstock and there were stages or hiking paths beyond the railroad's end. When the Nevada excitement extended eastward to the White Pine district, Crocker found that of 2,000 men he had hired and shipped up into the mountains, 1,900 had slipped away.

Crocker decided to try Chinese labor. The Asiatics were known to be hard workers, patient and docile, and infinite in number. His agents went to the China coast and shipped coolies over the Pacific by hundreds; as the experiment succeeded, by thousands. The coolies were known to the public as "Crocker's pets." Working with shovels, wheelbarrows, and one-horse carts, they moved the dirt.

The red soil of the foothills gave way to granite. The going became really tough. Several thousand feet of elevation were to be surmounted through a region gashed by gorges. There was not even a wagon road.

They whipped granite with hand drills and black powder. For the summit tunnel and two tunnels eastward, nitroglycerin became available. But it was little understood and mortally dangerous. Glycerin and nitric and sulphuric acids were hauled by teams to a factory at the summit and mixed on the spot. Only the fatalistic Chinese were willing to mix the brew, or use it. Often they went sky-high.

Sometimes the explosives shot out of the holes like charges from a gun, without disturbing the solid rock. And sometimes they disturbed too much rock. Far out in Donner Lake are some great chunks that were blown there by the railroad builders from a point high up on the mountainside. After one catastrophic explosion, so complete that a funeral was unnecessary, Charlie Crocker ordered his men to "bury that stuff," meaning the nitroglycerin. The work went on with the more old-fashioned tools.

But with picks and shovels and black powder and one-horse dump carts, the men under Chief Engineer Sam Montague and Construction Superintendent Jim Strobridge pushed on.

For many years after the road was finished, overland trains halted and passengers got out and gaped at "Cape Horn," an awesome spot where the railroad bed was built out from a cliff 2,500 feet above the American River.

"How will we ever carve a railroad down there, even the beginnings of one?" wondered Crocker.

"Leave it to me. I'll lower some Chinks down in baskets," said Sam Montague.

And that is what was done. The good-natured Chinese pick-and-shovel men were swung down to where they could peck at the rock and establish a trace for the crowbar and black-powder men who followed. By blasting and shoveling, the line was thrown into the hill at all except two points, respectively 100 and 200 feet in length, where heavy retaining walls were given the Atlaslike job of supporting the rails. In later years Cape Horn was supplemented by a tunnel, which railroad men nicknamed "Panama Canal" because it is such a nice short cut. Eastbound traffic takes the Horn and westbound the tunnel.

The westbound trains of the Overland Route rush today through a 800-foot cut in Bloomer Divide, just below Auburn, that has been left exactly as the pioneer road graders hewed it. A tedious job through cemented boulders, 85 feet deep, it had to be wrested out with black powder a little at a time. The native cement dulled the drills and kept a crew of blacksmiths busy. The steep sides of the cut have never disintegrated. The 500 kegs a day of gunpowder used by the gangs cost $2.50 a keg when work started, but soared to $15 a keg as the Civil War went on.

To cross the Sierra, fifteen tunnels were driven. Work on the tunnels was halted by winter, and late into spring the ground was found still frozen many feet deep. To avoid loss of precious time in summer, the engineer in charge of the work, John H. Gillis, kept three shifts of men at work day and night in 1866. One night he stumbled over 2 miles of rough terrain in the dark and laid out the east end of Tunnel No. 12 by the light of a bonfire. By midnight, he had traced out the portal and the men were at work.

Winter licked the tunnel men until 1866, but that year the job was attacked in a different spirit. Headings were underground by late fall and down there in candle-lit gloom the work went ahead. Forty-four snowstorms enlivened the ensuing months. Some 10 feet of snow fell during some of the storms, and snow tunnels 200 feet long were dug to keep the entrances open. But still picks and sledges rang on granite.

Hewing the topmost tunnel called for use of a hoisting engine. A locomotive that would do as a stationary engine was found in Sacramento. The engine, the "Black Goose," was dismantled, everything possible being

removed from it to reduce weight. It was taken on the line to Gold
Run, the end of track, and levered off the flatcar. Getting it onward
beyond the end of iron rail, through boulders, cliffs, and forests, was a
poser. But the railroaders had a bullwhacker known as "Missouri Bill."

Bill looked the situation over. "Give me a couple of months and plenty
of oxen," he allowed, "and I'll do it."

They gave Bill his bullocks. Then the "Black Goose" was jacked up,
and by the use of traveling jacks was moved 14 inches at a time to a
logging truck where Bill sat waiting. The truck had wheels 2 feet wide
to beat the mud.

After the load was bolted and braced on his truck, Bill spoke lovingly
if not quite refinedly to his ten yoke of oxen. He terminated his harangue
with a shrill yell and a crack of whip. The oxen strained to the yokes,
and the "Black Goose" was on its way.

All went well until a half mile east of Dutch Flat. There Missouri Bill
and his freight met a ten-mule team from the Comstock mines coming
the other way. The westbound mules took one look at the "Black Goose"
and stampeded. While their skinner set out after them, uttering senti-
ments that blasted the bark from the trees, Bill trundled his load along.
From that point onward, opposing traffic increased and there was hell
on the wagon road. Stagecoaches and emigrant wagons lost their animal
power, which stepped out of harness and went streaking for the heights
and the ravines. Finally, Wagonmaster Pratt, who trudged along beside
Bill, devised hoods for blindfolding the mules they met, and personally
helped lead the quaking animals past the black monster.

The farther up the mountain Bill and the "Black Goose" went, the
steeper became the grades, and the rougher. Wagonmaster Pratt went
ahead and had corduroy road laid for long stretches. After crossing the
divide at Emigrant Gap, the road to Crystal Lake was downgrade for
a while. But the weight of the "Black Goose" made this the hardest part
of the journey. With heavy logging chains fastened to great pine trees,
the locomotive was eased down. Cisco, one of the more permanent construction camps, was reached, and there Missouri Bill had himself set up
to a keg of beer and his oxen to a banquet of hay. From that point on
was a 2,000-foot climb without letup. After six weeks of labor, Missouri
Bill and his load broke out upon the summit. He drew a big cheer. The
locomotive was set up in the hoisting works above a shaft.

Before the CP had crossed the summit, the Union Pacific sent scouts
to see how the Westerners were coming along. The scouts reported that
CP would not cross its spiny divide for many months. That satisfied the

UP builders. They figured they would be at the California border before CP reached it.

Crocker and his group got wind of this. "Let's show 'em," said Charlie Crocker.

He and Montague and Strobridge sent across the mountains all forces not engaged in tunnel work, and put them to grading and rail laying on the eastern face.

The state road from the summit down to Truckee was steep and difficult, even for men of Missouri Bill's ilk. But over this rugged strip the construction forces hauled materials for 40 miles of track. Then came 3 locomotives and 40 cars. Blinding snowstorms kept gangs busy shoveling.

Crocker, who never was modest, described it to the Pacific Railroad Commission two decades later: "We hauled locomotives over (and when I say 'we,' I mean myself), and we hauled iron and cars and all that sort of thing and built 50 miles. We hauled the locomotives on sleighs, but some of them on logs because we could not get sleighs big enough for some of the engines."

In the effete present era a moving-picture company once tried to duplicate this feat. To save weight, it borrowed the tiniest locomotive it could find in any museum. With lots of man power, steel cables, tackle of the latest type, and a big Mallet engine to supply steam, they hauled their burden 500 yards and quit. Crocker's gangs, with ropes, oxen, and mules, hauled much larger locomotives through much worse weather and over worse trails, for 28 miles.

The railroad bed had to be carved out of rock, as usual, down the side of a long ridge. To create this shelf under winter conditions, domes were excavated in the snow, and the wall stones were lowered through shafts in the snow to the men working inside the igloos.

That snow! It sifted in everywhere. One of the engineers recorded, "I had an office and bedroom, which had to be shoveled out every time I returned to the mountains. The snow had to be shoveled out of the house before I could get into it."

The early Spanish padres, who had looked off toward those mountains from the plains below, had named them well: Sierra Nevada, Range of Snow.

4

The White Demon

BEFORE THE CENTRAL PACIFIC was built, snow in the Sierra Nevada had become famous and fearful. The Donner party's fate first advertised it. This group of emigrants reached California in the late fall of 1846 and went into temporary camp on the shore of a wooded lake which can be seen from the train windows today. The thirty-six men, women, and children were ill prepared for what was ahead—one of the extra-special winters which sweep down about once every score of years. Snow, soft and gentle, fell on the little camp; for days and nights it fell and it fell. Wagons were buried. Provisions ran out. Nobody knew anything about snowshoes, but finally one man made a pair and started over the heights for Fort Sutter. When he got back with help, most of the party had perished of starvation, murder, and cannibalism.

If the fate of the Donner party were not enough, hardships of subsequent emigrant outfits would have built up a tradition. And the efforts of mail contractors of the fifties to jam the mails through added to the awesome story. George Chorpenning tried it with mules, and John "Snowshoe" Thompson lugged 100-pound sacks of letters on his back and whirled over the mountains from Placerville to Genoa on 12-foot skis. The Pony Express tried bucking these winters in 1860–1861, also on the Placerville route. The fiery horses and their daredevil riders usually made it. But there were lapses. All too often snow avalanches and blizzards halted game steeds and game riders, seeming to prove that the Pacific railroad should be built along the low-level southern latitudes or not at all.

After many years of record keeping a few facts may now be offered to replace the legends and guesses of the pioneers.

In the years since 1907, no place in the world where records are kept has equaled the fall of snow that occurred on the west slope of the Sierra in Alpine county, at a weather station called Tamarack, between September of 1906 and June of 1907. The fall was more than 73 feet. The elevation there is 8,000 feet.

In that same period, at Donner Pass, 55 miles to the north and 1,000 feet lower, the snowfall of 1879–1880 had been recorded at 65 feet, and that of 1889–1890 had equaled it.

A snow gauge was set up on Donner Pass, the railroad pass, in 1870 and has been at or near the summit ever since. The snowfall varies from year to year. The whopping winter of 1879–1880, with 783 inches or 65 feet, was followed by a puny 12 or 13 feet in 1880–1881. Still and all, the average for eighty winters is there—409 inches, or 31 feet, 1 inch. Try ramming a train through that!

The Homeric winter of 1866–1867 was punctuated with the roar of snowslides. Most of these passed harmlessly, or with damage only to horses, mules, and equipment. But there were instances where camps were carried away, and the bodies of the men were not found until the following summer. It was June, 1867, before the forces down in Truckee could renew work up at the summit. Even in that month, the grade was still underneath 10 to 12 feet of snow. It would not melt for many days, so it was shoveled from banks and cuts by hand.

In spite of elaborate plans, the winter of 1866–1867 almost won the argument. With the total snowfall reaching 40 feet and the snow on the ground at the summit averaging 18 feet, all work had to stop except far underground. With spring, melting snows created a new issue. Slides carried away buildings and trestlework.

That problem was handed to Arthur Brown, superintendent of buildings and bridges. He was a good enough engineer and loved a tough problem. "Let's build a roof over the railroad!" he said. After numerous discussions with his directors, Brown was told to go ahead with the heroic solution. They would build out of the timbers of the forest a house 40 miles long, if necessary, and run the trains through that.

In the summer of 1867 the idea was tried out. The short sheds parried the snow that winter in good style. So in 1868, covering the railroad with a roof was undertaken in earnest. Twenty-five hundred carpenters and laborers were put on the job and six chugging work trains helped them. Six to eight feet of snow had to be shoveled away to clear the foundations. There were not enough sawmills to furnish the timbers, but the workers went into the woods and yanked out much of what they needed. Winter snow again overwhelmed them and stopped the labor, but in the spring of 1869 it was resumed until 65,000,000 board feet of lumber had been reared into a structure 40 miles long that wormed and eeled around ravines and ridges. A brakeman remarked, "I've railroaded all over the world, but this is the first time I've ever railroaded in a barn."

The sheds shut from view some lovely scenery and continued to shut it from view for several generations of train travelers. Not until very recent years were snowplows and other snow-fighting equipment built powerful enough to keep the tracks clear without the sheds. Year by year, however, the sheds have been coming down, until at present only a few miles of them remain.

Back of the graders, who were mostly Chinese, came the rail layers. These were usually white men. Lacking rail-bending tools, they developed their own method of bending rails by placing them over a fulcrum and jumping on them. They became precisionists at the art.

George E. Gray, chief engineer of the New York Central, and later of the SP, came west for a look while the Sierra line was being built, and he found that "the roadbed and mechanical structures are well constructed, ample provision being made for drainage, the crossties are of redwood and the whole laid with a rail of 60-pound weight per yard and set in wrought-iron chairs. Locomotives, cars, and machinery are all of the first quality and of the best material and are maintained in good order."

With 14,000 men working, the CP rushed onward, down the dry gullies east of Truckee and out upon the desert floor where cold changed to heat, but fiercely. On December 13, 1867, the first CP locomotive poked its brassbound nose and balloon stack across the state line.

What travel was like before the snowsheds was described in the Virginia City newspaper of early days. The ascending train was below Blue Canyon, and having a hard time of it:

Five locomotives and a huge snow-plow had arrived, and so your correspondent and passengers got aboard the locomotive Auburn, engineer H. Spence, and were made comfortable by that quick-eyed, strong-hearted man, who managed the huge machine with consummate skill. Hank Lancaster conducted the train, and after half an hour consumed in preparation, the signal was given for the charge at the unbroken snow bank which covered the track to a depth of nearly three feet. Two sharp whistles from the front engine, echoed by ten similar shrieks from the followers, and off they went. The snow was turned in huge furrows from the track, and the bright sun came out and seemed to make partly cheerful the heavy stillness which hung around the line of road, all undisturbed except by the puffing engines. Suddenly the snow began to increase in volume, the cuts became filled, the locomotives wheezed and labored, and directly the train came to a dead stop in the middle of a huge bank of snow.

The signal came to reverse, and haul back; half a mile down the track went the train, the advance was sounded, and with the speed of the wind the immense plow swept into the snow bank. The men on the plow swung their arms in the air with a frantic motion, the engineers each whistled a double-quick advance, every throttle-valve was pulled wide open and every pound of steam let in the cylinders, and the bank was again struck. A move of a few rods, and then another halt. So on, for hours, during which the hind engine became disabled and had to put back for repairs. . . . Not until dark did the engines force the plow to the wood shed at Blue Canyon. . . . The Central Pacific must be shedded—nearly every rod—to be rendered practicable in the winter.

The engines wooded up, the journey continued.

All Friday was passed, by Lancaster trying to force his train along, but not a mile was accomplished, and at dark the train backed to Alta for reinforcement. At midnight two more engines arrived, and early Saturday morning seven locomotives behind the immense plow rushed again to the fray. Passing the station with great speed, the bank was reached and gave way; curve, cut and trestle were passed, and a halt was not made until two miles had been accomplished. Bravo, Lancaster! Bully, Hawkins! Hurrah, Spence! Go to it, Masser Daily! Another back, two more runs, and at six o'clock the train made the sheds at Emigrant Gap, having accomplished four miles of track through snow that had drifted, and was from 5 to 20 feet in depth.

All through the construction days, for as far as its rails extended, the Central Pacific had been carrying passengers and raking in money. But the travel had been something to write to the papers about, especially in winter, and for many a day after the road was completed winter travel was still severe. A traveler bound from Sacramento for Virginia City wrote to that camp's *Territorial Enterprise* three months before the driving of the last spike:

At Auburn, an occasional flake of snow, of huge proportions . . . at Colfax the earth was covered, and each revolution of the engine "drivers" was more difficult. . . . The wind swept down the heavy canyons above, the two carloads of passengers settled down to a patient waiting; the youth at the telegrapher's office reported "Wires down in the mountains," and right then "trouble begin."

The long hours of the afternoon crept slowly on. . . . Conductor Dennison gazed at his flock of passengers pleasantly, and reported that there was no hope of progress until the coming day. And so it got dark.

There is no such thing as a comfortable position for sleep in a rail car seat—it is impossible.

Morning came, and found us in the midst of boundless wastes of snow. . .   Toilets were made of snow water and a finger comb. . . . Eight, nine, ten o'clock came, and then the order was given to take the train, with such passengers as chose, back to Sacramento.

All of which is railroading up a mountain the hard way.

In railroad language, the "Hill" of Sacramento Division begins at Roseville, 107 miles from San Francisco, at elevation 162. The snow territory begins at Gold Run, elevation 3,227, 45 miles east of Roseville. It extends from there up over the summit, elevation 7,017, and down to Sparks, Nevada, elevation 4,425. Until 1921 the Hill had 41 miles of single track, and travelers got what fun they could out of riding in semidarkness through the "longest house in the world." The single track is gone now. The whole Hill is double-tracked.

East and west of the summit the CP was carrying freight and passengers and earning revenue. Passengers and cargoes rode the intervening gap in the traditional manner via stagecoach, freight wagon, saddle horse, and pack mule.

The unsung heroes continued to be those humble Chinese laborers. The first batch of 50 brought from Hong Kong had done their work so well that before the CP was finished there were 12,000 of them on the payroll at one time.

No job was too hard or too dangerous for these sturdy sons of toil. From the Sierra to Salt Lake, and in succeeding years from San Joaquin over Tehachapi to the Colorado and the Rio Grande, they did their work. Their diet consisted of dried oysters, dried cuttlefish, sweet rice crackers, dried bamboo sprouts, desiccated vegetables, dried seaweed, peanut oil, rice, pork, and poultry. A feature of their camps was the barrel always kept full of lukewarm tea. Several times a day a Chinese mess boy would trot up to the big ex-whisky barrel and fill it with fresh tea from old powder kegs, carried on a pole across his shoulder.

The Chinese gambled and quarreled among themselves, but never with the white men except under intense provocation. When grading crews of the rival east-west builders finally met and passed each other on the Utah desert, the Union Pacific's Irish amused themselves by blowing up a few Chinese. The Chinese methodically mined the ground and sent tons of earth and rock cascading down on their tormentors, proving that they were able and ready to take care of themselves.

Union Pacific, the other half of the so-called "Pacific railroad," had broken ground at Omaha, then a town of less than 3,000 persons, in December, 1863. It promptly ran into financial paralysis.

On November 5, 1865, ready for another start, the Union Pacific again held ground-breaking ceremonies on the Missouri River, repeating the celebration staged by citizens of Omaha twenty-three months previously. This time UP meant business.

Ahead was empty country, with scarcely a hamlet except the settlements of the Mormons in Utah. From the Missouri River to Utah the region was "Nebraska Territory." Iowa was not a state. The land was bare of timber, save clumps of cottonwoods on the islands of the Platte River. Ties were brought from as far as Michigan, Pennsylvania, and New York, in some cases at a cost of $2.50 per tie.

The engine of 70 horsepower which drove the machinery at the company's Omaha shops was conveyed from Des Moines in a wagon. The Mississippi and Missouri rivers provided a way of transporting materials, but only for a few months of each year. The lengthening rails created a further problem, for the graders out there on the prairie were soon far ahead of the tracklayers. To supply one mile of track with rails, ties, bridge girders, fastenings, fuel for engines, provisions for men, and hay for animals required 40 freight cars. At one time there were 10,000 men working, and 10,000 draft animals. The job of building a railroad drank up money fast.

As the Union Pacific pushed out across Nebraska and into Wyoming, it entered the domain of the Sioux, Cheyennes, Arapahoes, and other nomad peoples. Between Fort Kearney, Nebraska, and Bitter Creek, Wyoming, surveying parties and construction gangs were in constant scuffle. As the toilers on the railroad were largely veterans of the Civil War, they were handy with their rifles and often dropped picks and shovels to defend themselves. The Army sent troops to quell the Indians, and the railroad's diplomats found a way to placate the elder chiefs by giving them free rides.

This was ancient buffalo country, and the shaggy beasts in vast herds sometimes blocked construction and upset telegraph poles.

Not Indians nor buffaloes, however, but a devious financial manipulation almost knocked the Union Pacific off its new tracks. In March of 1864 Durant had bought up a charter issued by the state of Pennsylvania in 1859 to a certain Duff Green for a "Pennsylvania Fiscal Agency," containing broad financial authorizations. With Oakes Ames and others, Durant brought this charter forward as a device for siphoning the Union Pacific's construction funds into the promoters' pockets. Under the name of Credit Mobilier of America, this outfit built most of the UP line. Ames, who went to Congress from Massachusetts, sold or gave Credit Mobilier stock to his fellow congressmen to stimulate cooperation in the legislative halls. This activity went on in gay style through the winter of 1867–1868 without reaching the public attention, but one Henry S. McComb, who had subscribed for stock but quarreled with Ames, was saving Ames's letters for a future disclosure. When the explosion came in 1872 it rocked the country, but by then the railroad was built.

By January, 1866, only 40 miles of UP road had been constructed. But at the end of 1867 the line had pushed westward from Omaha 550 miles. The remaining 534 miles to the tie-in with the eastward-lunging Central Pacific was accomplished in fifteen months, at a clip of more than a mile a day.

Another race against time was in progress. A unit of the present-day Overland Route between the Great Lakes and the Missouri was hurrying to close the gap west of the Mississippi.

The line traced back to 1836, when a score of Chicago villagers took out a charter ". . . to build a railroad out into the prairie country and on toward, if not to, the Mississippi near the lead mines at Galena, Illinois, and Dubuque, Iowa." In 1848, with 10 miles of track built outward from Chicago, the line went into operation with a 10-ton wood-burning locomotive and 2 coaches. This was the first railroad service out of the city which today knots together 40 railroads, including 23 trunk lines. By 1864 the Galena and Chicago Union, as the line was called, became the Chicago and North Western. Its 10 miles of track had extended to 960, and had reached the Mississippi.

While Central Pacific and Union Pacific moved toward a meeting point, C&NW leaped onward across the black prairie soil of Iowa to effect its own juncture with the eastern end of the Union Pacific. Its first train steamed into Council Bluffs, on the east side of the Missouri, on February 8, 1867. This closed that link in the Overland Route from the Great Lakes westward, and the juncture was made just as the Central Pacific, half a continent away, was topping the Sierra Nevada.

With Union Pacific striding westward at a quickening gait, the eagerness of the CP's owners was whetted for as big a slice of the intervening mileage as they could get.

In the spring of 1868, word came that the granite between the summit and Donner Lake on its east side had been conquered. From then on the going was easier. Crocker announced a program of "a mile of track every working day." In June the road was open to Reno, Nevada, a townsite staked out by the railroad men.

One day in the spring of 1869 Union Pacific's "Irish terriers" laid 6 miles of track in a day, and blew a lot of smoke about it. What happened then has become a part of the saga of American railroading. Central's "Chinese pets" were given the job of laying 10 miles of track in one day, and they did it. There is said to have been a bet of $10,000 between Crocker of the CP and Durant of the UP as to whether this could be done. Crocker and Construction Superintendent J. H. Strobridge made victory as certain as possible by grading and laying the ties in advance.

On an April daybreak CP's Chinese army marched forth to do this 10-mile job. They were armed with shovels and picks; their blue caps were jauntily pulled down over pigtailed heads. Two thousand white spikers and bolters moved out also. A train stood by, its cars laden with 2 miles of rails.

Up the track, one by one, came flatcars drawn by two-horse teams at a gallop. As each flatcar met another car, returning empty, a crew swarmed off, tipped their vehicle on its side, passed the loaded car on, and righted their own to the rails again. When the laden flat reached the end of iron, waiting hands thrust a beam beneath its wheels. Horses were detached. From each side of the car its rails were seized, borne forward, and dropped where spikers and bolters could knock them into place. Wooden ties meanwhile moved past in wagons on the right-hand side of the track-layers; water carts and tool wagons moved in procession on the left. Eight Irishmen did the unloading—all of it.

Before the sun was up, all were in stride. Two hundred and forty feet of rail in 1 minute and 20 seconds. Two hundred and forty feet in 1 minute and 15 seconds. That's about as fast as a man walks.

Six in the morning, and 2 miles of rail had been laid.

Distance was being swallowed now. Far at the rear an entire village of tents was also on the move. Dining rooms, kitchens, sleeping quarters advanced to the railhead. With noon, the white workmen made for the tables. The frugal Chinese, who had brought their food with them, squatted for noonday dinner along the line of track.

Afternoon produced more mileage, and every man involved in the business looked back over the long new snake of iron with satisfaction. Another hour was put in after supper, bending the rails for the great curve which completed the day's work. Ten miles and 56 feet of track— a thousand tons of rails—had been spiked down, gauged, and bolted. A locomotive ran back and forth over the new road while Dodge, the Union Pacific's chief engineer, looked on.

Out on the desert, in that springtime of 1869, the two roadbeds finally overlapped while their sponsors argued over where the joining point should be. Grading crews, working far ahead of the tracklayers, over-lapped by miles. But on May 10, at a shack town called Promontory, Territory of Utah, 690 miles from Sacramento and 1,086 from Omaha, the lines officially came together. The completion of the railroad aroused spe-cial enthusiasm in a citizen down at San Francisco named David Hewes, who had introduced steam shovels to that city and knew a big construction job when he saw one. He spent $400 for pure Mother Lode gold, paid $6 to have it hammered into a spike, $15.24 for suitable engraving on it, and $4 for a velvet box, and presented it to the builders. It gave a fine title to the occasion, but was kept by the railroad as a souvenir and the actual con-nection of the rails was made with an ordinary iron spike and sledge.

Stanford was there that day, representing the four partners. A wood-burning locomotive came up from the west and a coal-burner nosed from the east. "Jupiter" and "119" clunked cowcatchers with a kiss of iron. As Stanford whanged at the final spike, telegraph wires carried the blows to many cities—possibly the first "broadcast" ever made of a major news event. Bret Harte wrote a poem, and an artist, Thomas Hill, painted a picture into which he put a lot of people who were not there. And the chief engineers of the two lines, Montague and Dodge, shook hands.

So there was the Pacific railroad. The group who promoted its western or so-called "Central Pacific" end and jammed it through were a shaggy lot, definitely interested in doing all right for themselves, and some of them perhaps already thinking of the palaces they would build on San Francisco's Nob Hill.

In the course of time people asked how the Sacramento merchants had dreamed that they could accomplish their part of the project. "Because we weren't railroad men," was one explanation.

No, they were not railroad men, in the sense that Judah was, and they were not too much concerned with theories of public service, either. They were four hairy-chested individuals out to get theirs and making very sure they got it.

The first regular passenger train from Omaha to Sacramento rolled over the site of the "golden" spike a few days later. In its steam and dust an old era vanished, as leaves and papers are sucked up by a passing streamliner. The West of prairie schooner and Concord coach was a flipped page of history.

One day in 1942 some workmen piled off a flatcar at a point in the desert distinguishable from all the rest of the sagebrush and gravel by two rusty rails and a stone monument. From a coach on the work train a couple of officials and some newsreel men descended.

"Here's the spot, boys," said L. P. Hopkins, superintendent of SP's Salt Lake Division, who had a sense of ceremony. He tossed the section boss an iron spike which had been gilded for the occasion. The iron spike looked more or less like the golden one of 1869, which now lies in a bank vault in San Francisco. "Sledge her home."

The spike was knocked into place. Hopkins handed a claw bar to Herb Maw, governor of Utah, and said, "You first, governor."

Maw inserted the claw under the gilded spike and pried. The newsreel cameras ground.

"Now you, Smitty."

Executive Assistant (of public relations) Schmidt of the Union Pacific gave a vigorous yank too. So did the superintendent of the SP. The spike came up, a good deal of the gilt rubbed off.

"I pronounce the Promontory branch of the Overland Route unspiked," said Hopkins. To the section hands, "Take away the rails, boys."

They were not the rails that had been laid in 1869. Those had weighed 56 pounds to the yard. These were 10 to 25 pounds heavier. But up they came. The Promontory route had been the pathway of the main line until 1904, when the Lucin Cutoff was built; since then it had been a seldom used 120-mile branch far off the line, and now its iron was headed for World War II uses. A few of the more sentimental bystanders and section hands grabbed rusty spikes for souvenirs, the officials climbed back into the coach, and the last train from Promontory chuffed off.

All that is there now is the "Last Spike" monument, the all-pervading sagebrush, and the sand.

But eighty years before, it had been for its moment the most exciting and interesting spot on the globe.

5

Life in a Silver Palace Car

LONG BEFORE the United States came into being, the westward march of the American people had been on. From their first toehold on the Atlantic seaboard they had scrabbled, pushing along up the short, dashing streams and broad water gaps of the Appalachians; thrusting down into the hardwood country of the Great Lakes, the Ohio, and the Tennessee. And on the Big River, and the plains beyond, and the mountains behind those plains, and the deserts behind those mountains. Over the Rio Grande and the Pecos, or down the thundering Snake. Around the mile-deep Colorado in its red rock slot, or down the Columbia, or along the trickling Humboldt, and at last over Cascade Mountains or Sierra to the shores of the ocean.

The American spirit seemed to be possessed with four irrestible urges: to keep moving, to keep moving westward, to keep moving westward with accelerating speed, and to do it, if possible, while comfortably sitting down. So saddle horse and canoe, canal boat and steamboat, Conestoga wagon and stagecoach had all played their part in taking the firmly seated pioneer where he wanted to go. And now, at last, awaited the steam train, ready to contribute its comforts, speed, and splendors.

On May 15, 1869, regular freight and passenger service was inaugurated between Chicago and Sacramento. At first there was one passenger train daily each way. Westbound, it was the Pacific Express; eastbound, the Atlantic Express. Westbound passengers assembled at Council Bluffs from one of the three lines that operated from Chicago. They were ferried across the Missouri, and at Omaha—a town freshly created out of logs rafted down from the Minnesota and Wisconsin pineries—they approached the Pacific Express, which was to be their home for many days and nights.

At first sight of the head end of that train, the facilities looked promising and exciting. The locomotive was not very powerful by modern standards, but she was pretty. Steam dome and sandbox were either encased in brass or dolled up with brass caps and bands. Bell and handrail were brass. The cab was painted black or brown. Shiny brass got in its licks again as seam covering for the blue-black Russian iron jacket that covered the boiler. The thin steel box holding the oil headlight was gay with red, green, and gold arabesques, and the flowing name of the engine appeared on the cab, in the center panel. Driving wheels were a brilliant red. In some cases, cab and tender were decorated with works of art surrounded with gold leaf.

But the travelers had seen such locomotives as these on other roads. What they wanted to inspect and enjoy now were the luxuries of George Pullman's new Golden Palace cars. They were the last word in rococo. The seats were pretty firm; but grandfather was used to sitting on horsehair.

The start of the train was a moment of excitement. We're off! At a steady and rocky gait of 20 miles per hour, the plains were crossed. Dust rose in swirls; rock ballast was something for the future. But the passengers had many things to look at through the dust. There were moments of thrill when buffalo herds were sighted, a matter more pleasurable for the passengers than for the engineer. There were Indians to be glimpsed. There were eating houses to be invaded. There were the extraordinary situations of berth and lavatory, of undressing and dressing to be met and solved.

Imperceptibly, the High Plains gave way to the Rocky Mountains. Here was no dramatic outflinging of a panorama such as the Sierra summit would afford. But it was high, cold, barren, and exhilarating. Then the long slide down to Promontory, on the Utah desert, where a change of cars had to be made by both passengers and baggage. (The change was soon afterward shifted a few miles eastward to Ogden.)

The Central Pacific had reached no agreement with George Pullman. That would come soon. For the present, the western line presented its own wonderful contraption for the traveler's wonder and comfort—the company-owned Silver Palace car.

The first Silver Palace sleeping cars of the Central Pacific arrived in Sacramento June 4, 1869. They were built by Jackson and Sharp of Wilmington, Delaware. Contemporary guidebooks described the Silver Palace cars as "elegant," with "appointments of a home drawing room," assuring that one slept "amid the easy roll of the car as sweetly and refreshingly as ever upon the home bed." The fact is, they were wooden, frail, and by any standards except the prairie schooner's or the overland stagecoach's they were mighty rough-riding. But, like milady's rustproof corsets, they were elegant if bruising. Interior woodwork was of walnut and bird's-eye maple. Seats were upholstered in red silk plush. Backs of the seats and the woodwork generally were silver-mounted. Several oil lamps were suspended from the ceiling and small lamps were placed in recesses along sides of the car for convenience of passengers desiring to read while lying in their berths. Huntington was not too sure about the safety of these lamps. In 1875 he wrote to Uncle Mark:

"I had somehow come to the conclusion that we had all agreed that we had better use candles in all our passenger cars, knowing it was somewhat more expensive than oil, but used it on account of the greater safety involved. Cars that leave the track, or are smashed up by a collision are often burnt up by lamps that use oil. . . . But if you think the difference in cost is more than the greater safety, or that there is no more safety, let us go back to oil."

The cars were carpeted with Brussels carpet. There were sleeping accommodations for 46 passengers. Exteriors of the cars were gay with carved wood trimmings and bright paint. Vestibules were open. These cars were in service on the Central Pacific until 1883, when peace was made with the Pullman Palace Car Company and the Silver Palaces were transferred to that concern.

Central Pacific's fleet of locomotives, unlike the UP's, had balloon or diamond-shaped stacks and were named, besides "Governor Stanford" and "C. P. Huntington," "Hercules," "Samson," "Goliath," "Terrible," "Growler," and "Flyer." There were "Blue Bird," "Magpie," and five colors of "Fox." The ladies were there too—"Sultana," "Juno," and "Diana." Two of the earliest engines weighed 18 tons; later they got up to 47 and 50 tons. (A diesel freight locomotive for the mountains today weighs almost 500 tons; but the trains have grown too.)

Boilers of locomotives were made of iron plates and forgings, with the exception of the firebox and flues. These were made of copper plates and brass tubing respectively. Engine frames and most of the machinery parts were made of wrought iron, which was superseded by steel on locomotives built in the 1870s and later. In the 1860s, 1870s, and 1880s the bumpers and pilots were made of wood.

Behind one of these locomotives the string of Silver Palace cars jolted onward. Utah and Nevada's bitter flatlands were crossed, the Sierra climbed—and how refreshing the waters of Donner Lake looked, in occasionally captured glimpses through the cracks in the snowsheds. Sacramento was won four days out from Omaha, or seven from New York, and transfer made to a river steamer, which landed the traveler at San Francisco—until the rail terminus reached Oakland and the ferries took over.

A visitor to the West Coast wrote an article published in 1870, entitled "A Ride on the 'Hotel Train' of the Pacific Railroad," of which the following are excerpts:

> Every Wednesday a "Hotel Train" of the Central Pacific and Union Pacific leaves the Pacific Coast for Chicago on its 133-hour journey. All these hotel cars have names. Our train is made up of three Pullman Palace parlor and sleeping cars, four Silver Palace sleeping cars of the Central Pacific, two ordinary passenger cars and one baggage car.
>
> Each passenger on the hotel train pays $10 extra fare. Whoever does not pay this extra charge has no access to the dining car and other Pullman cars, but must travel in an ordinary car and eat at the station restaurants or out of his lunch basket.
>
> The most elegant of the Pullman cars cost $32,000. In some of them there are melodeons and pianos, so that musical ladies may play them while en route.
>
> These cars are heated in winter by pipes running under the seats, keeping the temperatures evenly warm at all times. The pipes are filled with salt water and are connected with a coal-burning stove at one end of the car, which heats the water evenly—an extremely practical arrangement. In winter, when the temperature is freezing in the high mountains, these cars are as pleasantly warm as a princely boudoir.

Service was rough and ready. T. R. Jones, who went on as a telegraph operator in 1872 and rose to be Sacramento Division superintendent, has left some reminiscences that preserve the flavor of the times:

> Only one passenger train each way was run daily over the division. This was composed of mail, baggage, and express cars, sleepers, smoker, and coaches. All the cars were painted yellow. The two passenger trains were through trains, but made stops at all stations and did all the local work. The second-class passengers were then called emigrants and rode in emigrant cars, somewhat better than stock cars, attached to the rear of through freight trains Nos. 5 and 6.
>
> All freight trains carried passengers in their cabooses. The depot at Sacramento had a long bar and a short lunch counter. A large number of passengers got off on the arrival of the train, most of whom went to the bar to get a drink while a few purchased and ate sandwiches.

The conductor was not in uniform. He was a folksy character in civilian clothes and slouch hat, usually called "Captain." The skipper of No. 1 was Capt. G. T. Witham. He had side whiskers and a pocket bulging with cigars that passengers had given him. He seemed to know every man on the train by his first name, and where he was going, before he took up his ticket. Other conductors often went through their trains smoking cigars as they punched tickets, but Cap Witham saved his smoking for later. He was very courteous.

When the Central Pacific was building, it often ran out of funds, and the privilege of building stations was given to caterers as a concession. Roseville, Rocklin, Auburn, Colfax, Blue Canyon, Summit, and Truckee all had privately built stations in which the concessionaires operated dining room and bar and the railroad sold tickets. No written deeds or leases existed—it was all a very informal arrangement with Charlie Crocker —but the concessionaires stayed until their places burned down. Then the company refused to allow them to rebuild.

"The wood sheds west of Blue Canyon," recalled Jones, "were located, evidently by design, at a proper distance east of the depot, so that while the engines were being wooded up the passenger cars stood in front of the depot." This gave the passengers opportunity to loiter and re- fresh themselves in the barroom until the engine was ready to start. "Everybody seemed satisfied and we who remember the old-timers of California and Nevada know that an oasis on the line could not be of too frequent an occurrence."

The management tried hard to preserve the niceties. General Super- intendent A. N. Towne, in 1878, addressed his sleeping-car porters as follows: "Hereafter upon leaving the terminals of your route you will *at once* notify each gentleman occupant of car of the location of the Wash-Room and Water-Closet for use of gentlemen, and at the same time give the location of the Ladies' Toilet, which must not be made use of by any gentleman. . . . This notice must also be given to each gentleman entering any car at any way station. . . ."

Many of the "gentlemen" were cowboys, Indians, miners, and gamblers —the latter making a habit of setting up their monte games and prac- tically roughing or forcing passengers to play, if indeed they did not simply assault them or pick their pockets. They made it a practice to swarm aboard the trains at various Nevada stops. A pitched battle by rail- road detectives finally brought these nuisances under some kind of control.

A very fancy excursion was the Pullman Special of eight brand-new sleeping cars which carried the Boston Chamber of Commerce to San Francisco in May, 1870, which was said to be the first transcontinental solid Pullman train. A daily newspaper called *Trans-Continental* was published in the baggage car. Its four pages of 10 by 7 inches had salutes for everybody aboard, including Albert B. Pullman, general superin- tendent of the Pullman Palace Car Company, who, "feeling a natural anxiety for the complete success of the eventful trip, had accompanied our train, in order that his presence, like Napoleon on the field, would be complete guarantee that all would be well with us." It isn't every Pullman traveler who can have Mr. Pullman along to check on the berth-making.

In 1876 a "lightning express" rolled the entire trip from Jersey City to Oakland, tying New York with San Francisco—including the ferry ride—in the record time of 84 hours, 17 minutes. That was a special train chartered by Jarrett and Palmer, prominent theatrical producers. The excursion party left New York at 12:40 A.M., June 1, and debarked at the foot of San Francisco's Market Street at 9:43 A.M. of the third day following. The mayor and dignitaries of the Western city met the excursionists as conquering heroes. Acclaimed, too, were CP's engineers Hank Small and Jim Wright, who piloted wood-burner locomotive No. 149 over the 879 miles from Ogden to Oakland Wharf in 23 hours, 45 minutes.

In 1880, Crofutt's *New Overland Tourist and Pacific Coast Guide* admonished the would-be transcontinental traveler:

Never purchase your tickets from a stranger in the street, but over the counter of some responsible company.

Do not lend to strangers or be induced to play at their game, *if you do, you will surely be robbed.*

Do not grumble at everything or everybody or seek to attract attention.

And finally, do not judge of the people you meet by their clothes, or think you are going west to find fools; as a millionaire may be in greasy buckskin, a college graduate in rags, and a genius with little of either, while in the breast of each beats an honest heart.

In addition to the luxuries of travel by the Express, which offered both first- and second-class or day-coach accommodations, the overland line offered its daily Emigrant and Freight. This last was something that really took endurance. It was as rough a ride as any crossing of the plains by buckboard, but it did in an hour what the wagon had done in a day. The plain unupholstered Emigrant and Freight in its time probably did far more than the lordly Golden and Silver Palace cars to upbuild the West.

Here are some extracts from rules and regulations for employees in effect in 1868:

The clock of G. M. Parker, 34 K Street [Sacramento], is the time by which trains are to be run. Conductors and Enginemen will compare their Watches with it daily, when practicable.

West bound trains will have the right to the track against East bound trains until they are twenty-five minutes behind their card time, after which they will lose all their right to the track. East bound trains will wait twenty-five minutes for West bound trains, keeping twenty-five minutes behind their card at each succeeding station until the expected train is met. Always allow five minutes for variation of watches, but the five minutes so allowed must not be used for running. If a train cannot reach a station on time to meet another, all the necessary precautions must be taken to prevent accidents. . . .

Passenger trains will not run faster than twenty-five miles an hour, except on special order, over any part of the road, and Freight Trains ten miles an hour East of the Junction [Roseville], and twelve miles an hour West of the Junction. . . . Special care must also be taken in case a train gets behind time and liable to be overtaken by a following train, to guard against accident. . . .

Enginemen and Firemen are particularly directed not to throw any wood from the Tender while in motion. If any wood is found too large for use, it should be thrown off at the next Station.

From his perch in New York, Huntington kept an owlish eye on the physical condition of the railroad he had done more than any other man to build. His daily letters to Hopkins were sprinkled with such admonitions as:

I would suggest that the trestles in the mountains be carefully watched, as I was on the back platform of the cars in passing over all of them, and some of them . . . [indistinct], showing at least that they were laboring hard. Now I understand that my engineers are looking after this, but I feel very anxious about it, for if a train should go down from the top of one of those high trestles it would cost us largely in money, and then we have a very great responsibility beyond the money part, in taking care of the lives of our passengers. . . .

Old Collis P., to the end of his days, was a railroader. Stocks and bonds and interest due, yes; but also, lamps and candles and trestles. No item was too small for his restless brain, and none too large.

The modern streamliner City of San Francisco, a handsome train owned jointly by Chicago and North Western, Union Pacific, and Southern Pacific, floats along in these effete times in a way to make the days of the palace cars and the emigrant cars, or even the one-generation-ago Standard Pullman, belong with the ox cart and the covered wagon.

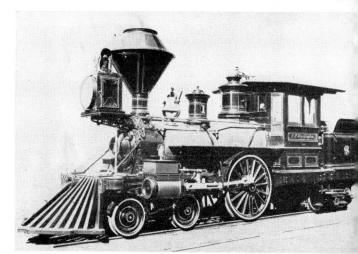

THREE FAMOUS OLD-TIMERS

Top. Pioneer of California rails, the "C. P. Huntington," now on exhibition in the station park at Sacramento. Like all early locomotives used in the West, it came around the Horn by ship. Length 29 feet, weight 39,000 pounds loaded. First used in April, 1864

Center. No. 149, which made a through run from Ogden to Oakland in 1876 and held the speed record for 30 years

Bottom. "El Gobernador," the monster of the steam world in the 1880s. Length 65 feet 6 inches (including tender), weight 190,000 pounds loaded. Too big for its times

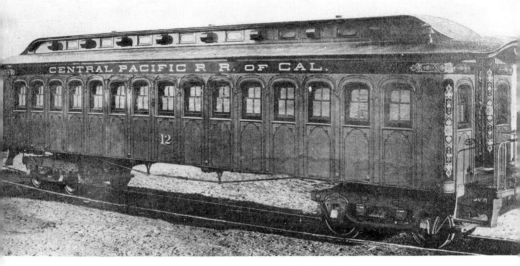

Top. Early-type passenger coach which reached Sacramento from the East on May 12, 1869, attached to President Stanford's special train returning from the golden spike ceremony. Plenty of paint, carved wood, and gold leaf, but thin cushions, a coal stove for heat, and candles or oil lamps for light

THERE'S YOUR OVERLAND RAILROAD, MR. WEBSTER!

Bottom. Locomotives of Central and Union Pacific meet for gold spike ceremony at Promontory, Territory of Utah, May 10, 1869

Chicago is left at 6:00 P.M. The tall corn of Iowa. The valley of the Platte, but nary a buffalo. Stations in Wyoming whose names, thank God, still preserve smell of horseflesh and creak of saddle and whistle of twirling rope and yell of charging Indian: Cheyenne, Laramie, Medicine Bow. Then, left of the tracks at Creston, Wyoming, a sign that may stir your pulses but probably won't: DIVIDE OF THE CONTINENT. Ogden, a few miles southeast of forgotten Promontory, where UP and SP territory join. Great Salt Lake, its 2,000 square miles reflecting a brassy sunset. Lucin Causeway, 32 miles from shore to shore. Self-consciously wicked little Reno, its neon lights still blazing at 2:22 A.M. (Would Joe Graham, who drove its survey stakes for the Central Pacific, recognize it?)

The Sierra Nevada, white under moonlight. The rugged canyon of the Truckee River. Truckee town, once a raw burg of saloons, cordwood piles, stacks of fragrant pine lumber and smoky roundhouse. Forty-nine miles and 2,486 feet up since leaving Reno, the summit tunnel. The west slope of the mountains as gashed and forested as ever, with nobody looking but the train crew. Old gold towns and old CP construction stations flitting by—Cisco, Emigrant Gap, Dutch Flat, Gold Run. Sacramento, where river steamboats used to churn with a commotion beaten only by New Orleans's, St. Louis', and Cincinnati's. Grain and fruit lands, salty marshes, a railroad bridge that put the big car ferries out of business; oil-refining, sugar-refining, smelting, and dynamite-making towns; and the rail trip is at an end at 7:40 A.M. of the second day. San Francisco lies over the water by one of the last blessed ferries on the bay, 40¼ hours from Chicago by rail westbound; less than that by 30 minutes eastbound.

And there is your overland journey behind you, and you don't think a thing about it, except that it's time for breakfast.

But to persons who had rocked around the Horn, suffering seasickness and cramped quarters and moldy food and boredom for months on end; or to persons who had rocked across the plains, taking on cholera and mountain fever and breathing dust and enduring thirst; and to both groups of persons who, arrived in the West, waited weeks and months for letters to their Eastern homes to be answered or sent-for goods to arrive—to all these, a Pacific railroad had seemed the most desirable thing the human mind could conceive. When the first train rolled down to the Coast in 1869, bearing letters and merchandise and people that had been in Chicago only five days before, the advent was utterly epochal.

It has been a long, long epic—westward, ever westward, begun in saddle leather or afoot and ending in foam rubber—the historic march from Plymouth Rock to Oakland Pier.

6

Playing Rough

BEFORE A RAILROAD is roadbed and rails and rolling stock and fuel and waybills and tickets—and for a long time afterward—it is money. Money in bunches.

Collis P. Huntington understood this from the outset. As soon as the Sacramento storekeepers compounded with each other to build the western half of a Pacific railroad, he had headed for New York and Washington. Let Charlie Crocker charge about the scene and boss the contractors and the construction gangs. Let Leland Stanford in barrel cuffs and boiled shirt lift the first dirt with a silver shovel and in due time aim a sledge at a "golden" spike. Huntington knew who was building the line, and to the end of his days he remained a long way from the line itself but as close as he could get to the places where a quick dollar could be raised.

The project needed all the help it could get from towns, counties, states, and the national government.

Stanford knew some of the ropes, and Huntington quickly mastered the rest.

In the year that saw the turning of the first spadeful of earth, President Stanford promoted, the California legislature passed, and Governor Stanford signed seven acts of benevolence toward the Central Pacific. The acts gave it rights-of-way, authorized cities and counties to invest in its stock, and enabled it to tap the state till for cash subsidies of $10,000 a mile after the first 20 miles were built. San Francisco was invited to subscribe a million dollars, subject to a popular referendum.

This measure raised a storm. Who were these upstarts, these amateur financiers of an interior town who arrogated to themselves the grants and privileges of the Railroad Act of 1862, and proposed to sell their stock to individuals and the community down in the Coast's metropolis?

San Francisco would probably have turned the proposition down as cold and hard as it turned down the public offering of CP stock, if the railroad vote-getting machine had not been realistic.

The methods used to grab that subsidy were crude. Money was simply handed out. Governor Stanford's brother Philip was observed going around in a buggy, shelling out greenbacks to persons standing around the polls and urging, "Now go to work for the railroad." San Francisco, in that year 1863, surprised itself by voting $600,000 to the enterprisers. From then on, the railroad was in politics. And in politics it stayed, until booted out.

The railroad was constantly beset by court actions, political attacks, and legislative cinch bills. Legal and political defense became as much a part of railroading as the building of sheds against the avalanching mountain snows. From defense the railroad moved to offense, which is approved military strategy. The railroad's various levels organized the politics and ran the governments of counties and states, and since self-preservation was involved, it did a thumping job of the business.

Huntington took a realistic view of his functions in Washington. He was there to get all he could for his railroad, and to fight or checkmate the Union Pacific. H. H. Bancroft, California historian of the 1880s, sent a reporter to take down Collis P.'s reminiscences while they were fresh in his mind. The railroad king's candor was complete, and he apologized for nothing and to nobody. Backing up was never one of his characteristics. Of the struggle with Congress in 1864 to get the Railroad Act loosened up, and of a certain clause passed in that year which limited the Central Pacific's right to build a mere 150 miles into Nevada, Huntington stated: "One hundred and fifty miles ought not to have gone into the bill; but I said to Mr. Union Pacific, when I saw it, I would take that out as soon as I wanted it out. In 1866 I went to Washington. I got a large majority of them without the use of one dollar. We still had our means, and wanted to get every vote, so I went into the gallery for votes—one head after another. I sat right there. I examined the face of every man, and I am a good judge of faces. I examined them carefully through my glasses. I didn't see but one man I thought would sell his vote."

Perhaps the railroad could have been built by no other type of man. At any rate, no other type then tried. To put through a transcontinental, or anyway a first transcontinental, you evidently have to be ready to play rough and to fight rough. You are embattled from the start. If a man or a mountain stands in your way, you persuade, buy off, surmount, blow up, or knock down the obstacle. You are tougher than anything or anybody about you. You gouge and you bribe and you choke.

About all that can be said for it is, "Well, anyway the West got its rail-road."

Financing that railroad and jamming it through was a bruising ex-perience, and probably reshaped the four Sacramentans as much as they altered the face of nature.

After arranging for the actual survey of Judah's proposed route east-ward over the Sierra, Huntington and his associates asked each other, "Why do so many railroad promotions fail? Why do so few of the men who start the ventures hang onto them?" Loose management and high interest charges swamped most projected railroads before there were any offsetting revenues.

Warned by these examples, the associates planned a course of close economy. "Hang onto every dollar," said Huntington, or words to that effect. "And every piece of string," added Uncle Mark Hopkins. "When we make a financial deal, push the interest payments as far into the future as possible," added Stanford. "Leave that to me," said the cagey Collis. And he succeeded.

The estimated cost of building from Sacramento to the state line was $8,500,000, and the original Central Pacific Railroad Company of Cali-fornia was authorized to issue capital stock in that amount. As plans grew more ambitious, the authorized capital stock was increased to $20,000,000. "Let's hang onto this stock," was Stanford's view. "The main purpose of the increase is to raise the authorized total of saleable bonds." When Congress gave the Central Pacific the right to build eastward beyond the California boundary until it should meet the Union Pacific, the stock was increased to $100,000,000. "Let's hang onto this, too," chorused Hopkins and Stanford and Huntington. Only Crocker wasn't so sure.

The Sacramento merchants shifted their financial thinking from the small deals of storekeepers to the large ones of financiers with surprising agility. They received $24,000,000 in loaned government bonds (for which they had promised to pay 6 per cent interest), and the bonds constituted a second mortgage on the road. The road's own bonds, sold in Europe or wherever money could be raised, were the first mortgage. To fill in when bonds wouldn't sell, or when interest on the line's own bonds had to be met, Huntington borrowed from New York sources on short-term notes, using the personal credit of the partners when necessary.

In addition to the monies raised by pledging their own resources, the partners picked up those county bonds from San Francisco as a gift (they got $400,000 in bonds out of the $600,000 originally voted), $550,000 in bonds from other counties, and $2,100,000 from the state of Cali-fornia. They received 9,000,000 acres as a Federal land grant in return for low rates on government shipments. Three-quarters of such land was probably worthless, but perhaps one-quarter of it possessed large ultimate value. All this was Central Pacific's. Later the SP captured its own Federal lands and local subsidies. As money raisers, the Sacramento storekeepers did quite well. But it took rustling and nerve. They pledged everything they owned, and by California law were liable as stockholders for all that weight of debt. Nobody would buy their CP stock because of the debt that went with it, even when they wanted to sell. They were stuck, and had to go on being railroad men even when they grew tired or frightened.

When the joint CP-UP enterprise had conquered the 1,776 miles between the Missouri and the Sacramento rivers, driving through some of the coldest, hottest, driest, roughest, loneliest terrain men ever labored in, people asked, "What has it cost in dollars?" The government's Pacific Railway Commission had estimated that the Central Pacific's portion of the great transcontinental could be built for $23,000,000, and that was about the amount the Big Four had received as a government loan. But was that what the Four had spent? Or was something left over? "I can't seem to remember," said Uncle Mark, in effect. "I've lost the books."

As the Sacramento foursome were not only owners of the western half of the Pacific Railroad, but partners in its construction company, they felt that the exact cost was a matter best kept under their own plug hats. To this day the expenditure is a matter of guesswork.

The four were a tired lot when the Central Pacific was completed and its trains running. "What shall we do with it now?" they asked each other.

Their Union Pacific contemporaries, aghast at the tottery financial structure that they had reared, all had got out as fast as they could.

"I'd like to get out, too," decided Charlie Crocker.

"I like being president of a railroad," confessed Stanford to his mirror.

"I wouldn't know what to do with a vacation if I had one," Hopkins probably mused.

As for Huntington, "I'm worn out," he stated a number of times. But he had a perpetual-motion machine within his breast and probably knew that he would never slow down, but run at top speed until he dropped.

So, beginning with 1869, their task swiftly changed: they had the railroad, but it was a road ridden with debt, and it was now up to them to run it and make it pay.

The Sacramentans had just built a raw, ragged railroad, and the mountains and forests were still bleeding from the onslaught. The quartet reveled in their sense of power, of stature. Monopolists? You bet they were, if they could make it stick. How otherwise would they get their necks out of that yoke of debt? Had they risked their personal fortunes, incurred personal liability for $24,000,000, simply to show that rails could be laid?

The partners, or three of them, went ahead and rounded out as much of a transportation monopoly as they could effect in their California heartland, and flung more bands of iron north, south, and east. It was during this process that the initial rails of the Southern Pacific Railroad Company of California, little brother (and, later, big brother) of the Central Pacific, came to be laid.

For a while, operations of the Central Pacific were conducted out of Sacramento, upstairs over the Huntington and Hopkins store. After the Southern Pacific—the road through the Southwest—was well launched, operational headquarters moved to a warehouselike structure at Fourth and Townsend streets in San Francisco. From there, or more particularly from wherever Huntington happened to be, the campaigns were pushed that finally carried not only to Ogden, but to Portland and New Orleans.

The financial and strategy-making headquarters of Southern Pacific was wherever Collis P. Huntington was, and that was in New York. For the railroad was a great borrower, issuing short-term notes even to meet the interest on its bonds, and Huntington had to remain near the lending sources.

Later the operational offices in San Francisco moved to a downtown bank building at Montgomery and Market streets, with Texas and Louisiana lines operating, as today, from Houston. For many years the severely furnished offices in San Francisco controlled the economic life and much of the politics of one-sixth the area of the United States.

Recognizing that only by controlling all competition could they manage their terrific weight of personal debt, the Huntington group pushed ahead. They got in on the Southern Pacific project, as will be shown. They picked up steamboat lines, giving them control of the Sacramento and San Joaquin river traffic, and with Union Pacific they started the Occidental and Oriental Steamship Company, an overseas line competing with Pacific Mail. Though O&O operated to the Asiatic coast, it could easily have been swung south to compete with Pacific Mail's lucrative freight business via Panama. The threat kept Pacific Mail nicely in line and enabled the railroads to have a say in coast-to-coast water-borne freight rates.

In the seventies the partners brought under their control the movement of almost all the freight to and from California and within the borders of that sprawling but not yet populous commonwealth. The rate schedules of the railroad reflected it. They were based upon the simple formula, "What will the traffic bear?" This control was kept for the next three decades, although the public thrashed about like mice in a trap. It was charged that the railroad's officials claimed the right to inspect shippers' ledgers, and that they raised or lowered freight rates so as to keep merchants and farmers and manufacturers just nicely in business, for a bankrupt business was a lost customer, while one that was enjoying undue profits was making off with something that the railroad had an inherent right to share.

The railroad maintained its control as it had won it: through suppression of competition and then through use of economic power, and wide, deep political manipulation. The America of that era was the America of the Drews, Goulds, Credit Mobiliers; of the carpetbaggers, the Grant administration, the Boss Tweeds. Anything went, or so it was thought. At all events, SP political power extended through bought politicians and bought newspapers into the legislatures, regulatory bodies, town and country governments, and frequently the courts. In the terrific tussle between the railroad, which had its hammerlock on the public, and the public, which had its shoulders to the ground, the majority of the newspapers proved cleaner than the courts. They were antirailroad, or they had no readers.

Yet there were moments when the leaders of what seemed to be a ruthless corporation had qualms about the indignation they had aroused. Huntington was often querulous about it. His letters show that he was simply out of touch with the public mind. He had understood it much better when he was a merchant in a country store. But in New York he was too far away, too aloof.

"Why is it that we have so many bitter enemies in Cal.?" he wrote to Hopkins in 1872. "There must be some reason for it. Do we do all that we can to quiet them?" His ideas of improving the public temper showed little wisdom. He knew of only two remedies: to buy off or to smite. Writing in 1876 of the great harm the newspapers in California were doing the company: "Of course I understand that you cannot prevent a lot of this stuff coming over here, yet I have little doubt but that a judicious expenditure of $50 a month to the right party would keep much of it back. I shall do all I can here, but I am getting tired."

The San Francisco *Daily Alta California* in 1874 estimated that about one-third of the membership of the current state legislature was composed of members elected professedly as opponents of the railroad. But did they stay that way? It was wonderful what an annual railroad pass for the family, a bit of flattery, or the promise of a job could do.

While the railroad's agents attended to the state capitals, Huntington attended to Washington. He was often caught with the goods and could be wryly humorous about it. Writing to the faithful Hopkins in the summer of 1876, "I was out to the park with Dr. Gwin [United States Senator from California] the other day and he asked me how much land we had given to Senator Stewart [William M., of Nevada, chairman of the Senate committee on railroads]. Of course I said none. He then said that Mr. Crocker and Colton were talking over some matters and that Crocker said, 'Huntington made a great mistake when he gave Stewart all that good land.' Oh, for a tower in some vast wilderness!"

The railroad's early lot had been to come out of its corner fighting, and a fighter it remained. The conflict with natural and man-made obstacles, the battles to raise money, the assumption on the part of many public officials that squeezing the railroad was fair sport, the struggles to beat or buy up competition, all created an organization that was more apt to be truculent than amiable, more suspicious than sweet.

Survival came first and the one sure way to survive was to keep fighting with whatever weapons came handy. For fifty years, one of the chief activities of the railroad was endeavoring to see that those that were elected or appointed to public office were most likely of the type to "treat it fairly." Meanwhile the public, confused and disillusioned, believed that the SP could turn prosperity on or off for a business or a community like water in a tap.

From angel to devil had been a descent accomplished almost overnight after the gold spike of 1869 had been driven.

But the workaday folk who ran the trains and the stations went on lifting babies down from car steps, helping with baggage, blowing steam whistles at horses drowsing toward crossings, returning lost articles, answering questions, and taking the abuse of travelers with reasonable good nature.

7

Double-heading the System

THE PLANS OF the Sacramentans included a terminal on San Francisco Bay. So, while building eastward, they also looked to their back door by assigning those final miles to an associate called the Western Pacific—not the present-day road of that name. Its line was led to Oakland over the lumpy Coast Range via Livermore (Altamont) Pass.

San Francisco, on its peninsula, was accessible by land only from the southward. By 1864 the southern approach was already occupied by a local line, the San Francisco and San Jose Railroad.

Stanford and his associates at first vigorously sought Goat Island in the middle of the bay for a terminus, to be reached from Oakland by a causeway and connected with San Francisco by ferry. Congress declined to give up the island. The Sacramentans already had an alternative. They had bagged the Oakland waterfront. That, they figured, would keep any future transcontinental contenders well fenced away from San Francisco, the prize. San Francisco was the gateway to the Orient, and everyone expected that immense freight traffic, arriving by sea, would be carried eastward by the new rails.

The strategists had a competitor for Sacramento–San Francisco business. This was the California Pacific Railroad, with a water-level line between Sacramento and Vallejo, a branch to Davisville (now Davis) and Marysville, and steamers on the bay. Its route was shorter than Western Pacific's, with no hills to climb, and it included an hour's pleasant boat ride on the bay. In 1876 Central Pacific was strong enough to acquire it, by means of some stiff in-fighting and rabbit punching. With California Pacific also went control of several minor lines north of the bay. With a train ferry over the strait at Benicia and a line down to Oakland, they had by 1879 a water-level route all the way from Sacramento westward. The Four also gathered in some bay ferries.

But there was the troublesome matter of the San Francisco and San Jose entering the metropolis from the south. It had merged with another line projected by San Francisco financiers—a paper enterprise under the name Southern Pacific Railroad Company. This seems to be the first emergence of that name in Far Western affairs. The Southern Pacific's announced program was to build down the coast and interior to San Diego and thence eastward. This was in anticipation of a reopening of the public lands grab bag. And Congress did open the bag, allocating to Southern Pacific a right-of-way and certain alternate sections of public lands within California, provided the road connected with a project known as the Atlantic and Pacific that was hoping to strike westward from the Missouri River to the Colorado.

The Federal cash and loans which had been granted to the Central Pacific and Union Pacific were not extended to the Southern Pacific. If Southern Pacific should succeed in opening the southeastern corner of California to a new transcontinental, the Central Pacific would have a competitor in its home state. The thing to do, perceived the Central Pacific's owners, was to acquire the Southern Pacific, and fast.

Southern Pacific was closely affiliated with the San Francisco and San Jose. The city and county of San Francisco had a large slice of SF&SJ stock. By promises, politics, and their rising prestige, the Big Four got the city's stock interest in the little rail line, and that gave them control of the paper SP as well. By mid-1868 the SP was in the Big Four's pocket. It and other small lines were made into a corporate bundle called the Southern Pacific Railroad of California. There were still some potent San Francisco names on its directorate, including those of Lloyd Tevis and Peter Donahue, but there were also the familiar and dominating names of C. P. Huntington, Charles Crocker, Leland Stanford, and Mark Hopkins. Huntington was president of the Southern Pacific and Stanford of the Central Pacific; Huntington was vice-president of the CP, and Stanford of the SP. Hopkins was treasurer of both. It looked as if CP and SP would have no trouble in working together.

The Big Four watched other frontiers also. The railroad-minded Congress of 1866 had extended land-grant aid to the so-called California and Oregon Railroad. In 1870 the Central Pacific group gathered this in.

Fifty miles south of Sacramento was the town of Stockton, and in 1868 a line called the San Joaquin Valley Rail Road had been organized to bring the future trade of the San Joaquin Valley—then a wilderness—to Stockton, which was at the head of a navigable channel leading into San Francisco Bay. But the SJV, like all railroads of the time, was sketchily financed, and against the maneuvers of the now expert Sacramentans it did not have a chance. However, a few miles of track were laid under its name south from Lathrop before the company was gathered into the Central Pacific network in 1870.

These goings-on began to frighten Californians, so an independent line was started southward up the San Joaquin Valley, to be known as the Stockton and Visalia.

Stanford, Hopkins, and a party of CP engineers decided to see the upper San Joaquin for themselves. They made the trip on horseback. That valley, 250 miles long and 100 miles wide, is today a productive area of distinction. Its acres of grapes, melons, vegetables, fruits, cotton, sugar beets, grains, hay, livestock, and petroleum derricks support a chain of cities. Its farms on the watered east side are a continuous checkerboard. But for most of the year the valley, if left to nature, is sere and arid, and so it had been through geological ages. As the party rode out on horseback, camping where night overtook them, only the most powerful imagination could foresee the future. Except for an occasional sheepherder or squatter, population was nil. The towns between Lathrop and Los Angeles were Visalia, Bakersfield, and Tehachapi. Tehachapi had one store and a saloon, Bakersfield about the same. Still, it would not do for a rival railroad to have access. Such a road might extend onward to Southern California and bring in an overland rival. So the Stockton and Visalia, too, was brought under the Central Pacific flag.

Construction of a CP spur up the San Joaquin started on December 31, 1869, seven and a half months after the juncture of the CP with Union Pacific. The take-off was Lathrop, a railroad station on a stub of the so-called Western Pacific. S. S. Montague was still chief engineer of the CP enterprises. Lott D. Norton was construction engineer over much of the valley line and laid out the townsites. Traffic to Modesto was inaugurated in November, 1870; to Merced fourteen months later; to Fresno and Tulare in 1872. Those were mere townsites staked out by railroad surveyors. Each townsite, as the rails pushed up the valley, became a temporary backing-up point for stage lines that used to operate from Sacramento, but now were being pushed south.

The stagemen and teamsters, in spite of past defeats, took the oncoming railroad skeptically. When Delano was reached in 1873, teamsters looked on the bell-clanging locomotives, spat, and vummed that a team of eight oxen could "outpull any of them derned puffing machines." A bet was made. Bullocks were hooked up to the drawbar of an engine. There was a crack of black-snake whips at one end of the contest, a beep of whistle at the other, and the eight oxen were yanked bawling over the ties and cinders.

By November, 1874, the railroad was operating to Sumner (now East Bakersfield).

That the Central and Southern Pacifics were soon to be merged began to be rumored about 1870. The Big Four denied it. But in the following year, the public discovered that the Contract and Finance Company, the construction unit which Charlie Crocker had operated to build the CP, had taken over the building of the Southern Pacific from Gilroy southward. George E. Gray, however, was chief engineer, not Montague, and a letter from Huntington is still extant urging that A. N. Towne be not appointed general manager of the SP (he was already the able general manager of the CP) lest the public discern the single ownership of both companies.

Work on the Coast Line went forward in two prongs. One came to a languishing end in the foothill hamlet of Tres Pinos. The other got as far as Soledad, 63 miles below Gilroy, where construction ceased during hard times.

In the spring of 1872 there arrived in San Francisco a delegation of St. Louis men intent upon enlisting the aid of the Golden Gate city in bringing the Atlantic and Pacific onward.

The A&P (not the tea and grocery firm) had been incorporated as a proposed trunk line to run along the thirty-fifth parallel from Springfield, Missouri, to some point on the Colorado River opposite California. A&P's inspirational figure was John C. Frémont, explorer and first Republican presidential candidate. The A&P had shown early strength by achieving entry into St. Louis. Congress had granted it public lands on terms similar to those extended to the Central Pacific.

San Franciscans set up a Committee of One Hundred to meet with the A&P men and talk things over. The upshot was a return delegation of San Franciscans to St. Louis. It was discovered that part of the A&P route lay through the Indian Territory, where treaty rights would interfere with land-grant titles. So the San Franciscans declined to take chips.

Were the Big Four by this time greedy grabbers, or public benefactors who simply had to go on building railroads in California and beyond because no one else had the strength or nerve to do it? Human motives are complex. William Hood, a chief engineer who knew the Four well and admired them exceedingly, weighed the subject in later years and declared thoughtfully: "After succeeding in building the Central Pacific, instead of being financially wrecked as freely predicted, and as they themselves feared, the ambition seized the four associates to build a great system of railroads to develop the Pacific Coast. . . . It is inevitable in such a case that a monopoly for a time of ownership of railroads was necessarily created, and the only way to prevent it was for the associates to stop building railroads. . . . California would have been many years longer without a complete railroad system if these associates had failed to devote their energies and to continually risk their fortunes in railroad construction."

As the Big Four pushed their Central Pacific spur southward up California's interior valley, the times were far from rosy. How bleak they became will be shown farther along, in Huntington's correspondence with Hopkins. The "hard times" were both national and coastal. Mining activity along the Comstock Lode in Nevada had passed its first flush period and was in the doldrums. It was to revive sensationally within a few years, but no one knew that.

Coupled with the decline in business to Nevada was disappointment over that expected sea traffic from Asia. The Suez Canal, opened at this time, shifted the world trade routes and shrank San Francisco's tonnage.

Meanwhile the Big Four had a mutiny in its ranks. Charlie Crocker decided to quit. Unlike Stanford, who liked the limelight, and Huntington and Hopkins, who could only flirt with the idea of retiring, Charlie found it easy to relax. He offered his share in the partnership, together with the minor interest of his brother E. B., for $1,800,000, and took from his old associates three notes for $600,000 each. He retained a big chunk of Central Pacific stock which he had received as dividends from the railroad construction companies. Charlie was now free to sit around and enjoy himself. It galled Huntington and Hopkins to see such fun being had by one of their number, while they remained toiling and worrying.

In 1872 Huntington thought he was good and ready to sell out, too.

A sales agreement was drawn up by which Huntington and Hopkins agreed to deliver their holdings in CP and SP and all affiliated interests to whoever would pay $33,000,000 for them. The deal was put up to Mills and Ralston, reigning San Francisco bankers. But Mills and Ralston backed away, frightened by the personal obligations the partners had incurred while building the CP. Huntington and Hopkins had to stick.

Huntington himself was bowed by the weight of other financial ventures that were chiefly his own—the Chesapeake and Ohio railroad and the Newport News Shipbuilding Company.

As a result of these burdens, and the total lack of eagerness of any of his partners except Hopkins for plain hard work, Huntington frequently clashed with his associates in private; and was in a mood to take another member into the fold, a worker, when the right man should show up.

The man who did show up seemed to be just the answer. He was "General" David Doulty Colton, a blustering, ambitious fellow who had come to California in the gold rush and served a term as sheriff in Siskiyou County. His red hair and big fists were prominent in many a political fracas. He had been one of the seconds of Senator David C. Broderick when that politician was slain by Judge David Terry in the hills south of San Francisco in a pistol duel of the fifties. Colton's military title was from a youthful connection with the state militia. He was taken into limited partnership by the railroad group as a general handy man and for a while the papers called the group the "Big Four and a half." He built a mansion on San Francisco's Nob Hill, where Stanford, Crocker, and Hopkins erected flamboyant piles after the railroad moved its headquarters to San Francisco. (Huntington later bought Colton's edifice but seldom used it.) For a while Colton rode high, handling construction work and a lot of politics for the railroad, but he died abruptly in 1878 of a knife stab or a fall from a horse, and the "Big Four and a half" (the press had never been able to think of Charlie Crocker as really out of it) was collapsed back into a Big Four again.

Rails continued to advance up the San Joaquin, though slowly. Huntington kept his eye on the southeastern or Colorado River corner of the state. There were two points, Needles and Yuma, where the river logically could be crossed and the state entered by rivals. There was also one course, down the deserts from Salt Lake, by which the barrier river could be flanked.

The CP rails reached Goshen Junction. From Goshen Junction onward up the San Joaquin Valley, CP became SP by name; for now the tracks were in territory designated as SP's by charter and land grant. What kind of a line the SP was going to become had not been determined even by its owners. That it was going to lunge for Yuma, El Paso, and New Orleans was not yet foreseen, unless possibly in the recesses of Huntington's keen brain.

8

The Fearful Price of Riches

THE BONE-WEARINESS at this period of at least one of the Big Four may be gathered from some correspondence that has come to the authors of this book. Made available by Huntington's son, most of it has not been published before.

There was a point in his affairs at which he gladly would have unloaded his someday-golden Southern Pacific Railroad Company on any taker. He sought to unload on Tom Scott, who had tried running the Union Pacific after its progenitors got out. "At what price will we sell our SP to Tom Scott?" he wrote Hopkins in 1872. His letters and telegrams during the era leading up to the panic of 1873 vividly reveal the strain that that dour, almost pathetic, but genuinely heroic figure was under in trying to meet interest payments on the CP's bonds and keep the concern afloat.

NOVEMBER 12. Must have more money!

NOVEMBER 16. Draft received from Stanford. Came just in the nick of time.

NOVEMBER 20 [telegram]. Money market close here. Not possible to borrow a dollar in N.Y. I must have five hundred thousand dollars. . . . If I do not, everything will come down.

NOVEMBER 20. Tom Scott in again to talk about buying SP.

DECEMBER 13. Received telegram from Tom Scott a few days ago asking me to come to Philadelphia to talk up SP matters, but I thought it would be better for him to come here to buy than for me to go there to sell. So I answered that my engagements were such that I could not leave. . . .

DECEMBER 30. Since writing you yesterday I have been out to see if I could borrow some money to pay Jan. interest and as yet have not been able to get any.

JANUARY 5, 1873. Tom Scott was in my office and talked trade for the SP. Offered $15,000,000 for it but I told him that we would not take it, but we would take 17. . . . He is to be in my office again on Tuesday next and I think there is an even chance that we can make a trade. But I would not say anything about it, or if anyone there should say it was rather talked of I would deny it. . . . I am bound to get out of debt in the next six months, if I get out of everything else in doing it. . . .

FEBRUARY 7. I am not well. . . . I am about used up.

FEBRUARY 15. . . . Let us sell anything that we have that will bring money. I am doing all I can to close the trade with Scott. . . .

FEBRUARY 27. I have not seen or heard from Scott for several days although I have written him. Everything is so demoralized at this time I am fearful I shall not be able to make this trade   In the money market things look bad. I am doing all I can to get things straight and think I will succeed, but I am not well, and I do not think I have had twelve hours sleep in the last three weeks.

Call on me for the least amount of money possible.

FEBRUARY 28 [to Stanford]. I have made up my mind to get out of the active business, and am bound to do so. . . . And while I know that you want to hold on to the CP as you told me until you could get par for your stock, allow me to advise you to sell with the rest. Not but what I think you will realize par, if you hold, but that you have enough, and so why not retire and enjoy it?

MARCH 3 [to Hopkins again]. We have very large amounts to pay this spring and where the money is coming from I do not know.

MARCH 4. Herewith I send Mem. of bills and notes payable with about $2,000,000 to be added for July interest, which makes a fearful amount ($5,500,000) although I have no doubt it will be paid somehow, but you must not call on me for any money, as I cannot send you any, but will have to have some from you.

MARCH 7. Now we owe a fearful amount of money and want it now. So do, as soon as you get this, make up your mind what you will do . . . do not sleep night or day until it is done.

MARCH 8. I have not heard from Scott since I wrote you last. In fact, not, I think, for two weeks. . . . I see no other way out but to sell to Cohen and others [San Francisco capitalists Mills, Ralston, Sharon, Tevis, Russ] and get as much cash down as we possibly can. We must have money and that soon and I can't get it here. I have never known so blue a time for money here before.

There must be something done, and that at once.

I am not really able to be at my office today and shall return home soon.

MARCH 10. . . . You know that when I have made up my mind to do a thing dollars and cents have but little to do with it. And I have got tired and am going to quit.

MARCH 10. Fisk and Hatch [the brokers] have just been in and say they must have some money on our account. . . . Maybe things would look better to me if my health was better, but there has been a kind of nervous unrest come over me, and I cannot sleep. I do not think I have slept any for the last seventy-two hours. . . .

MARCH 11. . . . Scott was in the city last week but did not call at my office, and it looks a little as if he was playing with us . . . if we do not trade with him we must trade with someone, for we have to pay, now, between this and the first of June three and three quarters million dollars, a little over half of it in gold.

So you will see the necessity of doing something on this at once.

MARCH 13. Looks as if there would be a general break-up.

MARCH 14. I am satisfied that we have made a mistake by holding on to our stock as long as we have, as it is worth to us to raise money on little more than blank paper. . . .

MARCH 15. *WE MUST HAVE MONEY.*

MARCH 17. . . . Unless I get some sleep soon I shall break in some way.

MARCH 19. If something isn't done soon we shall all go to hell together.

MARCH 26. Tried in vain to borrow some money today. . . . Have not seen Tom Scott though he was in N.Y. He is hard up, borrowing heavily. Guess that deal is off.

APRIL 4. Can't sell bonds or borrow a dollar.

APRIL 7. A terrible smash seems imminent.

APRIL 10. What we are all coming to the Lord only knows. As things look now there is no more hope of raising one dollar for the July interest than there is of getting it from the moon. So for God's sake stop spending a dollar except the least amount possible to operate the road and send the rest here to pay bills and interest coming due.

APRIL 12. I have just received from you $20,000. Small but good.

APRIL 16. Interview with Pullman suggesting consolidation of CP and UP roads. Personal liability prevents sale of CP stock but consolidation under UP charter avoids liability. . . . Consider the matter and telegraph if you approve. . . . Time is narrowing and something must be done.

JULY 10. I want to sell the SP.

SEPTEMBER 11. . . . I have never known such a fearful time in N.Y.

as we have had in the last few days. All confidence seems to be lost in R.R. bonds. Fisk and Hatch have been called on for nearly all their loans when they had R.R. bonds up as collateral. . . . *You must send money.*

SEPTEMBER 13 [after listing several closings]. All the failures here have been on account of the default of some railroad.

SEPTEMBER 15. I have just telegraphed you that you must send me at least $25,000 a day for twenty days. It is doubtful if we can get through with that. . . . [More failures listed.] So look out for breakers.

SEPTEMBER 16. You may well believe that yesterday and today have been rough days. *Do all you can* for me here.

SEPTEMBER 18 [Telegram]. I must have half million dollars telegraph transfer tomorrow. Send this if possible, and immediately. Don't fail.

The nation had been plunging ahead too fast, building too many railroads with too little cash. The hard times of the 1870s were a stomach-ache caused by too many financial green apples. The paroxysm known as Black Friday occurred on September 18, 1873, when Jay Cooke and Company closed its doors.

SEPTEMBER 18. This has been the wildest day on the Exchange in this city that I have ever known. The House of Jay Cooke and Co. gave notice at the Stock Board at eleven A.M. today that they had suspended. And since then the news boys in the street have been calling the extras of this failure and that . . . no one is safe in a panic like this. God only knows where we will land. Help me all you can.

SEPTEMBER 19. Fisk and Hatch suspended payment today. Terrible panic here.

In this bleak hour, Charlie Crocker bethought himself of the notes the other three partners had given him for his interest in the mighty venture, and he bobbed up in Huntington's office at 9 Nassau Street.

SEPTEMBER 26. Charles Crocker was in the office yesterday. I did not talk business but think the best thing we can do is to let him come back into the Co.

Can you and Stanford get up a ring to whom you can sell the So. Pac.?

SEPTEMBER 26. Mr. Crocker has just left the office. We had a long talk. He said he wanted his money. I told him we were to have a property fight with the government and that we could not pay him until the fight was over. He said it was our fight, and not his. . . . He then said he would come back now and take his position just as though he had not been out and give Stanford, Huntington, and Hopkins $100,000 each in something that was good. And this I have telegraphed to you that I would do it.

SEPTEMBER 27. Charles has been in today and seems rather pleased at the idea of coming back. I do not like it, but see no other way out. . . .

SEPTEMBER 29 [telegram, Huntington to Hopkins and Stanford]. Crocker will not pay the amount named. by you. Would rather have his pay. If we cannot pay him I would rather trade with him, as it is the best he will do. Of course he will make millions by it, but if he comes in and works with us, why should he not?

SEPTEMBER 30 [telegram, Hopkins and Stanford to Huntington]. Trade as you approve best with Crocker.

OCTOBER 1. I have agreed with Mr. Crocker that he come back and take his position in the company the same as though he had never been out. He gives you and Stanford and myself each $100,000 in some good paper security. I think So. Pac. bonds would be as good as anything.

So Charlie, the wayward, was back, and the partners were a quadrumvirate again.

The struggle for cash to meet bond interest continued.

OCTOBER 29. I have been out for two days trying to borrow $48,150 for small notes due. To have such notes protested is utter ruin. I could not get a dollar from any monied institution but picked it up of friends in lots of about $5,000 of each person and gave my personal obligation for it, and at that I had to use, say, $14,000 of money that belonged to Huntington & Hopkins Co. and then the last note was taken out of the hands of a notary at 4:20, just in time to save a protest.

I would not go through another panic like this for all the railroads in the world.

But Uncle Mark, although he could not always produce cash, suddenly lifted Huntington's spirits with some figures about the Central and Western Pacific railroad companies and their branches. He revealed that the Central Pacific and its branches had earned a gross income in 1873 of $13,871,089.82, net of $8,281,649.67, and a profit above interest on bonds of $4,767,292, equivalent to 8 per cent on the capital stock. The first dividend, of 3 per cent gold, was declared and paid. The earnings of some $8,250,000 for the panic year compared with $5,171,192.05 for 1871 and $7,207,284.63 for 1872. The company owned and operated 1,219 miles of main line and branches. Responded Huntington:

> NOVEMBER 24. Yours of Nov. 14th received. The figures are large but I have got used to large figures and I have more faith that all will be well than I had one year ago, as our debt is growing less. . . .

Four months later he wrote to his old friend and hardware partner, "It is well to remember that there is a limit to what man can do. . . . *The fact is, Mr. Hopkins, we are, and have been, for a long time, giving more for money than it is worth.*"

The italics are Huntington's. But he was destined to drive himself relentlessly down the iron track for another quarter century.

9

The Railroad Throws a Party

NORTHERN CALIFORNIA, from the head of Sacramento Valley
to the head of San Joaquin, is a long oval saucer or gravy dish tilted
slightly upward toward north and south. When the Sacramento men had
built their route across the Sierra Nevada east of Sacramento, and swung
south with their second major line, the Tehachapi Mountains at the
head of the San Joaquin Valley presented opposition that in some respects outdid the Sierra.

Bill Hood, assistant chief engineer under Sam Montague, eyed the
problem, which was how to get a train 2,734 feet into the air up a grade
that looked as if its engines and rails would have to be fitted with cogs.

"I'll have to make a few miles into a lot of miles," he decided, "to
whittle down the grade."

It took Hood about a year to get geared for the assault. Then, starting
from the village of Caliente at an elevation of 1,291 feet, the line made
a swerving U-turn up the face of the mountain. At the sixth milepost the
graders could look down and see little Caliente a mile away in an air
line. Four tunnels had been bored up to this point, and a fifth, the
longest on the hill, was then begun. Number 5 proved to be a heart-
breaker, but when it was holed through, Hood had characteristic news
for his assistants—there were going to be thirteen more tunnels, boys,
only thirteen more.

Above this No. 5 tunnel, Hood began the first of two giant circles.
Into the side of a ridge he burrowed, swung upward, and crossed directly
over the point where tunnel No. 9 was just bored. That maneuver gained
77 feet. When the little trains of Hood's day went chugging into the hole
and, after a while, crossed directly above their recent point of disap-
pearance, it was spectacular enough, but today's trains add still another
quirk. It is not uncommon for the double-header locomotives of a

modern freight to be passing over the tunnel just as the caboose of their train flits inside.

Boring the San Fernando Tunnel (not one of the eighteen Tehachapi tunnels) was another man-killer. Softness of material, and water seepage, created all kinds of difficulty. The mountain was attacked from four faces. Shafts were sunk to give adits between the two ends. The work was pushed night and day by 4,000 men and 300 animals. When daylight broke through the big hole, and tracks and trains followed, there was an epic celebration and Bill Hood, later made chief engineer, was well on his way to becoming one of SP's immortals.

A reporter for the Los Angeles *Evening Express,* in the wonderful language employed to describe railroad operations of the time, wrote:

> On entering the dark abyss of the long tunnel, a feeling of complete separation from sublunary places seized one and the time dragged very heavily during the Cimmerian passage. It took the train just ten and a half minutes to go through. . . . Leaving Newhall, we passed several stretches of fine looking land, well timbered, presenting here and there very handsome groves, and soon entered the Soledad region, a wild, weird, and seemingly inhospitable section.
>
> Reaching the end of the track at noon, we were met with one of the most picturesque sights imaginable. Before us, formed in a line on either side of the road bed, was an army of about three thousand Chinamen standing at parade rest with their long-handled shovels. Every one of them was covered by a big basket hat, and the long line of head roofs presented a curious picture.

In recent years it was decided that Bill Hood's line could stand a little face lifting. A couple of those tunnels could be done away with; they never had been of quite standard size anyway. So the SP started rearranging and tidying up the Tehachapi scenery.

Carryalls moved in, capable of lugging 24 yards at a haul. A quarter million yards of earth and rock were moved along a strip of 2½ miles. A special pumping plant down on the Santa Clara River tossed water up to wet down the earth for solid fills. Two of Hood's tunnels were replaced with open cuts, curvatures were reduced from 10 degrees to four, five curves were eliminated completely, and the rest were spiraled with "compensated" grades and superelevated—banked on the outside for speedy modern traffic.

But the workers had to stop now and then and marvel at the handiwork that Bill Hood and his basket-hatted Chinese had left behind them.

While Hood grappled with his Tehachapi Mountains, Huntington in New York flicked his eye over the map and became concerned about a pass east of Los Angeles, called the Cajon.

A geological fault between the San Gabriel and San Bernardino mountains, this was the natural ramp between the plain where Los Angeles slumbered and the upper desert which led on to Salt Lake City. What if a railroad connected with the Union Pacific at Salt Lake and built southwestward and down the Cajon to Los Angeles (a thing that, years later, decidedly occurred)?

Huntington discovered that a man of ideas and action, Senator J. P. Jones of Nevada, was toying with the same thought. Jones was selling stock in a narrow-gauge line that he had built from Santa Monica on the ocean as far as Los Angeles, and he contemplated scaling the Cajon and continuing onward to some mines at Panamint, just west of Death Valley. He called his line the Los Angeles and Independence. His stock salesmen made no secret that atop the Cajon the Jones line could very well branch off around Death Valley's east side and push for Salt Lake.

The Big Four bore a grudge against Jones. The senator had been trying to put a tax on their 7,000,000 acres in Nevada. Colton was ordered to Washington to demand an amendment to the SP's land grant that would give SP the Cajon Pass.

This precipitated a row between the SP and the people of Los Angeles. A door-to-door canvass was started to raise funds to help the Jones line. San Bernardino, too, was angered. "Join hands with our natural allies [the LA&I] and carry that Narrow Gauge through the Cajon Pass at a gallop. Time is everything, the Southern Pacific operates against us," urged the local newspaper.

Meanwhile the Nevada senator, a maker and loser of many fortunes, was enjoying one of his flush periods. He hired a young civil engineer, James U. Crawford, away from a line called the Texas and Pacific and sent him into the San Bernardinos in a hurry. Crawford scouted the Cajon by horse and buggy and concluded that he could climb the pass with rails in 20 miles, cut an 1,800-foot tunnel through the upper sandstone, and come out on high-lying country at a point where the Calico mountains are skirted by the usually dry but sometimes brawling Mojave River—the site of Barstow today.

In November, 1874, stake-driving started. Reported Crawford: "We are camped on a summit of the Cajon, about 31 miles north of San Bernardino. It is very cold. Snow among the pines reaches down close to our camp. Bears are numerous, and frequently interrupt our surveying."

At this date the Southern Pacific was laying its plans for tunneling and looping its way up the Tehachapis about a hundred miles off to the north-west.

In December a party of SP engineers and surveyors passed through Bakersfield on their way to do battle for the Cajon with transit and sledge. They reached the pass and set up their instruments.

Crawford was there ahead of them with thirty-three laborers, who were at work grubbing out trees and blasting rock. Trestle footings were set up, and living quarters for winter—an item which his SP rivals neglected.

Rain began falling. It continued for three days. When it rains in the San Bernardino Mountains, salt flats become quagmires and gulches become sluiceways. Wind and snow drove down from the north. Then came a blizzard, one of the worst any of the old-timers remembered in those heights. Crawford's snug huts saved the day for the Jonesmen. The poorly protected SP crews fell back toward warmer quarters below the mountains. The gale increased and their retreat became a rout. It looked like complete victory for Senator Jones. But Huntington thought otherwise.

"I will do my best to cave him [Senator Jones] down the bank," Huntington bleakly wrote to Crocker.

Came August, 1876, and its Black Friday of the twenty-seventh—a date which made history in the West, for it marked the downfall of Comstock speculations, the ruin of millionaires, and the collapsing of many dreams. Jones was one of the victims. Work on his Cajon Tunnel stopped with the workers' picks 300 feet into the rock. As debacle spread, subscribers to the LA&I were forced to cancel. In that unhappy hour, Virginia City, on top of the Comstock Lode, caught fire and burned to the ground. That finished Senator J. P. Jones. Though he made more millions in another day, he was unable to hang onto the LA&I. Huntington bought him out for $100,000 cash, a $25,000 note, and $70,000 in SP bonds. The Cajon Pass reverted to the sagebrush, waiting for stronger hands to seize and utilize it. When such hands did reach, they belonged to the Sante Fe.

For the moment the Big Four had what they wanted. Their CP, with its San Joaquin Valley Division, held the interior basin far upward toward its head. Their SP stood guard over ocean-fringing counties. Their California and Oregon held the ramparts at the north. On the eastern front they had the Union Pacific pinned against the Wasatch Mountains in Utah. There were a couple of Achilles heels at Yuma and Needles, but Needles was not threatened at the moment. That left only Yuma to be considered.

The importance of Yuma was made plain by certain activities down in San Diego, in the extreme southwest corner of California. San Diego long had dreamed of a railroad. In the days of the so-called "Jackass Mail," which lugged the public's letters on muleback along the Mexican border in the fifties, the little mission city had been identified with a main route of overland travel. Since then, it had been ignored. But in 1872, there had arrived in San Diego the already mentioned Thomas A. Scott, recent president of the Union Pacific and currently vice-president of the Pennsylvania. He proposed to give San Diego its place in the railroad sun by connecting it with a line from the East through Yuma.

Scott's Texas and Pacific, later called the Texas Pacific, had been chartered to run from Marshall, Texas, along the thirty-second parallel. Texas had given Scott substantial land grants, and westward of the Pecos he had obtained land donations from Congress. Buying up some predecessor companies in Texas, Scott set to work. His line was completed from Marshall to Dallas in 1873.

To forestall Scott, the Big Four did not wait for Bill Hood to climb Tehachapi Pass, but started building at once from its top to a point where rails could be pushed toward Yuma. Los Angeles was to be left off to one side.

Los Angeles was at the time a drowsy Mexican-style town with a few thousand persons. Its transportation needs were served by steamers and sailing vessels into nearby harbors, and a 22-mile local railroad from the sea.

Dazed from the blow that had befallen when Jones lost the Cajon Pass, Los Angeles still found strength to make one more try at becoming a main-line station. Its leading citizens wrote to Stanford asking for an interview. A railroad representative was appointed to receive them. Two delegates pleaded earnestly. The railroad demanded 5 per cent of the county's assessed valuation as a bonus for bending its route their way. That seemed high. Before delegates Newmark and Downey got through, they cornered Huntington. In the end the railroad received a present of about $600,000 in cash and bonds, along with the little Los Angeles and San Pedro Railroad, and in return it undertook to swing to Los Angeles by building 25 miles of main line northward out of Los Angeles, and 25 miles eastward.

Bill Hood meanwhile smashed away at his Tehachapi Pass barrier. By 1876 there was his railroad, laid up like a Hindu rope-climbing trick. There was still a lot to do before SP would be a transcontinental. Ahead was the turbulent Colorado River, with Yuma and Apache Indians on the other side. The land-grant authorization limited SP to the California boundaries, and Tom Scott and his Texas and Pacific were plunging onward. There was also, perhaps, still some doubt on SP's part as to what its own ambitions were.

Huntington made up the outfit's collective mind. They would drive east before Tom Scott could get west of Texas.

They had been in that kind of a race before—against the Union Pacific. Scott should have been forewarned. Even Charlie Crocker was back in the foursome, who did not have the cash to pay him off anyhow. Charlie had lately driven another spike, on September 5, 1876, linking the rails north out of Los Angeles with those coming south from San Joaquin Valley.

A veteran cast were the engineers, the superintendents, the foremen, and the Chinese load-lifters and Irish spike-bangers who by now had whipped both Sierra and Tehachapi. Ahead of them was the formidable Colorado Desert.

The engineers and construction gangs watched while Charlie drove that spike and prominent citizens of San Francisco and Los Angeles pledged lasting regard for each other, but now there was work to do. Laying rails as they went, they moved out beyond the vineyards and sheep pastures, surmounted San Gorgonio Pass, and looked down the long 200-mile slant that leads deeper and deeper, until it is several hundred feet below sea level, on its way to the upraised sandy banks of the Colorado. For the Colorado, off yonder, is no longer buried in a mile-deep slot. It has emerged from the Grand Canyon and is here a sort of natural overhead aqueduct held away from the below-sea-level sink by low hills.

It promised to be rugged going. Desert sandstorms and alkali dust would inflame the throats and eyes. Water would be scarce. Heat would be searing. There would be times when the work would halt simply because iron tools could not be handled.

Tom Scott watched from afar. He wanted to make certain the SP would stop at the river. Other funds lacking, Tom turned to Congress for a cash subsidy. Huntington thwarted him, offering to Congress to build his SP over Tom's proposed route eastward if SP could have merely the land grant in the territories west of Texas—and never mind a subsidy. Huntington's offer knocked Scott off balance without deciding Congress either way. Congress had no desire to see the Huntington crowd in control of both the central and southern routes. By now it was suspicious of all railroad enterprises. The Union Pacific's Credit Mobilier and other scandals had led to a cautious do-nothing attitude on the part of the lawmakers.

Out on the desert the war with nature was waged in earnest. "Have you steamers in the Colo.," wrote Huntington to Hopkins in January of 1877, "so that they will run with us when the rail reaches the river?" The west bank was reached in May. Beyond, from Yuma to El Paso and onward across Texas, was the region which Scott had cut out for his Texas and Pacific. "Scott is making a very ugly fight," wrote Huntington to his old crony, "and doing more mean things than I have ever supposed one man could be guilty of, but I think we will live to see the grass grow over him."

Tom Scott's line in actuality was bogged down 1,200 miles east of the Colorado, but he decided to get a spade into the ground on his bank of the river without loss of time. There was a difficulty. Yuma was on an Indian reservation and the nod of the military commander was required. General McDowell gave Scott that nod, but almost immediately turned it into a shake of the head and asked the Secretary of War for a ruling. That brought Scott and Huntington to the War Office in Washington on the run. First SP, then T&P, got an authorization; then both were revoked.

The United States Cavalry had a regiment across the river on the Fort Yuma side that was keeping one eye on the Indians and one on the railroaders across the stream. But eyes can close, or they can grow bleary. The railroad men crossed over in a boat, suggested that they had un- limited provisions, including liquor; sighed at the thought of all those men of Uncle Sam dragging out their lives so far from home and pleasure, and proposed a party.

The party lasted for four or five days and it got better every day. When it was over, the officers rubbed their eyes, saw a wooden cantilever bridge over the river, closed their eyes again at such a nonsensical mirage, and opened them once more. Yes, a bridge. And that tattoo of sledges on iron spikes wasn't just a morning-after ringing in the skull, though there was plenty of that too.

Rails were being laid. A month later, work trains rolled over the bridge. Troops at Fort Yuma stopped them. But the civilians of the region raised a howl that reached clear to Washington and the bedeviled Secretary of War once more issued various contradictory orders.

The SP builders halted at Yuma, to wait for the weather and Con- gressional tempers to cool. They got encouragement from an unexpected source. William Tecumseh Sherman, General of the Armies, who had once done a little plunging ahead himself on his march through Georgia, wrote a letter to the SP stating admiringly: "I cannot neglect the oppor- tunity to thank you for having built a first-class steel railway across the Great Desert of the Colorado River. . . . A railroad east and west through Arizona is a great civilizer, and will enable the military authorities to maintain peace and order among the Indians, as well as the equally dan- gerous class of robbers who have so much increased in numbers and bold- ness."

Huntington was at work upon cabinet and president. He also directed that the legislatures of Arizona and New Mexico be approached in the matter of territorial charters. On October 9, 1877, he got an executive order from President Hayes authorizing the operation of trains in the forbidden land.

That whipped Scott, who unloaded.

Huntington had rid himself of one adversary only to face another. His new foe was the slippery Jay Gould.

10

Bayou and Prairie

FOR AN UNDERSTANDING of the east-to-west and west-to-east rail-laying race that now was shaping up, let us swing back for a moment to the other end of the line. Back in Chapter 1, we left Texas and Louisiana men of the early 1850s struggling to build local lines of large but vague ambitions. The Opelousas was grading toward the Atchafalaya River 80 miles beyond the Mississippi; the Buffalo Bayou line had reached the Brazos. In all, eleven railroads of sorts had been built in Texas prior to the Civil War, including a hundred miles of the Texas and New Orleans, someday to be an SP unit.

With $2,994,235 to spend, the Opelousas had ordered locomotives and 4,000 tons of rail and started early in the fifties to buck its way westward from Algiers, across the river from New Orleans.

Railroading in the United States was scarcely twenty years old at the time, so the Opelousas' undertaking was strictly pioneer stuff. The region ahead was low, swampy, thickly forested, full of reptiles and mosquitoes, and ridden by fevers. A year of the struggle and Col. Jim Gibbs resigned and went home, but his associate, G. W. B. Bayley, continued to push the line along. He headed it for Lafourche; for Bayou Terrebonne; and three years after the start at Algiers the 5-foot-6-inch-wide railroad was 66 miles long and had broken into Tigerville, now Gibson.

As examples of what Bayley had been up against, he had had 700 men at work during the entire summer of 1855 building roadbed and laying track through Chacahoula Swamp, a distance of 12 miles, where the road was largely laid on piles and later filled in with dirt and shell lugged from Algiers. The men worked in mud up to their waists. Heat, malaria, and bad drinking water laid them low in droves. When the work was done, not a foreman had escaped serious illness.

But in 1857, the railroad tumbled into Brashear City, 80 miles from its birthplace. Its terminus stayed there for twenty-one years.

As if to mock the toilers, scarcely had they gained Brashear City than the Mississippi found a soft place in its levees 28 miles above Algiers and boiled out over the countryside, wiping out the tracks and keeping trains from running for five months. A couple of years later the Bayou Lafourche, which connects the Mississippi with the Gulf, likewise went rampaging through its dikes and scattered the little railroad over the countryside. It took three months to pick up the pieces.

But from then on the road had a few years of peace. It transported passengers from New Orleans to Algiers on a steamboat and freight on barges. The 20-ton cars were hauled on and off the ferry transfer boats at the foot of St. Ann Street, New Orleans, by a team of gaudily decorated Spanish mules. To and from Algiers, the little engines hauled them over the bayou country. The peace came to an end in the spring of 1862 when the Union fleet threatened the mouth of the Mississippi.

What can happen to a railroad in wartime was promptly disclosed. Citizens of New Orleans burned the barges, lest the Yanks grab them; the Union forces seized the steamboat *Ceres*, and then the railroad. The Yanks commanded the railroad to operate as usual; the high-spirited Southerners indignantly declined to be told what to do. Others took their places, and just about wrecked the locomotives; and a company of Confederate Rangers from St. Martinville ambushed the line at Boeuf station.

"Surrender," they yelled, "in the name of the Confederate States of America!"

"Hell, we're already on your side," yipped the engineer.

The Rangers took over all trains and equipment from that point west. They smashed track and burned bridges. Then Union troops recaptured the road. When the owners got their railroad back at the end of the war, it was a wreck.

A. S. Seger was president of the line by that time. Pretty soon he had a railroad running again. The Opelousas line's engines, gaily named "Natchitoches," "Texas," "Terrebonne," "Sabine," "New Orleans," "St. Mary," "New Iberia," and "Tiger," went steaming up and down the track, routing the ducks and alligators and sending echoes flying. But there just was not enough business to keep the line solvent, so in 1869 it was sold by the United States marshal to one Charles Morgan. He was quite a man—every bit as big and able as any of the Big Four who were just finishing their Central Pacific over the Sierra.

Back in 1835, Morgan had taken the side-wheel steamer *Columbia* and chugged down the Mississippi, out into the rolling Gulf, and onward to the island which has become Galveston, Texas. That was the first steamer ever to churn the Gulf. So Morgan, whose interests fifty years later were to be merged with those of the Southern Pacific, was doing business with

Texas before the Alamo and the battle of San Jacinto. Morgan was in the transportation business when Huntington was only thirteen years old and earning seven dollars a month as a hired man, on a neighbor's farm in Connecticut; when Charlie Crocker was twelve and selling papers in Troy, New York; when Uncle Mark Hopkins was a blade of twenty-one growing a fuzzy beard and clerking in a New York village store; and when Stanford was a ten-year-old complete with bare feet and a fish pole, back home in Schenectady.

The career of Charles Morgan is more closely remembered in connection with steamships than railroads, but that does not make his caliber as a railroad pioneer any the less. After operating the first steamer between New Orleans and Galveston, in 1835, he followed with two more. His fleet, *Columbia, Constitution,* and *Comanche,* developed a real carrying trade along the Gulf Coast, and in the end he was credited with building and owning over a hundred vessels—more than any other man in American history. During the gold rush he operated ships to Panama and Nicaragua. During the Civil War all his vessels were commandeered by one side or the other. That did not put him permanently out of business. The war over, he started to build up a fleet again. His plans widened. He soon had ships running directly between New York and Galveston. He also saw the possibilities of Houston and in 1875 he did the first important dredging to make a ship channel out of the Buffalo Bayou.

One of Morgan's competitors in the steamship business of the Gulf Coast before the war was Thomas W. Peirce, a Boston capitalist. After the war, Peirce threw in with Morgan and helped to rebuild his steamship business and to augment it with rail lines. The combination proved profitable, and when the steamship magnate died in 1878, he left an established rail and steamship setup for Huntington to gather up, and he left Thomas W. Peirce to become a Huntington right hand.

When the Opelousas Railroad had reached Atchafalaya River, it was Charles Morgan's boats that connected with the railhead. When Morgan bought up the Opelousas, he extinguished it as a corporation and made it his personal property. Morgan provided through rail-and-boat service from New Orleans to Brashear, Galveston, and elsewhere on the Texas Gulf Coast. A few years later he sold out to a Louisiana outfit, which named itself Morgan's Louisiana and Texas Railroad and Steamship Company. Morgan had given the public good service and his name was an asset. His successors took up again the early dream of the old Opelousas Railroad—the laying of track with an eye to a possible Texas connection. In 1878 this grading and tracklaying began.

In charge was Julius Kruttschnitt, a young engineer of courage and promise. He started a career that led, eventually, to the operating director-

ship of all the Harriman lines, and to the chairmanship of the Southern
Pacific Company. As construction man for the extension of the "Apple-
sauce," Kruttschnitt's first struggle was with a savage yellow fever epi-
demic which broke out in New Orleans, claiming as many as 350 victims
a day. The disease crept along the line, strewing death and panic. Communication by steamer with Texas ports ceased. Supplies could scarcely
be brought in. Somehow, Kruttschnitt kept pushing along. Lafayette was
gained in 1880. The Atchafalaya was bridged at Berwick's Bay by a
structure 1,835 feet long, erected on pilings thrust down into water
80 feet deep. The railroad took on a familiar adversary, the Mississippi,
in 1882, when the barriers went down south of the juncture of the Big
River with the Red, filling the whole basin of the Atchafalaya and swamp-
ing the tracks for a 50-mile stretch. The new bridge held.

Construction did not stop at Lafayette. It pushed on in various directions, picking up connections. One was with the Louisiana Western Railroad, building westward from Lafayette to Orange.

In Houston, Col. A. M. Gentry and some associates, presumably all
of them also colonels, in 1856 had organized the Sabine and Galveston
Bay Railroad and Lumber Company. Their objective was the forest
country of east Texas. When the Opelousas outfit came chuffing out of
New Orleans toward the Atchafalaya River and tied in with the Morgan
steamers at Brashear City (now Morgan City) for that final 200 miles
down to Galveston, the Houston promoters in 1859 turned their enterprise into a concern called the Texas and New Orleans Railroad Company,
shifting their plan to a new one of building eastward to a meeting
with the Louisiana railroad at the Texas-Louisiana border. They whooped
along, laying 5-foot-6-inch gauge of their own, putting down a little
over a hundred miles of it, and reaching Orange in 1861.

One day in 1876 a young Texas and New Orleans engineer named N.
R. Olcott got to musing, and with his pencil sketched out a couple of
circles, a sunset, and a pair of rails. The idea interested him. He took the
sketch to W. C. Averill, his superior in charge of building the T&NO.

"Say, Bill, some day this little old railroad is going to be a link in a
through line to the Pacific Coast," said Olcott. "When that happens, this
sketch may come in handy."

The sketch rode through all the hazards of files and pigeonholes and
did not get lost. It is the Southern Pacific medalion or trademark today.
For boxcar uses the design has been simplified. But for menus, tickets and
travel folders, letterheads and official documents, the whole thing is
there. Rails to the sunset, onward they stretch, with the addition of
a fine, ballasted track and six ties and the words "Southern Pacific
Lines."

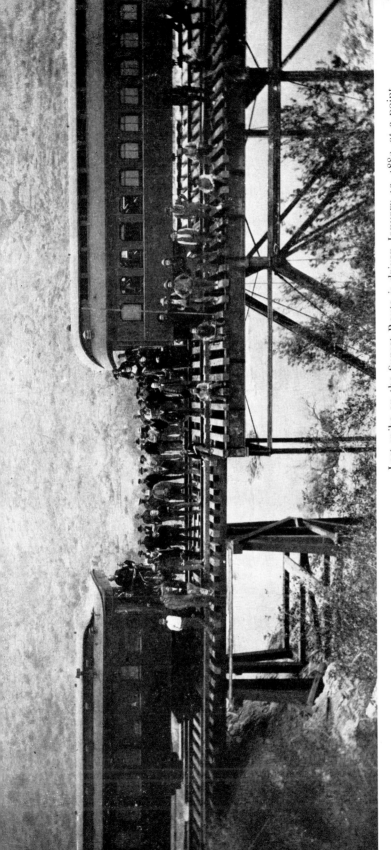

SOUTHERN PACIFIC WINS THE RACE!

Last spike on the Sunset Route is driven January 12, 1883, at a point two and a half miles west of the Pecos River. Spike driven by Col. Tom Peirce, president of the Galveston, Harrisburg and San Antonio, an early SP affiliate

Top. Early freight at Painted Cave, station on the old line crossing the Pecos at its mouth. This line was abandoned in 1892 when first high bridge was built

OVER THE PAINTED MESAS

Bottom. 'Way up there! Southern Pacific's historic first high bridge over Pecos River in southwestern Texas was 321 feet high and 1,515 feet long. Opened to traffic in 1892 and replaced by new high bridge in 1944

The earliest antecedent of the Southern Pacific system in Texas had been the Harrisburg Railroad and Trading Company, the handiwork of one Andrew Briscoe, a citizen of Harrisburg, to get a railroad going from that town toward the Brazos River. The year was 1840. He did some grading and he bought some ties. But a threatened military invasion of the republic of Texas by the republic of Mexico put Briscoe's Harrisburg Railroad and Trading Company on the shelf.

Another Texas line deeply embedded in the SP system of today was the Houston and Texas Central, which started life as the Galveston and Red River Railway. Its charter, dated March 11, 1848, was two years the elder of the Buffalo Bayou, Brazos and Colorado, the road which later became the Galveston, Harrisburg and San Antonio. The Galveston and Red River did not get its rails laid and trains running, however, until the BBB&C or "Harrisburg Railroad" had won the proud right to blow the first locomotive whistle in Texas. When money had been raised and the dirt did fly for the Galveston and Red River, it took two years and seven months to build 26 miles, and by this time the start of construction was from Houston, not Galveston. The great Texas city of the future was starting to feel its oats.

As now constituted, the Southern Pacific system in Texas is the largest and oldest railroad system in the state. About forty independent lines are fused into it, of which one was the first constructed in the state, and five were among the first ten.

There was another road organized in Texas which expired before it ever made any history, but its stock certificates still occasionally show up and their possessors feel that they are entitled to recognition by the present-day Southern Pacific. They aren't, for there is no connection; but the name of that embryo railroad, by coincidence, was Southern Pacific, too. It was originally known as the Texas Western, sometimes as the Vicksburg and El Paso. The Texas legislature labeled it Southern Pacific Railroad Company in a charter renewal on August 16, 1856. Twenty-seven and a half miles were constructed up the Red River, and the line owned two boxcars, a flat car, and three yoke of oxen. The oxen hauled the cars uphill and then rode down on one of the flats by gravity. One of the bullocks became known as "Bull of the Woods" because of a habit of charging off into the tall trees instead of sticking to his railroading. One way and another the road reached a length of 35 miles and was looking for laborers when the Civil War broke out. S. G. Reed, who spent forty-nine years in the traffic department of the SP lines in Texas and who wrote a scholarly book, *A History of the Texas Railroads*, located an advertisement of this early-day project (not related, we repeat, to the SP of today) in the New Orleans *Picayune* of October 19, 1861:

SOUTHERN PACIFIC RAILROAD
1000 SLAVES
Wanted by Hire or by Purchase

We will purchase or hire, for a term of five years, Five Hundred or a Thousand Slave Laborers, to work on the Southern Pacific Railroad, in Texas—immediately west of Shreveport, La.—in a region secure and protected from invasion or molestation during the conflict which shall exist between the two sections of this country. . . .

This company has a magnificent land grant from Texas i.e. 10,240 acres for every mile of road the company constructs, for the distance of 800 miles from Shreveport on the eastern, to El Paso on the western boundary of Texas. In times like the present, the company cannot command cash to pay for labor essential to the rapid development of the company's interests; but for a term of year(s) by hire or by the actual purchase, this company will make the most liberal and advantageous arrangements with slave-owners in Kentucky, Missouri, Virginia, Maryland, North Carolina or elsewhere. . . . Families entire will be taken, either by hire or by purchase. . . . The late Congress of the United States passed a bill, at its last session donating to this company, through Arizona, New Mexico and California some 13,000,000 acres of land, and a loan of thirty-six millions of dollars, to be repaid in postal and other services. This bill passed the House of Representatives, was amended in the Senate and only failed to become a law, for the want of time and the startling political events familiar to the nation.

The advertisement, signed by one Jeptha Fowkes, general and financial agent, failed to produce the slaves and also failed to produce the promised "protection from molestation or invasion." The nearest connections which the line ever had with Southern Pacific of the present day was through transition into the Texas and Pacific, the line which Collis P. Huntington fought and whipped from hell to breakfast. Of that, more later.

Civil war left the Buffalo Bayou, Brazos and Colorado bogged down at Alleyton, 80 miles from Houston. In 1867 the road was penniless, and it was sold and resold, ending up in 1870 in the hands of previously mentioned Thomas W. Peirce and others.

Peirce had been a member of the Boston firm of Peirce and Bacon. They had an extensive business with Texans in cotton, hides, and sugar. When war broke out between the states, they operated fifteen packets between Galveston and Boston. Peirce first appears in Texas railroad chronicles as a director of the Houston and Texas Central, another

SP forerunner, in 1857. He was a man of honor. When the BBB&C went broke and he bought out former associates in that line, he petitioned the legislature, asking for a new charter, stating that the associates had dipped into their own pockets for $300,000 to build, buy new equipment, bridge the Brazos River, and restore the line to usefulness and respectability; adding, "although not legally obliged to do so, we have agreed in writing to pay amounts due by the old company to employees and . . . other debts."

Under "Colonel" Tom Peirce's management, the BBB&C became once more a line with fire in its heart and places to go in its eye. It was given a new name, the Galveston, Harrisburg and San Antonio, and its charter authorized it to build clear to the Rio Grande—if it could get there.

A man of piety, Peirce was nonetheless a staunch admirer of a fast horse, and is said to have won two engines for his line by betting on a horse race against another railroad magnate. He put the engines on the rails at Columbus on the Colorado (the Texas river of that name), and pointed his line for San Antonio. It arrived there in 1877, the same year in which the Southern Pacific rammed and jammed its way over the Colorado at Fort Yuma.

San Antonio, which had been yearning for a railroad for years, promptly knocked off work. The *fiesta* lasted two solid days and nights. President Peirce invited all the prominent citizens aboard his private car for a free ride to Marion. He soon discovered that everybody in the town was prominent. Anyway, they were all on board.

At Marion they met the excursion train bringing 250 of Houston's distinguished citizenry, and all continued back to San Antonio, which promptly stepped its celebration up several notches as Governor Hubbard proclaimed, "We can rejoice in the near approach of the day when Texas shall have two million people and when it will rank with New York and Pennsylvania as one of the greatest and most populous states of the Union." Overlooked was the fact that the road lost a subsidy of half a million dollars, offered by San Antonio if the rails reached that city by March 1, 1875. They had not, because yellow fever had broken out during construction.

When the first regular train was operated into the new San Antonio terminal, Colonel Peirce occupied the cab with John Sullivan, the engineer, and heaved fuel under the boiler. He was entitled to feel enthusiastic over things achieved and other good things ahead. He had just bought out his associates and turned a large slice of his interest to a new partner, Collis P. Huntington, who was roaring out of the West with a through line from the Coast.

11

Highballing for Texas

FOLLOWING THE GOLDEN SPIKE of 1869, linking the Central Pacific and Union Pacific railroads, the original managers of the UP had got out as fast as they could. The money had been made in construction. Let others have the grief of running the road. "I'll try it," Thomas A. Scott had offered. The weight of UP's debt had proved too much. That was where Jay Gould had stepped in.

This interesting gentleman was never a railroader. He was a stock manipulator. Whatever he touched tended to wilt. He conducted his operations from New York. He rose to national prominence by operations in the gold market, in street railways, in telegraphs and steamships. From the UP he moved, line by line, until he had a network of roads south to the Gulf. An outlet to the Pacific appealed to him. But the way was blocked by four outfits possessing strategic rights-of-way—Southern Pacific, Santa Fe, Atlantic and Pacific, and Texas and Pacific.

When Scott handed his Texas and Pacific over to Gould, the latter dropped in on Huntington in New York and suggested that the three get together for a talk.

"They are two of the worst men in the country and I do not like to meet them together," wrote Huntington to Hopkins, shudderingly.

It must have been a rare meeting. Gould and Huntington decided to work together. It was a peace that would last only until one caught the other with aces under the table. They agreed to build west from Austin, east from Yuma, and bring their roads to a junction somewhere in Texas and divide the through traffic revenues in much the same fashion that central route revenues were being divided between UP and CP.

And a hidden ace is exactly what Huntington produced. Not relishing a division of Texas business with Jay Gould's T&P, he obtained a large interest in that other line, the Galveston, Harrisburg and San Antonio, in about 1880. This was Col. Tom Peirce's line and, if the SP could tie into it, there would be a pathway straight from San Antonio to New Orleans. The thing to do was to bring Peirce's line westward to a junction with the eastward-smashing SP before wily Jay Gould could lay the rails of his T&P.

The rivalry between Huntington and Gould—and Peirce and Gould —to get a line first across west Texas was not the only battle. There was also a hot fight between the Huntington-Peirce and Gould interests to drive a line south to Mexico. The obsession to have a line into Mexico was powerful with Huntington. Gould, with his International and Great Northern Railroad, reached San Antonio in February, 1881, pointing for Laredo.

Peirce had just started building westward from San Antonio. He was coy about his destination. His rails were merely moving off somewhere, and those who cared to guess where were free to do so. Mystified, Gould set his rails marching out of San Antonio parallel with Peirce's. This must have been one of the few times in history when a railroad actually pushed off into never-never land without knowing even what country it was making for, if any. So the two wayfaring outfits continued, for about 25 miles, until Medina River was reached. Then Peirce dived for El Paso, and Gould for Laredo.

But Peirce had a scheme up his sleeve. When he reached Spofford, 133 miles west, he launched a 35-mile branch to Eagle Pass. That disclosed his hand. Eagle Pass on the Rio Grande was a good place for an international bridge, and there Huntington and Peirce built one, owned jointly with the Mexican International Railroad. It was November, 1882, when Peirce reached Eagle Pass, and Gould had already been in Laredo for more than ten months. But Huntington and Peirce felt that they had kept Gould baffled and busy.

East of the Colorado River at the Arizona-California border the Southern Pacific graders faced territory that for years had been making transportation history with pack mules, freight wagons, and stagecoaches, all operating through a series of running fights with Indians and bandits.

The Butterfield stage route had come on the scene briefly in 1858. It got a government mail contract and put on strap-slung, or "thoroughbraced," Concord stagecoaches, running between the Missouri Pacific railhead at Tipton, Missouri, and San Francisco. One trip over the 2,759 miles was reeled off, eastbound, in twenty-four days and some hours. While the railroad was now a-building, pack mule and freight wagon were still the main cargo carriers of the region.

When SP started building eastward from Yuma, in November of 1878—winter months were best for that sort of thing—in the whole

252 miles onward to Tucson there were no towns nor settlements except, somewhat to the north, a store and blacksmith shop that constituted Phoenix, and the two tiny hamlets of Tempe and Florence.

The Southern Pacific followed the Gila River to a place known as Adonde Wells, up heavy grades over the Mohawk Mountains, and down to old Maricopa. Beyond, Engineer Hood had the fun of tracing with steel rails what may still be the longest railroad curve in the world—5 miles in length, followed by a tangent, or arrow-straight piece of track, of 47 miles without a bend.

The immediate objective was rowdy Tucson. That town, the only walled city (other than wooden-stockaded) that ever flourished in the United States, had about 2,000 persons. The coming of the railroad gave them a chance for a whopping *fiesta,* and miners and ranchers pitched in. So, too, did the Sixth Cavalry, which was posted there. As the first train approached on March 20, 1880, the military gave it a salute of thirty-eight guns and the cavalry band brayed lustily. The 5-foot walls broke out the banners of all nations.

Charlie Crocker was on hand and drove another "last spike." No record of that Tucson celebration would be complete without the oft-told anecdote of Pete Kitchen and his telegram to the Pope. The celebrators felt an intense urge to communicate the glad tidings of the railroad's coming to someone, and after Mayor Leatherwood had wired the President, the governor of Arizona, and the mayors of San Francisco, Los Angeles, and Yuma, someone suggested the Pope. But nobody knew where he lived.

A messenger was sent out to the ranch of Pete Kitchen, an old settler, to ask Pete's Mexican wife.

"His Holiness lives in Rome, Italy," came back the word.

So a telegram was duly dispatched: "The Pope, Rome, Italy. The Mayor of Tucson begs the honor of reminding His Holiness that this ancient and honorable pueblo was founded by the Spaniards under sanction of the Church more than three hundred years ago and to inform Your Holiness that a railroad from San Francisco, California, now connects us with the Christian world. Asking your benediction."

A reply was slow in coming, but someone slipped out of the barroom in which Mayor Leatherwood, Pete Kitchen, and their cronies waited, and in due course a telegram was brought from the railroad station. It read: "Am glad railroad has reached Tucson, but where in hell is Tucson? The Pope."

The railroad pushed on from Tucson, a military escort accompanying the construction gangs over a portion of the route. For this was Apache country. Over the eastern boundary of Arizona and into the lower corner of New Mexico went the SP, racing against time, against Scott's successor,

Jay Gould, against mounted Indians who whirled up out of the horizon like dust clouds, took a searching look, and whirled away again.

A lonesome land. No place for a superstitious man. Among these red and tan and chocolate mountains, these wide horizons and dry mesas, a grader or a rail bender longed for the cool pines and rushing streams of the Sierra.

But the bosses said "Onward"—on to El Paso—and so the rails pushed east.

From Tucson eastward there were only the handful of stage stations and, a considerable distance northward, the villages of Silver City and Mesilla. The line was opened to what is now Benson in June, 1880; through what is now Willcox to Lordsburg by mid-October; to Deming December 15. And suddenly, on May 19, 1881, here they were in El Paso, which was a sun-baked village of adobe houses, of cantinas where the beer was warm and the tequila was plenty hot. This was as far as SP, acting under territorial charters, was privileged to go; but the SP bosses had an answer for that also. They would continue building east, under the name of the Galveston, Harrisburg and San Antonio, the Texas line in which Huntington had purchased an interest for the SP about 1880.

So the change from SP to GH&SA was only nominal. Still in general charge of construction was J. H. Strobridge, who had built the Central Pacific over the Sierra under Crocker years before.

East of El Paso there were a few struggling settlements in the Rio Grande bottoms and then that string of stage stations again, with a scattering of military posts, to Marathon 254 miles onward. Between Marathon and Del Rio, 197 miles, all was vacancy awaiting the coming of Roy Bean, his saloon, and his "law west of the Pecos." Del Rio to San Antonio, 169 miles, was also pretty much just open sky and broad Texas real estate.

It was Huntington against Gould in earnest. The mountainous nature of the country southeast of El Paso made only one route feasible for rails, and that was through a pass from Sierra Blanca westward. That put fever into the race. Huntington relied on Peirce to whip Gould. He now definitely purposed to run the Southern Pacific through to San Antonio over Peirce's rails and onward via Houston to New Orleans. He supplied Peirce with material and men. The route was worked out by Hood, and the construction was performed under the eye of the veteran Strobridge. Many an Irish rail juggler and Chinese shovel hand had been with the Central Pacific in its conquest of the Sierra Nevada.

"We'll give a cash bonus to every man who sticks with the job," offered Strobridge.

W. H. Monroe, who five years before had laid the last rail that connected Los Angeles with San Francisco, was a construction contractor working out of San Antonio at the other end. Against such veterans, Gould did not have a chance.

A little beyond Del Rio the rails from the eastern end edged along the tall limestone cliffs of the Rio Grande. Here the going became slow. Footings were blasted out. After crossing Devil's River and climbing mesas, the route dropped into the canyons of the Rio Grande again. Grading proceeded to the point where that river was joined by the Pecos.

The original bridging of the Pecos was performed in 1882, exactly at the point where Pecos and Rio Grande merged. It was necessary to tunnel for the take-off, bridge the stream, and tunnel again in order to ascend from the chasm. And just east of this second tunnel, the gangs working west met those working east. The rails were joined at 2 P.M. on January 12, 1883, and Tom Peirce, president of the GH&SA, drove the "last spike" of this section. First through passenger trains over the Sunset Route between New Orleans and San Francisco whipped out of their respective cities on February 5, 1883.

The first shipment of freight that went east on the new transcontinental consisted of fifty barrels of port wine consigned by Arpad Haraszthy and Company of San Francisco to F. Hollander and Company of New Orleans.

Within a few years, engineers were scanning the canyon of the Pecos farther upstream for a location that would shorten the line and reduce grades. Jim Converse, chief engineer of the lines east of El Paso, went into the field. When he came back, he announced: "I've got something really spectacular. We'll build a high-line viaduct that will skip the descent into the Pecos Canyon altogether, and practically swing the railroad through the clouds."

He figured that he could eliminate the two tunnels, reduce maximum curvatures from 10 degrees to 5 degrees, and shorten the line by 11 miles. He got a clear board. Converse's problem was to get across a space 2,180 feet wide and stay 321 feet in the air. That called for a structure higher and more massive than railroaders had ever before tackled. When finished, Jim Converse's bridge was such an eighth wonder of the world that the railroad put an extra charge of fifty cents on all passengers taken over it. Tickets included "Pecos River Bridge toll." A newly set up Texas Railroad Commission challenged the authority for the charge, and it was withdrawn.

The thing went up in eighty-seven days and was opened for traffic in 1892. There was the bridge, airy as a cobweb and high, almost, as the moon—3,500,000 pounds of metal, over which trains were to advance like performers on a tight wire. Seventeen years later, because of increased traffic loads, it was reinforced with another 2,250,000 pounds of steel, and shortened by 665 feet. In 1942–1944, the bridge was replaced with a long cantilever steel structure, and that is where hot-shot and fancy drag, high-liner and varnish string skim today. In 1949 workmen moved in on the older structure with torches and cutting tools. Down came the weather-beaten steel that had once formed the highest bridge of its kind in the country. The pieces were numbered and then shipped away over the railroad they had served so long, to make a sea voyage and rise again as a highway bridge over a canyon in Guatemala.

The Southern Pacific had followed more or less closely the line as surveyed by the T&P. This, upon completion of the road, was the foundation of a unique law suit instituted by the Texas and Pacific in the United States District Court at Santa Fe, New Mexico, in the early 1880s. The beaten line claimed that the Southern Pacific had kindly built a road for it through Arizona and New Mexico upon a right-of-way granted it by Congress, which it appreciated, and it now demanded possession. A brilliant staff of attorneys on both sides enjoyed a legal field day. The Mexicans of Sante Fe and the Indians of nearby Taos looked in through the courtroom windows in wonder. But when oratory was over and judgment rendered, SP retained the tracks.

Evidently the "manifest destiny" that young Olcott sensed when he sketched that trade mark for the original Texas and New Orleans line has really been at work. The little Morgan's Louisiana and Texas line, successor to the Opelousas; the Texas and New Orleans, building eastward from Houston; the Louisiana Western filling in the gap between Morgan's railroad and the T&NO; and the Buffalo Bayou line that later became Tom Peirce's Galveston, Harrisburg and San Antonio, pushing west from Houston—these lines all were ready to furnish continuous travel onward to New Orleans as soon as the rails laid eastward by the Sacramentans met Tom Peirce's at the Pecos.

Huntington's dash across Texas involved more than rail laying. It involved the picking up and gathering in of about two-score lines, and the sweep of the man's imagination is staggering as one contemplates the diversity of geography and variety of interests that he was able to grasp and bend to his will. But on one occasion he almost met his match. While rampaging around amid the mesas and bayous, he collided head-on with the interests of the amazing female capitalist and Wall Street figure, Hetty Green.

Hetty was one of the richest women in America, and when on the warpath or the dollar trail she often sent her son Ned to represent her. One day he made one of his appearances, which became a Texas legend. He arrived in the town of Terrell to set up business as president of the northern branch of the Texas Central after Huntington had acquired the southern half. He showed up without announcement at one of the local banks and presented a certified check for $500,000, signed by his mother. As that sum was twice the resources of the bank, there was some hurried wiring to New York for identification.

"Have him remove his hat. If there's a large mole on his forehead, he's Hetty's son," was the gist of the reply. Green took off his hat, the mole was there, and he got the money and was forthwith made a vice-president of the bank.

Hetty was a woman of large prejudices. One of the prejudices was directed at Collis P., and for a long while he does not seem to have been aware of it. But there it was. They clashed in Texas over possession of a trifle of trackage called the Waco and Northwestern Railway. This had been owned by the Houston and Texas Central when that road went into receivership during Huntington's control. As Mrs. Green had had a number of her shrewd pennies invested in H&TC, she blamed Huntington for the downfall of that enterprise—holding that he hadn't kept the line up, had made wrecks inevitable, and had invited damage suits. When Huntington sent Kruttschnitt to bid in the sliver of the H&TC known as the Waco and Northwestern, Hetty lay in wait for him.

The day came in December, 1892. The place was Waco. Kruttschnitt, as general manager of the Southern Pacific Lines in Texas and Louisiana, was present with a war bag of $1,250,000. That such a sum would be needed for bidding in the 54-mile streak of rush seemed hardly probable. Present was a representative of the Rock Island, a man named Gold who represented an undisclosed party, and E. H. R. "Ned" Green, the one-legged son of indomitable Hetty.

Kruttschnitt opened the pot. "Eight hundred thousand," he bid.

Rock Island raised him. "Eight hundred and fifty thousand," offered the Rock Island man.

"Nine hundred thousand," chirped Gold, the unknown.

Kruttschnitt, beginning to feel bruised, made it a million. Rock Island made it $1,050,000, and then Hetty's son moved in. "I offer one million one hundred thousand!"

Gold added another $50,000. Green raised him by the same amount, and Kruttschnitt, almost unable to believe his ears, shook out all that was left in his bag. He made it $1,250,000, and probably wondered what he would say to Huntington, if Huntington gave him a chance to talk at all.

"I make it $1,255,000," blandly announced Green.

Kruttschnitt was through, but the others parlayed Green up to $1,365,-000 before the road was knocked down to him. Kruttschnitt left the meeting somewhat numbed, as everyone usually was who had ever been knocked on the head by Hetty Green's well-swung umbrella. In the end, though, Huntington got the line. He convinced the courts that Hetty was not entitled to the 481,000 acres of Texas land that she thought went with the railroad, and the upshot was conveyance of the Waco line to the SP interests for $1,505,000.

To round out the record, the El Paso and Southwestern joined the system in 1924. The EP&SW, extending from Tucson, Arizona, to El Paso, Texas, and to Tucumcari and Dawson, New Mexico, had its beginnings back in 1888 as The Arizona and South Eastern Railroad Company, and built a line from Fairbank to the copper mines at Bisbee, Arizona.

By 1902, it had reached El Paso, Texas. Other interests had begun a railroad extending north from El Paso in the early 1890s. At the turn of the century, the line was pushed northeasterly to meet the Rock Island from Chicago, and so the Golden State Route came into being in 1902.

Today your Sunset Limited, current model, rolls out of New Orleans Union Station on the swift 2,069-mile journey over SP's Sunset Route.

This train, the only streamliner in the SP's collection that still retains the word "limited," represents to the fullest extent what the mid-century passenger railroad man has been able to fancy in his finest dreams. The five all-steel trains knock five hours from previous runs, and do it with style, beauty, and considerably more luxury than the average traveler ever finds in his own or anybody else's home. New Orleans furnishes the *décor* of the dining room and lounge. The French Quarter walks right into the scene. Texas gets in its licks in the coffee shop, which is done in longhorn heads and cattle brands. The sleeping cars are all-room affairs with roomette, bedroom, or bedrooms en suite. Foam rubber chair-car seats with upholstered leg rests also notify the passenger that a new day has dawned. The train leaves New Orleans a half hour after midnight. It whisks over the 4½-mile Public Belt Bridge and enters SP operational territory at Avondale on the west side of the Mississippi, scoots through the water hyacinth and Spanish-moss bayou region and sugar country of lower Louisiana, flirts with the magnolia and live-oak-hidden homes of Bayou Teche, disturbs the egrets and ibises in the cypresses, leaves the French names behind and picks up the Spanish-named country, moves out upon rice, cotton, and corn lands, and begins to gather up oil derricks.

Modern Texas and its current history really began near Beaumont, just over the Sabine and a few miles north of the Gulf, in 1901 with the uncorking of Spindletop, the first fabulous oil strike of the state. The train picks up its pretty ruffles and swings along into Houston, the chief rail center between New Orleans and the Pacific Coast.

So the panorama of the big state floats past: sugar, and oil, and ever more oil; the Brazos River; cotton; rice; the beginnings of the great grazing lands. The little Alamo, where Texas was born and Davy Crockett died, struggles for air in the heart of a modern San Antonio. The sometimes mighty Rio Grande is reached at Del Rio, and Old Mexico is just across the international bridge.

The region changes: treeless plains, sagebrush, and Spanish bayonet move in. The train rolls across the Pecos River on a new bridge 321 feet high. Maybe the ghost of Judge Roy Bean, who used to dispense liquor and lynch law west of the Pecos, waves from the canyon bed below.

This is outdoor country. The sky is broad and not many roofs shut it out. The train climbs; at Paisano it reaches 5,074 feet above the sea. It is a land of yuccas, and cowboys in the saddle. Here is El Paso, with Carlsbad Caverns off to the right and Mexico to the left.

The two routes, Sunset and Golden State, merge and plunge westward, with an alternate line of the SP winding off for Douglas and Bisbee, and your fast train for the coast clipping along via Tucson. An alternate route west of Tucson, between Pichaco and Wellton, makes Phoenix also a main-line town. From Tucson, it is down the valley of the Gila to Yuma, with squaws selling trinkets on the station platform. Soon appear the Colorado River; Salton Sea; Palm Springs and the girls in their sun tans; Beaumont Summit, where desert gives way to almonds, apricots, peaches, grapes; the orange groves and real-estate signs of the San Gabriel Valley; and the Union Station of Los Angeles, located amid palm trees and patios like a movie set.

12

Here Come the Zulu Trains

SOUTHERN CALIFORNIA had been only moderately affected by the gold rush. Activity had centered several hundred miles to northward. Two decades later, there still wasn't much in and around Los Angeles.

When the SP decided to be gracious in the mid-seventies and put the town on its main line, Los Angeles had only 10,000 or so inhabitants. It was a three-quarters Mexican pueblo, with adobe houses scattered among pretty vineyards and olive trees. Its streets were dusty, unpaved, and strewn with litter. It had, however, a horsecar line and a short local railroad to the sea. It had daily stagecoaches that set off up the coast and tri-weekly coaches for San Diego, Bakersfield, and Prescott. It had a rough-and-ready hotel or two, and a bank.

Sheep, honey, and wine making were the industries, with a little grain, walnut, and fruit growing. The citrus industry was almost as much in the future as the unheard-of oil, tourist, real-estate, and movie industries.

The opening of the overland railroad, though it took place far to the north, created stir in all quarters. Seventy thousand persons a year began to arrive on the West Coast. They fanned out from Sacramento and San Francisco by wagon and by steamer, and some turned to the southern end of the state. A boom started, flattened with the nationwide panic of 1873, but developed again as the Southern Pacific was completed southward through the San Joaquin and as it pushed onward for the Colorado.

For a short time, Union Pacific and Central Pacific had a monopoly of such rail traffic as there was between the Missouri and the Pacific. In Union Pacific's case it was not an entirely satisfactory situation, because Central Pacific and its affiliates were spreading north and south, whereas the UP was bottled up between the Missouri and the Wasatch Mountains of Utah, dependent upon other lines at both ends for through business. And all over the prairie country, little upstart railroads were making muscles and threatening to spring westward to the Pacific.

So UP swelled its own muscles, and by 1884, through a connection via the Oregon Railroad and Navigation Company, gained access to Portland and the Coast independently of the Central Pacific.

That seemed to make it all the more incumbent upon Huntington and his partners to hold California against all comers. Since there were only two really logical river crossings into Southern California, at Needles and at Yuma, they felt reasonably safe.

But off across the intervening territories, picking up a little bankrupt trackage here, building a little there, SP's rival of the future for southwestern business was creeping onward from Kansas.

The Santa Fe system of the present day was chartered by the Territory of Kansas in 1859 as the Atchison and Topeka Railroad. It received a land grant of about 3,000,000 acres and started construction work in 1868 under the enlarged name Atchison, Topeka and Santa Fe.

A sharp tussle with the Denver and Rio Grande, won by Santa Fe's construction gangs, had given it the important Raton Pass over the mountains of New Mexico north of Santa Fe.

Pushing on over the Sangre de Cristos, the Santa Fe reached its namesake city with a spur early in 1880, and Albuquerque and Deming a few months later. A branch was tossed onward to El Paso. At Deming the Santa Fe made connection with the Southern Pacific.

The Atlantic and Pacific, which went bankrupt in the panic of 1873, had been reorganized as the St. Louis and San Francisco ("Frisco"). Its nickname indicated its ambitions. Santa Fe bought half the Frisco, with its valuable right-of-way along the thirty-fifth parallel from Albuquerque to the Colorado River. Huntington and Gould—Gould by this time having the Union Pacific—hurriedly bought the Frisco's other half. But Huntington's interest in the Frisco was not big enough to offset Santa Fe's. Huntington hustled SP's construction crews out upon the California desert to lay those long-postponed rails between Mojave and Needles. The Santa Fe pushed onward from Albuquerque, reaching the Colorado opposite Needles in 1883.

There on the west bank the SP seemed to hold the portal securely. If Santa Fe wanted to do business in California, it would have to do so on SP's terms. Santa Fe seemed to settle down opposite Needles for a nice long stay.

But Santa Fe was only pretending to be peaceful. Its management had built the Sonora Railway, a line that had been creeping leisurely up the west coast of Mexico from Guaymas on the Gulf of California, helped along by Mexican subsidies. Santa Fe, by building the Mexican line and announcing the intention of completing it up to a connection on United States soil, served notice that it would soon be squarely on the shore of the Pacific—south of the border, it is true, but in a position to slash rates at will on freights to and from the Pacific seaboard. That was a shocker for Huntington. It was only a preliminary.

Santa Fe had already done a hopscotch jump and started a railroad from San Diego northeastward for San Bernardino, called the California Southern.

San Diego had been disappointed about a transcontinental railroad almost as many times as the swallows had come back annually to the Mission San Juan Capistrano. But this time the townsmen once more dug up some cash and added some land, and urged Santa Fe's little California Southern to do its best against big SP. The California Southern built through Temecula Canyon, which looks tame but isn't. No sooner had California Southern got its trains running in the direction of San Bernardino than down came a flood through the Temecula and out went the tracks. It looked as if San Diego was never going to have a transcontinental, and as if Santa Fe was forever going to be just short of constituting itself one—especially as SP had touchily announced that no railroad was going to cross its tracks.

But Santa Fe sent in a fighting construction man who laid the iron between San Bernardino and Colton and jammed a crossing frog over the SP tracks at the latter point. The rails from San Diego were also relaid on safer ground. And there was San Diego, on a railroad again—a road that ran clear to San Bernardino, 136 miles away. With that achieved, all Santa Fe had to do to reach the Western ocean was acquire trackage between San Bernardino and Needles. Practically anything could happen now, and did.

Back of San Bernardino is the Cajon Pass. The SP had gained apparent control of the Cajon when it bought out Senator J. P. Jones of Nevada and his little Los Angeles and Independence, that narrow-gauge from Santa Monica to Los Angeles with its ambitions to continue onward to Salt Lake. But SP had failed to fill the Cajon with the ties, bridges, and rails. While building north from San Diego, Santa Fe had also been into the Cajon with surveyors and graders. Now it followed with ties and iron. The end of 1885 saw the pass open to Barstow, 78 miles from San Bernardino and several thousand feet aloft. At the other end of its operations, Santa Fe had built from Kansas City to Galveston and to Chicago.

Between Barstow and Needles was a waste of 170 miles, part of which was paralleled a little to the north by SP's Needles-Mojave line. But Santa Fe, which now had the whip hand, offered SP a deal—a reciprocal lease, Santa Fe taking the Needles-Mojave tracks and SP taking the Santa Fe–built Sonora Railway from Nogales to Guaymas and its United States connection between Nogales and Benson. Huntington accepted—it was the best he could do. As swaps went, he had got a lot of Mexico for a lot of California. In September, 1884, a Santa Fe train tootled over the Mojave landscape, its wheels churning up the alkali dust of a California desert, and in November, 1885, a transcontinental train set out at last from San Diego. The SP had a rival in its bed.

The rival lost no time reaching for a preliminary share of the bedclothes. It got them in the shape of some little local lines tapping Los Angeles.

The stage was set for a rate war that drastically altered the character and destiny of Southern California and the entire American Southwest.

When Central Pacific brought its first overland trains through to California in 1869, the first-class fare between Chicago and San Francisco was $130. By 1873 this had been cut to $118, and second-class was $85. But in 1886, when SP and Santa Fe squared off for a fight, this rate structure fell in.

SP struck first. It whacked the passenger rate for a traveler from the Missouri River down to $100. Santa Fe met the cut. Suddenly the United States awoke to the fact that two great railroads were offering to haul passengers from points west of the Missouri out to the Coast for as little as $15, and then for only $12.

SP met that Santa Fe slash. Santa Fe enthusiastically dropped to $8. SP resoundingly went to $6. All this happened between breakfast and lunch on March 6, 1887; in fact, before lunch was over, the rate was $1 a head. It bounced back promptly to $40 second-class and $50 first, but the job was done. Word had got to the prairies of Illinois, Iowa, and Kansas, the mines of Pennsylvania, the counters of New York that the snow-free winters and ocean-cooled summers of Southern California could be had at bargain rates. Farmers and their families, and city folk too, started for the southwest in droves.

The railroads soon had thousands of so-called "Zulu cars" which operated in freight trains, carrying one member of the family as caretaker for the family's livestock and belongings. The rest of the family usually rode in passenger cars at the low emigrant rates. Santa Fe had three and four trains a day roaring for Los Angeles, and SP dumped into that amazed town 120,000 arrivals in the single year. The majority rushed out into the surrounding countryside; about 40,000 stayed right in town.

Little San Diego, which had had a population of 2,600 in the middle sixties, and about 7,300 in 1872, found 50,000 persons surging up and down its streets.

Among these participants in one of the whoopingest land booms in history were, of course, the real-estate sharks from all quarters. Every newcomer was a prospect for a ranch, a business site, or a block of town

lots. Flags fluttered and auctioneers spieled. Townsites sprang up everywhere. There were bands, free picnics, tightrope walkers, all the tricks
that had been tried out in Minneapolis, Chicago, Kansas City, and the
other boom cities of the nation.

Sixty new towns were laid out within three years. Real-estate transactions
for one year totaled more than $200,000,000. SP's famous old Arcade Sta-
tion was opened with a grand ball and civic celebration in 1888. By that
date Los Angeles county had 100 new towns, platted and beflagged and
their streets all named.

Besides trains, and rails to run them on, Southern Pacific pumped
financial steam into this promotion. It had land bureaus in New York,
New Orleans, Omaha, and points in Europe. Its settlement agents and
lecturers spread out. Prospective settlers were sold "land seekers' tickets"
which permitted the fare to be applied to the purchase of some of that
Federal land that had been granted to the railroad. "Emigrant houses"
gave a week's free board. There were excursion parties. Carloads were
filled up with sight-seers gathered town by town, each party personally
conducted by a persuasive orator.

The emigrant trains were sociable affairs. People soon got acquainted.
They shared with each other from their food hampers. They washed
clothes, cooked steaks and coffee on the stove at the end of the car. They
had sermons and songs and they broke out the banjo and the violin. Often
they hopped off and got married. It was just like prairie-schooner days,
without the five months' journey, the cholera, and the Indians. SP had a
hundred emigrant cars running at one time, and they all were jammed.

And if the cars had hard seats, there were always the elegant Pullmans.

In a short while the beautiful railroad rate war exhausted itself. By
1889 the railroads had traded as many of their land-grant acres for cash
or promissory notes as they could unload, and they called the bargain
fares off. That gave Southern California a chance to digest its overload of
population, which consisted of about 137,000 permanent new settlers.

Slightly groggy, Southern California proceeded to calm down for a bit.
Two-thirds of the townsites, that had been laid out for 2,000,000 persons,
went back to the jack rabbit and the ground squirrel, though only for a
time. There were to be more booms and yet more booms until, in another
half century, the 2,000,000 population would be there, and quite a lot
more.

Cheap railroad rates, frenzied promotion, and chain-acting individual
enthusiasm, plus a pleasant setting and an admirable climate, had put
Southern California on the map.

The booms, with their necessary lulls for the gathering of new breath,
never ceased. SP carefully nurtured them. Farm advisers on the company

staff aided farmers along its lines in the tillage of soil and cultivation of crops. In 1901, SP established special spring and fall one-way "colonist fares." From Chicago to the Coast this fare was $33, and from Missouri River points $25. From 1901 to 1916 Southern Pacific brought 794,824 people west on colonist fares. The number of colonists carried by SP into the West and Southwest was equivalent to 70 per cent of the increase in population.

Union Pacific did not get in on the two-ringed circus of the eighties. But it reached Los Angeles in due time. It had a line in southern Utah, and Senator William A. Clark of Montana, a copper millionaire, started to build one of his own. Opposing construction forces battled in Meadow River Canyon in a good old Western tussle; whereupon a compromise was reached at the brass-hat level and UP and Senator Clark became joint owners. The Salt Lake line pushed from Salt Lake City down across Utah and Nevada along part of the route once contemplated by that other mineral-rich senator, John P. Jones of Nevada, in the 1870s.

The Salt Lake line came striding down Cajon Pass in spite of the Santa Fe's presence there, securing trackage privileges over Santa Fe's steel, and arrived on the shore of the ocean at the turn of the century. Today its streamliner City of Los Angeles toots into Union Station right beside Santa Fe's Chief and SP's Sunset Limited, Golden State, Daylight, and Lark. Any thoughts Southern Pacific ever had of monopolizing Southern California seem as antediluvian now as the dinosaur tracks down by the bank of the Colorado.

There are more railroad employees just in Los Angeles today (about 15,000) than the entire population numbered before the railroads took hold and the rate wars began. The population of San Gabriel Valley is now some 3,000,000. The visitors and new residents who come into Los Angeles by rail are passed through a union station that handles upwards of 60 trains a day. Opened in 1939, its architectural and functional features, supplied jointly by Southern Pacific, Union Pacific, and Santa Fe, nicked those lines for a total of $11,000,000. The layout handles 15 morning trains in 70 minutes.

The hour of concentrated activity is 7:30–8:30 P.M., when five transcontinental gallopers, SP's Sunset Limited, Cherokee, and Argonaut, Santa Fe's Super Chief, and Union Pacific's Pony Express, all pull out.

The Zulu trains don't run any more, and the word for them is forgotten. But, like clipper ship and prairie schooner, they contributed their share.

13

High Iron past Shasta

THE SHASTA ROUTE of Southern Pacific was born in Marysville, California, a bustling little river city of the fifties and sixties that rivaled Sacramento as a center of early-day railroad fervor.

Marysville, about 52 miles north of Sacramento, was well along on the stagecoach and teaming route to Oregon, and its gaze tended in that direction. In 1865 its citizens incorporated a California and Oregon Railroad Company to build to Portland. The plans for the road were sketchy and the terrain ahead was formidable; but railroad building was in the air, and before long the California and Oregon had a promise of land subsidies. The line started laying its first requisite 20 miles of track.

Stanford, Huntington, Hopkins, and Crocker could have told the Marysvillians something about that—to the effect that the first 20 miles are the hardest. The Sacramentans permitted the men of Marysville to play at railroading until money gave out. Then a number of incorporations and consolidations took place, in which the question of who swallowed whom becomes secondary to the fact that the CP eventually swallowed all. By 1870 the California and Oregon was a part of the Central Pacific system, and CP had 90 miles of patched-together railroads that wound northward from Sacramento. The road skirted granite quarries, oak forests, sheep ranches, and vineyards and ended nowhere in particular, with Portland still 600 miles and a week's hard stagecoaching away.

CP's Contract and Finance Company took over the job of building to Redding, about 100 miles onward. Work proceeded cautiously, for these were times of money trouble, and Huntington wrote to Hopkins in 1872, "I think we had better go slow for some time and build [on the California and Oregon road] only when the government compels us, unless you know where the money is coming from. I certainly do not."

A projected line to meet those northward-creeping rails interested several Oregon personalities. A row broke out among the Oregonians, resulting in a split into two factions, each taking the name of Oregon Central Railroad Company and each breaking ground at Portland in 1868. The faction backed principally by Portland men started its line on the west side of the Willamette River. A Salem group favored the east side.

Into the struggle among the Oregonians waded Ben Holladay, fresh from exploits of another nature. Holladay was one of the titans of an era that was fast fading—the era of dashing teams and thundering stage-coach wheels. A Kentucky farm boy who climbed to the overlordship of half the stagecoach routes of Western America, including the old Over-land Mail between the Missouri and the Sacramento, he had been the ruler of an empire of a thousand coaches and wagons, five thousand horses and mules, and an army of whips and hostlers in the middle sixties, but had heard the shrill toot of the oncoming locomotive and had sold out all his stagecoach holdings to Wells Fargo in 1866. He had turned to Oregon for a new world to conquer, and was sure he beheld it in the projected north-and-south Coast railroad.

"Let me in on this," roared Holladay. The east-siders let him in. They won the nod from the government, and were required to have their initial 20 miles of line in operation by Christmas Day, 1869.

The first rail was laid October 26. Exulted a Portland newspaper, the *Daily Herald,* "Scores of curious persons looked on at the first railway engine ever fired in the Willamette Valley. The engine moved majestically over the rails, filling the sanguine with delight at the fulfillment of their hopes, and the doubters with chagrin at the failure of their prophesies."

A pretty good performance for a locomotive whose boiler was just a trifle bigger than a wine barrel, and whose tender was filled with half a cord of wood.

Twelve miles onward was an imposing job, the erection of a 370-foot bridge across the Clackamas River. And time until Christmas Day was growing short; it was already mid-November. The bridge went up, its timbers yanked out of the nearby forests and still so green that the birds were practically singing in them. But there they were, a bridge. The last stick was almost in place when high water hit. Everything went downstream. But Ben leaped to the challenge. While rebuilding was pushed, the locomotive "J. B. Stephens" was hurried across the river on a barge, and rail laying continued on the farther side.

Ben Holladay was everywhere, exhorting, driving—a regular Charlie Crocker, with a thousand times Charlie's original transportation experi-ence. And Ben won his race against time. On December 23 at four-thirty in the afternoon, the last spike in the twentieth mile was driven home, and the next day the locomotive tooted its way across the restored bridge and onward to win the Federal subsidy. It pulled a baggage car and two passenger coaches, which had been constructed on the spot from Oregon timber. An elegant lunch, with champagne, was served to all. The engine rattled onward to Parrot Creek, about 6 miles south of Oregon City.

The roadway, cut out of the living forest of straight, tall firs, looked like a canyon with green walls and moss-covered cliffs. No ballast had gone into the roadbed and the way was rough, but never was a better time had in Oregon. And by September 29, 1870, the rails were laid to Salem in time to bring visitors to the Oregon State Fair. The railroad itself, however, was the big show. According to the words of a local newspaper, "The toot of the locomotive whistle at any hour of the day never fails to start crowds of sightseers toward the tracks, and the arrival or departure of a train calls out hundreds of people who never saw that style of wagon before."

Holladay had trains in operation between Portland and Eugene by the end of 1871. The stages there took over, completing the remaining 345 miles to Redding, California, in five days. The railroad pushed on to Roseburg, Oregon, reaching that town at the end of 1872, and reaching the end of its financial rope likewise. The double bridging of the Clackamas, the expense of converting Oregon trees into coaches and ties and flatcars, the lack of traffic in the sparsely settled region, and the cost of doing business with the Oregon legislature—bluff Ben Holladay said that item had cost him $35,000—had combined to bust him, as the cost of railroad promotion and construction busted many another man before and since. Ben's funds had been largely raised through sales of bonds to German capitalists. When he admitted defeat, the German bondholders took over.

They put the affair in the hands of one Henry Villard. Villard had been dispatched from Germany to look out for the interests of European bondholders of the Oregon Steam Navigation Company, an outfit organized in the sixties to provide transportation by boat up and down the Columbia River. Out of Oregon Steam Navigation, Villard built the Oregon Railway and Navigation Company, which in time brought the Union Pacific to Portland. In later years he became president of the Northern Pacific, completing that transcontinental line to Portland in 1883.

Villard, in 1876, approached the Big Four with a proposition that the Oregon and California be bought up by the Big Four's California and Oregon. The Big Four, who had probably long expected just such an offer, but who knew that time was in their favor, preferred to play possum. Villard obtained funds elsewhere, resumed road building south of Roseburg in 1881, and reached Ashland in 1884. There he went broke, joining the Holladays and so many others whose railroad-building reach had exceeded their grasp. The O&C went into receivership and tumbled into the hands of the Southern Pacific by lease in 1887.

At the south, work had been halted at Redding since 1872. But with the receivership for the O&C looming, the Californians picked up their tools. North of Redding the gorge of the Sacramento River, here a rushing mountain stream, was hopped, skipped, and jumped seventeen times. Hornbrook, near the California state line, was reached in May, 1887, two months before the Southern Pacific took over the Oregon enterprise.

The heavy job of hoisting a railroad up over the Siskiyou Mountains then began. SP pushed construction both from Hornbrook north and from Ashland south. Eighteen bores were made, of which the summit tunnel of 3,108 feet was the longest, and the mountains were crossed at an elevation above the sea of 4,135 feet. There were 100 miles of curved track in a distance of 171 miles. Curvatures reached up to 14 degrees on a maximum grade of 3.3 per cent. Those curvatures and grades were to plague the line for years. Eventually, a shorter route with gentler curves and grades was found by swinging east of the Cascades for a portion of the trip.

On December 17, 1887, in the south end of the railroad yard at Ashland, the traditional "last spike" of the original or Siskiyou line of the Shasta Route was whanged into place. Charlie Crocker swung on it to the cheering of a deputation brought from Portland and the California cities by special trains. The old-time stagecoach journey of seven days between Portland and Sacramento had been cut by steam to thirty-eight hours.

In promoting the Shasta Route to the traveling public, the railroad added to its construction feats by performing a neat job of mountain-boosting. It raised Mt. Shasta—at least by the printed word—to 14,444 feet. That had a fine ringing sound, it read well on posters, and passengers used to look out the train windows in awe, murmuring, "Think of it: Fourteen thousand four hundred and forty-four feet." The United States Geological Survey people weren't so alliterative, and with their theodolites and levels knocked the fine peak down to 14,161. It still looks the same from the train.

14

Huntington Again—Close View

THE VOLUMINOUS LETTERS and telegrams made available to the authors by Archer M. Huntington of New York and Connecticut, now a man beyond four-score years, cast many side lights on his doughty and omnipotent sire. In almost daily correspondence with the faithful Hopkins, Collis P. is seen to be not only frequently badgered and at bay, but remarkably resilient and ready for each new scrap. To Uncle Mark he completely unburdened himself, and was by turns tender, irascible, fussy, bossy, and beseeching.

He relied on Hopkins to make it clear to the other partners that he regarded Hopkins and himself as the key men. In 1866 he wrote tartly:

> JANUARY 3. I think it would be well to have Crocker understand that we, you and I, have something to say to what should be used. If it had not been for you and I, my opinion is that the Central Pacific would have gone to the devil before this. . . .

He also pays his respects to the hardware store:

> I quite agree with you, that you and I have enough to attend to outside the hardware business, but as long as we have it, it must be attended to, but I am still of the opinion that if we should hire Mr. Hammond, or give him an interest in the store, it would be the best thing that we could do.

Before the railroad was finished over the Sierra, he was homesick for the hardware business:

> MARCH 29, 1867. . . . Could not sell my interest and walk out of the old store without dropping a tear.

He scolds even his crony Mark Hopkins, on occasions:

APRIL 1, 1872. . . . I got no telegrams yet in relation to Goat Island [in San Francisco Bay, which the railroad men wanted for a terminal], but hope you are doing all that is necessary to be done. Although I must say that it does not look much like it.

Concerning the withdrawal of Charles Crocker and his brother E. B. from the enterprise in 1870, in return for about $3,500,000 in interest-bearing securities, their CP stock to stay pooled with that of the remaining trio for ten years, Hopkins wistfully writes to Huntington:

OCTOBER 17. . . . This gives them a *productive* fortune of a vast sum, and a reasonable expectation from C. P. stock of many millions more, so yoked with our interest in like property that we must realize their expectations, or do worse for ourselves.

While it leaves us the *hope* of an equal fortune, without their presence in our councils—the *certainty* of continued years of anxious toil, and the *uncertainty* of how well, and with what net results we may work out the problem of financial success. . . .

Huntington, who all his life wondered what kept him driving, replied:

OCTOBER 26. . . . The outlook is certainly not a pleasant one, and to your inquiry, why do we take their cares, perplexities and risks, when we have more than enough, I have no answer.

By 1871 Huntington, too, thought he was ready to sell out. He wrote to Uncle Mark:

DECEMBER 5. . . . The more I think of it, the more valuable my interests on the Pacific Coast look to me, and if I had some boys growing up, I hardly think I would sell any stock in the C. P. and S. P. at par, but as it is I know no reason why I should wear myself out as I am doing for the sake of getting more money, even if the amount should be untold millions, and have made up my mind to sell if I do not realize above 50% for my stock.

Now that the decision was made, Huntington plunged ahead:

AUGUST 23. . . . The more I think of it I am inclined to the opinion that we had better close out all our R. R. interest. . . .

SEPTEMBER 14. . . . Please give me yours and Stanford's views about selling the So. Pac., the price, and the best way to bring about a sale.

Late in September, 1872, a pair of San Francisco millionaires, D. O. Mills and Lloyd Tevis, showed up in New York ready to talk about buying the SP. The plan, Collis Huntington informed Mark Hopkins, was for the Big Four to keep very much in the background and appear to oppose the sale while letting others conclude the negotiations. "I certainly mean business," concluded Collis.

He suggested a hidden ball trick to Stanford. "Tevis was in again last night on the SP matter. He seems inclined to trade but says Mills thinks $15,000,000 too high. . . . Now I would suggest that you would say that if you could have your way you would not sell for, say, $40,000,000 but if your associates want to do so, for the sake of quiet you will do what they do."

But Mills and Tevis and their associates backed out, so Huntington had to turn elsewhere for the customer he never found.

DECEMBER 10. It is just possible that I may make sale of S. P. and if so it may be done almost any day and I hope everything connected with the co. will be put and kept in a very sunny condition . . . I would suggest that you say nothing to anyone there about it. . . .

By 1873 it was part of the Central that Huntington and Hopkins were eager to unload. The idea was to make it look as if Huntington and Hopkins were willing, but that Stanford wasn't. In this way the price could be jacked up.

FEBRUARY 28 [to Stanford]. *You must hold firm* that you will not sell C. P. at less than par.

MARCH 1 [to Hopkins]. . . . You understand that we will share alike if the sale is made, but Stanford should hold for par, and nothing less. . . .

The deal with the group of San Francisco millionaires came to naught —there was too much personal liability in the Big Four's Central Pacific holdings; too much horse trading and slick work all around in the Southern Pacific matter.

Los Angeles' narrow squeak from being by-passed by the transcontinental is shown in a letter of September 27, 1872. Huntington left the location of the line to his associates, but added, "It certainly looks as though we would have the best line to go back of L. A. [that is, avoid

the town by swinging many miles to its east], but then we would surely
have that town working against us, as she probably would do anyhow
as soon as we have spent our money among them. But if we do make up
our minds to go East of the town I think we should first get a vote on the
subsidy and beat it and then we could say you would not help us and we
had to take the cheapest line, etc."

There are frequent flashes of Collis P.'s opinion of Stanford, whom he
considered lazy and with whom he finally had a resounding rupture.

JANUARY 23, 1872. . . . Trading is not one of Stanford's strong
points. . . .

MARCH 15, 1873. I write to say that if there is anything done there
you must do it. Or, if Stanford does anything it will be only because
you go with him and push him to the front.

There is also the husband, wanting to know what his wife is saying
about him:

JULY 7, 1873. Mrs. Huntington sent you a cypher dispatch. What
was it about?

The record does not show.

He was having his troubles with Congressional investigation committees, as tycoons have been having before and since.

FEBRUARY 17, 1874. . . . if we could keep them out of our business
I would do so. You can see by the questions that they were disposed
to be mean, and if I had known more I would have told them more . . .
as I have never counted the stocks or bonds which were my portion I
could not tell. And I hope it will not be necessary to let them know
who are the C. and F. [Contract and Finance] Co. What they expect to
do, I think, is to make out that the C. P. and C. and F. Co. are one
and the same. . . .

In spite of his woes and worries, the old hardware dealer was still
deeply concerned with the business progress and management of Huntington and Hopkins at 54 K Street, Sacramento.

JANUARY 24, 1874. Some time since I received an order from Mr.
Watson [of the hardware store] for wire netting. He also enclosed a
circular from Evans Co. of Chicago, in which they proposed to make

the wire cloth of *best quality, English Steel Wire* #17—8 mesh, for 26¢ per square foot:

This price was so much under any I had ever been able to purchase that it looked very suspicious . . . I gave them the order, they to send me sample one foot square. . . .

I have no hesitation in calling it iron wire.

If you have men conducting the affairs of the company, in the shops, or elsewhere, whose judgment is so much at fault as to the materials they are working with I think it time your attention was called to it.

The same close scrutiny of detail could detect the mishandling of an ordinary traveler's piece of baggage, and "Uncle Mark" heard from it.

MARCH 31, 1874. The C. P. has been sued for a trunk valued at $1,038.05, and I find on inquiry that it was lost in the fall of 1872, and I find further that it was sold by the U. P. at Omaha on the 21 of this month as unclaimed baggage. Now if our company has called on the U. P. for it, and was told that they did not have it, then I suppose that it will be their loss. But if we have never put out a tracer for it, or asked them for it, then it is the loss of the C. P. Co., *and ought to be their loss.*

Passes bought a lot of favors, but Huntington tried not to waste them, as evidenced by this:

APRIL 9, 1874. I have given a Mr. Bogart a letter to you. . . . He is a note broker. Handles large amounts of paper. May want him to handle ours. Gave him a pass. He takes his wife but pays her fare.

From the quality of a foot of fly screen and the loss of a trunk to a scheme to capture a whole steamship line at a bargain was but a nimble leap.

APRIL 6, 1876. The Pacific Mail Steamship Co. is in trouble and it would be a very good time to take it into camp if we had the right parties to work with. I think the whole concern could be controlled for a million and a half.

The attitude of the press never ceased to bewilder him, and his heavy bear's paw was always up to smite.

FEBRUARY 20, 1873. Yours of the 11, 1873 is received with clippings from the papers of the enemy. Why is it that we have so many bitter enemies in Cal? There must be some reason for it. Do we do all we can to quiet them? I think not. . . . And that we need not buy them either.

I am keeping the papers here as quiet as I can.

On May 2, 1872, he urged Hopkins to spend "any amount necessary to subsidize the press" with relation to the grab for Goat Island. "Of course this is not be mentioned in Cal."

He tried sweet reason:

MARCH 26, 1872. . . . I spent two hours with [Horace] Greeley last Sunday night and hope to get some good articles in the Tribune in a few days, but maybe not. . . .

He also tried playing on woman's wiles:

OCTOBER 12, 1873.—Is it not possible for you to devise some means for stopping the Bulletin and Call [of San Francisco] from publishing false tables of figures against C. P.? There is no doubt but that they are hurting us. . . . I think if Mrs. Pickering [wife of an editor] could be reached it would be well, as she is very envious of Mrs. Stanford, and has much to say, and, I have no doubt, has much to do with the bitterness of her husband.

Huntington, although he claimed, "I am not much on paper," tried his own hand occasionally at penning a favorable piece. In 1875 his plans for a shipbuilding plant at Newport News took him south with frequency. He told Uncle Mark in some pride:

NOVEMBER 19. I am getting many articles published in the Southern papers without cost, by getting Southern men to offer them as their own promotion. The last time I was in Richmond I left two articles. I shall soon bring the S. P. of Cal. more to the front than I have. You will see the importance of our keeping under cover, for if it were known that the articles were written in this office they would have but little, if any, influence in the south.

Yet it is money, he decided, that talks loudest:

MARCH 31, 1876. I think you had better pay $50,000 to get the Press [favorable to us] than not to have them.

But a year later he cried, discouraged:

MARCH 31, 1876. I do not think there is any other concern in the world that has so many personal bitter enemies as the parties that built the Central Pacific Railroad. When will it be otherwise? Oh, would that I could retire from the field!

His affection for his hardware and railroad partner becomes genuinely tender at times. Being younger and tougher than Mark, he continually cautioned him:

MARCH 16, 1874. I am very sorry that you have been sick, but hope that this will find you quite well. I am fearful that you have too much to attend to. It is well to remember that there is a limit to what man can do. I have not been well for some weeks past. Have been nervous. Have not slept well. The Chesapeake and Ohio matters have plagued me very much, and I would like so much to get out from under the load that I am carrying. *The fact is, Mr. Hopkins, we are, and have been, for a long time, giving more for money than it is worth.* [The italics are Huntington's.]

Before many months he was definitely alarmed:

JUNE 23, 1874. I would like very much to see you. . . . And as you are not feeling very well the change will do you good. So do take Mrs. Hopkins and get aboard the officer's car, and start. And that is all there is to it, for you need not make another effort but just stay on the car and you are soon here.

Now you not only owe this to me but to yourself, for you have stayed at your post until you are all worn down with work, . . . You know I am not much on paper, but I have thought much of you lately, and I think I know just what you want, and it is to get out of California for a few months, or even weeks, and I believe it will add years to your life. Life is too short at the longest to have any part of it cut off by carelessness on our part. Telegraph me when you leave Cal. Please give my regards to Mrs. H.

But the faithful Mark was no more to be torn from the grindstone on the West side of the continent than Collis was on the East.

As it turned out, Uncle Mark had only three years and nine months more to go.

15

The Old Kings Step Down

THE BIG FOUR were living the good life as they saw it. Crocker's San Francisco mansion, a riot of arched windows, mansards, and chimneys, with a tall tower for capstone, swiftly became the visible symbol of its owner's wealth.

Mrs. Hopkins wanted a house which would be even more showy, and went after Uncle Mark until he let her have her way, and the ultimate result was a dwelling of such turrets, gables, bays, ells, couchant lions, and Gothic-arched conservatories as the West had never dreamed of. Hopkins, strolling past the unfinished building shortly before his death, is said to have exclaimed, "What damn fool built that house?"

Stanford's house rose, bay window upon bay window, upon a 2-acre lot next door. Marble steps climbed from California Street to a circular entrance hall, glass-domed 70 feet aloft. All was plush, walnut, and elegance.

The California newspapers made the most of these extravagancies. It was charged that Stanford, Crocker, Hopkins, and Colton had crowned the hill with edifices costing seven millions, at a time when the railroad was pleading starvation. Huntington winced at these reports. He tried his hand at a piece of journalistic composition and pretty clumsy it was, but he found a New York paper, the *Banker and Capitalist*, to print it:

A paragraph is going the rounds of the so-called "news"-papers to the effect that four of the Central Pacific managers in San Francisco have built for themselves palaces on top of the California Street Hill, costing them from two to three millions a-piece. Of course this is a ——— mistake. It is evident some editor or typo has added a cipher or two to the amounts to make a good sensation item. Gentlemen recently from San Francisco say that the railroad residences, like so many other "palaces" of the far west, are much more splendid in the papers than in fact. They are all wooden buildings, and with the grand furniture, pictures, libraries, etc., may have cost from $200,000 to $300,000 each. Furthermore they represent a net profit of a little real estate joint speculation, whereby a comparatively worthless knob was transformed into the best building site in the whole city.

Huntington sent this bit of his handiwork to Hopkins with the sarcastic note: "Friend H————: As I suppose you do not want to sell your house, I thought it would be well to reduce the price a little." Huntington also wrote testily to Colton:

I notice that you write about people telling lies about us. By the way, is there not some reason for them—these lies people tell about us? Or, in other words, have we not done some things it would have been better not to have done? As the doing of them have made our neighbors jealous of us. A man may climb a pole in a crowd in his ordinary garb and nothing is thought of it. But if he paints the rear of him vermillion before he goes up the crowd might take it as an insult.

By 1884 the Central Pacific had taken in more than $277,300,000 and expended $239,600,000, leaving upward of $37,000,000 as surplus and profit. The young Southern Pacific was booming along, earning three millions a year.

The Federal government was beginning to ask what arrangements were being made to take care of that Federal advance of $24,000,000 to the CP, with its mounting interest.

The railroad associates pointed out that they had conveyed freight, supplies, mails, and military munitions and passengers, in a period of seventeen years, for $20,000,000, when at regular rates the service would have cost the government $160,000,000.

Still, the government pointed out that it was talking about something else. It was talking about the $24,000,000 and interest. It wanted to know what would be done when the due date came around.

The associates left that wrangle to Huntington. He had never failed them, and they were pretty sure that he would find a way to take care of this question, too.

In 1878 Congress passed the Thurman Act, a bitter pill for the CP and the UP, for it required them to go about setting up a sinking fund into which they were to put 25 per cent of their annual net earnings toward liquidation of Uncle Sam's little bill. The railroads fought that through the courts, and lost. The next stage was to make the "net earnings" look small. The Central Pacific managed this by diverting as much business as possible to its other lines, which suggests one reason for the rapid growth of the southern route. Another and potent reason for the growth of the southern route lay in the fact that half of the Central's revenues tended to go to the connecting Union Pacific, whereas over the SP to southward the proprietors got everything. At all events CP and SP were now not only one system, but also within a few more years were known to the public by one name—Southern Pacific. (The present Southern Pacific Company is a legal entity that emerged a few years later, succeeding Southern Pacific Railroad Company.) The younger line, with a terminus on the lower Mississippi and increasingly excellent credit, became the dominant holding.

Before the close of 1884 the associates owned and controlled more than 5,500 miles of railroad, including all the lines that ran into San Francisco, Sacramento, Stockton, and Los Angeles. They had the entire broad-gauge system of the state centralized under one management.

Such a system could be, and often was, a tyrannical thing. But had the scattered system been in a dozen different hands, its development might have been sporadic and feeble. Or a Jay Gould might have stepped in.

In 1884–1885 all joint interests of the original Four, including those rail or steamship lines originated by or acquired by the Central Pacific, passed to a company called Southern Pacific Company, a new corporation. With the ships of its Morgan Line to carry freight between the Gulf ports and the Atlantic, the southern route was a true transcontinental transportation system even if the whole thing was not accomplished all the way on rails. Southern Pacific was the name to build up, Central Pacific the name to subordinate.

But a curious part of the reorganization was that it was done by special act of the legislature of Kentucky, and for many years to come that state was to be SP's official "old Kentucky home." The Kentucky act in effect gave the SP the green board to operate railroads or do practically anything else except run a lottery or bank, or lease, own, or operate any railroad within the state of Kentucky itself.

This offered many advantages for Huntington and his associates. Under that Kentucky charter of March 17, 1884, the company could increase its capital stock at will without further permission or concern of the hospitable state. The liability of the company's stockholders was limited (it had not been, under California law). And Huntington had another railroad in that vicinity which was his own venture, the Chesapeake and Ohio. This also may have influenced the choice of Kentucky as a place of incorporation. By lease dated February 17, 1885, the historic Central

Mansion of Charles Crocker atop San Francisco's Nob Hill

MARBLE STAIRS AND BAY WINDOWS

Residence of Leland Stanford on Nob Hill just above San Francisco's Chinatown and financial district. Both structures were destroyed in 1906 by earthquake and fire

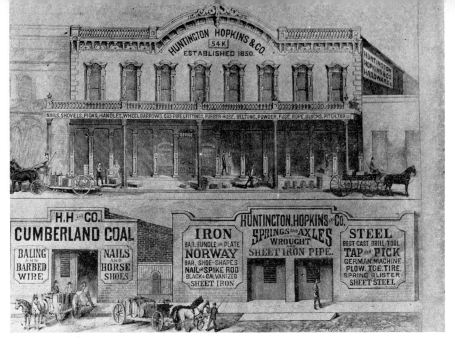

Top. The Huntington, Hopkins and Company hardware store in Sacramento, long known as "54 K Street." General offices of the Central Pacific were on the second floor from 1861 to 1873

NAILS AND SHOVELS TO SOARING TOWERS

Bottom. The wild, weird dream-house of Mrs. Mark Hopkins (old Mark never found it appealing or useful). Site today of San Francisco's Hotel Mark Hopkins and the "Top o' the Mark"

Top. Bill Hood's loop on the Tehachapi grade in 1876. As engine comes out of tunnel, another train passes overhead

WHIPPING THE TEHACHAPI

Bottom. Construction gangs turning out for work in San Fernando Mountains in 1875 when Southern Pacific was extending toward Los Angeles. It was largely a pick and shovel job

UP AND DOWN THE TEHACHAPI

Diesel-powered freight descending the Tehachapi grade meets a cab-ahead-type steam locomotive and freight ascending

Pacific Railroad Company became part of the system of the new Southern Pacific Company. So, at about the same date, did the three corporations named Southern Pacific Railroad Company, operating under charters from various states. Similar leases took care of other subsidiaries.

Huntington had still bigger ideas. He offered to toss his Chesapeake and Ohio into the pot and create an all-rail route system under one management from ocean to ocean. But by this time, "Uncle Mark" Hopkins had passed on, and Crocker and Stanford declined to come in.

At a directors' meeting of the new company, on February 18, 1885, Stanford was named president, Huntington and Crocker vice-president and second vice-president, respectively, Timothy Hopkins (Mark Hopkins's foster son), treasurer; J. C. Stubbs, traffic manager; A. N. Towne, general manager of the 3,004 miles of Pacific system lines west of El Paso and Ogden; and A. C. Hutchinson, manager of 1,692 miles of so-called "Atlantic system" lines east of El Paso.

For the next six decades, the stockholders of SP, or those who held their proxies, turned to Kentucky for the annual meeting.

To carry this phase of the story into modern times, the Kentucky headquarters, after a number of shifts, in the 1930s reached a place called Spring Station. There, at a curve of the road, in a little frame house with two chimneys and six square white pillars—just the sort of a house where somebody's grandmother would enjoy sitting on the porch and knitting—Southern Pacific "lived" a comfortable rocking-chair existence until 1947. It paid Kentucky about $100,000 a year in taxes in return for a spot to call "home."

But one day Kentucky informed the railroad that it owed $4,369,268 in personal property taxes for 1944, on an assessed valuation of $873,-853,756 worth of company stocks and bonds. Similar assessments were proposed for prior and subsequent years. With shrill, excited cries the company attorneys pointed out that all railroad property lay outside the state. While hearings were on, the Kentucky tax commission handed in another bill for $1,864,354 of income taxes for 1942, 1943, and 1944, and the state contended that income taxes in corresponding amounts should also be paid for subsequent years. The total amount of the state's claim was in excess of $20,000,000. That was enough. Southern Pacific paid Kentucky and Woodford County $4,001,693.90 in settlement of all tax claims, looked sadly on the home that had cost such a whopping rent, and moved its files and corporate address to Delaware.

The ranks of the Big Four had begun to thin.

The first to go was Mark Hopkins. He died on March 29, 1878, slipping off to sleep on a couch in his car at a siding in Yuma, Arizona, where he had gone to inspect the advancing rails of the Sunset Route. His mansion on San Francisco's Nob Hill was unfinished. The business affairs of his widow on the Coast were taken over by his foster son Timothy, and the Widow Hopkins, with Uncle Mark's millions in her purse, went east and married a youthful interior decorator named Edward T. Searles. Story had it that the marriage was brought about by the sly hand of Collis P. Huntington, who saw a way to obtain voting control of Uncle Mark's Big Four quarter interest, and who told first the widow, then the youthful decorator, that each was secretly enamored of the other. Anyway, Searles got the widow and Huntington got the proxies.

Charles Crocker died on August 14, 1888, at the fine new Del Monte Hotel which he and his associates had erected in a fairyland of natural beauty on the Monterey peninsula. He left a capable son, Charles Frederick Crocker, hard at work in the railroad organization.

Leland Stanford was to remain five more years, until June 21, 1893, but he had lost a beloved son in 1884 and was more interested in founding a university in the boy's memory, and moving back into the political limelight, than in running a railroad.

Huntington, the man who had wanted to quit back in 1872, who had written to Hopkins in 1874, "I would like so much to get out from under the load that I am carrying," remained grimly in harness. From his plain, cluttered office at 23 Broad Street, New York, he ran more and more railroads, took on more and more interests. A hard, lonely, severe, implacable man, he sat with a black silk skullcap perched on the top of his bald head and continued pulling strings, amassing power, piling up millions. After attaining national eminence, he summarized his own attainments in an interview: "I have never failed to do anything I started out to do. I could whip any boy in school, old or young. I excelled in geography. I never studied by books. I knew more geography than all of them. I was good at mathematics. Grammar always beat me, and has ever since."

Besides the SP, which he ruled from his office in New York with an iron hand, he had his Chesapeake and Ohio. The state of Virginia had nearly bankrupted itself in the endeavor to build a line of improvements from Hampton Roads, on lower Chesapeake Bay, to a connection with the navigable waters of the Ohio River. Huntington had taken hold of this and persevered when others withdrew, completing it to Memphis, 1,040 miles. After reaching Memphis, as one of a syndicate he built the Louisville, New Orleans and Texas from Memphis to New Orleans, where it connected wth the Southern Pacific to San Francisco. If anyone wanted to make a transcontinental journey on an all-Huntington system, from Newport News to the Golden Gate, he now could do it.

He was also interested in the United States and Brazil Steamship Company, the Old Dominion Steamship Company, the Pacific Improvement Company (through SP) and the Morgan Line, which operated some of the best freight ships running out of New York at the time and which later became the "Hundred Golden Hours at Sea" steamship service of Southern Pacific, flourishing until 1941.

He was president of the Pacific Mail Steamship Company, which he had picked up as previously told, and he was sole owner of the great shipbuilding plant at Newport News. The Mexican International Railroad was under his thumb. He owned the Kentucky Central and he controlled the San Antonio and Aransas Pass Railroad, the Houston East and West Texas, and the Houston and Texas Central. Docks at Galveston were constructed at his signal. The Pacific Improvement Company, of which he was an owner, held title among its other properties to a proposed railroad in Guatemala.

The New York *World* estimated in 1890 that there were thirty-five fortunes of $10,000,000 or more in the United States. It rated Huntington with $40,000,000, placing him after John D. Rockefeller, William W. Astor, Jay Gould, Cornelius Vanderbilt, and William Vanderbilt. It gave Stanford $30,000,000 and the estates of Mark Hopkins and Charles Crocker $25,000,000 each.

The lives of the last two of the original four were filled with private feuding. Huntington always had been impatient of Stanford's restful attitude toward railroad business—an attitude which the high-tension Huntington could not imitate. And when Stanford picked up a United States senatorship with the aid of the railroad machine, displacing Huntington's man to do it, the feud broke out in the open. Huntington angrily set aside Stanford as the SP's president and took the title which he had in name, but never in fact, relinquished years before.

Stanford died in 1893 while serving his second term as senator, two years after the opening of Stanford University on the sunny fields of his Palo Alto stock farm. Soon after, during the probate of his estate, the thorny question of those Central Pacific loans of the 1860s again came up. To what extent were the Big Four, or their estates, liable? The Stanford share could amount to $14,000,000.

The government swept down upon the widow, Jane Lathrop Stanford, with an injunction that would prevent distribution of Stanford's estate until the Central Pacific debt became due and was paid. That would have closed the little university which the Stanfords had built 30 miles south of San Francisco as a memorial to their son. Huntington watched coolly while the widow fought the case. The decision went to the Stanfords and the university. It was equally a victory for Huntington.

The sum due the government, as finally computed and paid in July, 1908, was about $58,813,000. By meeting the bill, Central Pacific and its successor and guarantor, Southern Pacific, preserved a status unusual among major American railroads—it never defaulted on a debt. That fact would have pleased Huntington, even though he had fought hard to save his railroad the money. But by 1908, the man in the black skullcap was past caring.

On August 13, 1900, death came to the last of the Big Four. By then the Southern Pacific system was operating more than 8,000 miles of railroad extending from Portland, Oregon, to Guaymas, Mexico, and from Pacific Coast cities to Ogden and New Orleans. With its steamship lines from Gulf ports to Havana and New York, it was then the longest and one of the major transportation systems of the country.

"I have always had a good time all my life," Huntington had said in his later years. "I have always been plotting—always had something to think about. I cannot remember when I was not doing something useful." At the time of his death an estimated 150,000 families supported themselves by his enterprises.

What became of the assemblage of interests gathered and watched over by this self-driving, often bone-tired railroad builder? Two-thirds of it went to his widow, one-third to his nephew, Henry E. Huntington. And then the widow and the nephew married. Ultimately the money found public usefulness in the notable library founded by Henry E. Huntington in San Marino, California.

As for the Huntington SP stock, it was gathered in early in 1901 by a rising new titan of the rails whom Huntington had known along "The Street," but perhaps never dreamed of as his successor. This quiet little man now took over.

16

And Then There Was Harriman

AT FORTY-NINE he was unknown to the public. At sixty-one he was dead. Within the eight-year span from 1901 to 1909, Edward Henry Harriman, son of a Long Island Episcopal minister, mastered and wielded control over the whole sprawling Southern Pacific railroad system. Yet such was the scope of his operations that the SP represented only a spur track, so to speak, of his transportation domain.

Huntington knew Harriman. The two had scurried up and down Wall Street and its environs for years, and during the last four years of Huntington's life Harriman had been the Union Pacific's boss. But Huntington would probably have been the most surprised man in the world if his crystal ball had told him that this tight-lipped, natty stockbroker was one day going to sit behind his Southern Pacific desk and that he was going to pour millions upon millions, and then still more millions, into rebuilding Huntington's railroad.

Whatever it was that had kept Harriman from opening the throttle of personal achievement until he was almost fifty, once he started he really opened up. In 1897 he was up there visible to all, riding high on the engineer's cushion, because in that year he moved into control of the bankrupt Union Pacific as the representative of a syndicate of bankers.

"But who is he?" people still wondered.

"I seem to remember," said others. "He's the fellow who put over that railroad deal in 1884 when he picked up a little shabby New York State railroad line, dusted it off, painted it up, waved it under the nose of the New York Central, and then snatched it back and sold it to the Pennsylvania."

"Oh, yes," said still others. "Wasn't he linked with Kuhn, Loeb and Company, Gould, Vanderbilt, and Fish in the affairs of the Illinois Central?" So it was recalled that Stuyvesant Fish had sponsored him in the

IC, and some Dutch investors in the line had shown marked confidence in his handling of their interests.

"And in 1887," remembered others, "he had shown up at a meeting of the Iowa Central, a line leased by Illinois Central, and by some smart parliamentary tactics had upset the great house of Drexel, Morgan and Company in a proxy showdown. Morgan was hopping mad!"

"That's right. And in 1890 he penned a report on the financial outlook which led the Illinois Central to duck into the storm cellar in time to escape the 1893 financial tornado."

But still, to the public at large, Harriman was only one more derby hat in the crowd. Few persons realized how much was under that hat.

Union Pacific went into receivership in 1893, just as Harriman had foreseen many businesses would do. In 1897 the UP was still in receivership, its physical plant in a bad way and its financial prospects particularly unhappy because the government debt, incurred in the sixties, had grown to about $53,000,000.

"The line needs one hundred millions to put it on its trucks and drivers. Maybe I can raise the money in Germany," said Jacob Schiff of Kuhn, Loeb and Company.

Retorted Harriman, "Why go to Germany? I can get it from Illinois Central." The Mississippi Valley line by that time had fine credit and, sure enough, would lend UP what it needed at lower interest than the Germans wanted.

That opened Schiff's eyes to Harriman's prowess. "Let's work together," said Schiff. They got up a syndicate and took over the busted UP.

"What you fellows have picked up," said Gen. G. M. Dodge, the engineer who had originally built the UP, "is two dirt-ballasted streaks of rust." Stations along the mountain grades, warned Dodge, were tumbledown shacks, and most of the equipment fit for the junk pile. Jay Gould had certainly been around there.

But Harriman, who was buying all the UP stock he could pick up, had a special train rigged with an observation car for his use. Seated on its rear platform, he had himself backed by daylight over the entire UP system. He scanned every detail that his busy eye could take in, returned to New York with a solid, impressive report, and took it to his directors. The fact that a Wall Street man had really gone out and studied his railroad made a big hit with the moneyed people—they had never heard anything like that factual report. They voted the diligent man $25,000,000 for new cuts, tunnels, bridges, and rolling stock. When the big new locomotives and big new freight cars arrived on the line and began operating over the reduced grades and curves, business so perked up that by June, 1900, two and a half years after taking charge, Harriman was able to declare a UP dividend. He had meanwhile tried to buy Central Pacific from the SP and fit it organically to the UP, of which it was a geographical extension, but SP wouldn't sell.

Huntington died two months after the UP declared its dividend. Harriman went to the rugged old SP chieftain's funeral. He observed there the Huntington widow and the nephew. Whether he scented a romance or not, he evidently smelled out the fact that the Huntington estate would soon be willing to part with its SP stock. As UP had restored its own credit, he mortgaged it for $100,000,000, and with that for a war bag he started buying out the Huntingtons and others. Within seven months he had about 37.5 per cent of SP. By the summer of 1901 he controlled one million shares, or 45.49 per cent. In April he had placed himself in the chair of SP's executive committee. In September he took over the presidency.

But here was no Gould, blighting everything he touched. Here was a man whose touch was energizing and vitalizing. The silent Wall Street broker, who had been all over the UP lines on a train running backward, took the SP's Julius Kruttschnitt of San Francisco back to New York with him and sat him down and picked his brains, until Harriman the broker knew to the last bolt and tie what Kruttschnitt, general manager of the SP, had craved for years: for Kruttschnitt wanted a better railroad.

"How much do you need to start with?" asked Harriman.

"Eighteen millions," mentioned Kruttschnitt, getting ready to leave.

In two hours with SP's directors, Harriman obtained the first eighteen millions of a huge betterment program for the delighted Kruttschnitt.

"Spend it in a week, if you can," Harriman ordered.

Kruttschnitt did not spend it in a week—he was not raised in that kind of school—but he poured it out in a good lively way. Three big projects went through within a couple of years. One was a series of tunnels and nearly 10 miles of track-straightening out of San Francisco. Another was a 60-mile cutoff between Burbank and Montalvo in the Los Angeles region. A third was an attack on Great Salt Lake itself. When the Lucin Cutoff of 103 miles was finished, in 1903, it left the original Central Pacific line far to the north.

Between these feats Harriman put on his spectacular razzle-dazzle, the fight in 1901 with Jim Hill and J. P. Morgan for control of the Burlington and the Northern Pacific, but that gets beyond the boundaries of this story. Harriman lost that brush, but he made history in Wall Street while doing it; he brought down the wrath of the Theodore Roosevelt administration on the whole national railroad setup, and he helped pave the way for the drastic reforms of the Hepburn Act.

By 1907, Harriman was in control of Illinois Central, Union Pacific,

Southern Pacific, Oregon Railway and Navigation, Oregon Short Line, and the new line from Salt Lake City down to Los Angeles and tidewater. He had steamship lines, coal fields, oil fields, and street railways.

"What this country should recognize is that the 'community of interest' principle between many of the railroads really exists," he declared. By this he meant that each railroad should buy up stock in others in which it had traffic arrangements or whose competition it dreaded. Through the "community of interest" policy of investment of railroad funds in other railroads, he soon had control of important chunks of New York Central, Baltimore and Ohio, Chicago and Alton, and Santa Fe. When an anxious government, worried by this trend toward monopoly, posed him the query, "You might spread not only over the Pacific Coast, but spread out over the Atlantic Coast?" he replied tersely, "Yes."

Maybe he would have done it. Other men, including Huntington, had dreamed of a closely integrated coast-to-coast all-rail transportation system, but none was so close to putting it over as E. H. Harriman. But, however big his plans, and however practical, they ended with his sudden death on September 9, 1909. The ambitious, late-starting man had been scorching the ballast too fast.

Yet, in his brief run, this enigmatic Wall Streeter had developed into a remarkably sound railroader, speeding up his trains, increasing their loads, their frequency, their convenience.

He had ruled Southern Pacific for only eight years. He had expended on it a rousing $240,000,000.

When Harriman took hold of the SP, veteran officials of the line were not slow to point out the grades and curves that had been unavoidable in the construction days, and had not been eliminated in subsequent years for lack of money.

"Straighten the line and reduce grades!" ordered Harriman briskly.

That suited the veterans. Kruttschnitt pointed out to him the long curving sweep of the line around the north end of Great Salt Lake. This curve added 44 miles to the distance between Sacramento and Ogden.

"Get it out of there!" commanded Harriman, rocketing over the rails in his special train.

So, in March of 1902, the work began of establishing trestle and fill across the broad inland sea. November of 1903 found the causeways extending from the east and west shores coming together near the center of the lake. Although the depth of the lake along the causeway reaches only 32 feet, its appetite for rock proved almost insatiable. Twenty miles of fill and twelve miles of trestle went into the project. The unstable bottom had gulped not only astronomical tons of rock, but often threatened the piles and construction tracks themselves. "Keep dumping," insisted Harriman. "Fill it up!" And filled it became. The new route was opened to traffic in 1904, two years after work started, and the cutoff as a whole extended for 103 miles between Lucin and Ogden, leaving the spot at Promontory, where CP and UP had joined rails in 1869, far off the new railroad map.

A souvenir of the big construction job was a tiny "town" left by the railroad out in the middle of Utah's inland sea. Camps for construction workers had been built at intervals along the trestle and one of them, formerly "Camp 20," grew to be known as Midlake. It lasted for forty-one years. Once it had a population of 30 souls. The town was a row of houses set atop piling. The platform area was about 80 yards long and 40 feet wide. The single track which passed over the trestle fanned out into three tracks through Midlake—main line, siding, and spur. "Main Street" was the track of the Overland Route.

At Midlake trainmen received their orders and section men made their homes. Three lady telegraphers also called it home. But the three girl brass-pounders were shifted elsewhere in 1945, when centralized traffic control from the shore line went into effect, and Midlake became one more Western ghost town.

Today the Lucin Cutoff is a weird, out-of-this-world ruled line that cuts straight across the uncanny inland sea. It is the epitome of desolation and lonesomeness. Yet there is a certain beauty about it. Frank Call, who is a labor inspector at Ogden but used to be a section foreman along the track that spans Great Salt Lake, discovered some of this beauty one day and began picking up bits of the salt crystals that formed on the trestle piling and in the grains of sand in the fill.

"I noticed that the sand on the great flats was round instead of sharp like ordinary sand," he reported. "I looked at some through a microscope and what I saw was amazing—each grain of sand had become a beautiful pearl." From the government geologists in Washington, D.C., he learned that these sands are called "oolites" and each grain contains a fossilized single-cell plant. He sent a cluster to the museum in Salt Lake City and soon was sending them to schools, universities, and other museums.

Peppered through the rock he found petrified cone coral, and in the mud off the flats he found selenite, which crystallizes in pentagon-shaped designs. Much of this is fluorescent, throwing off yellow, pink, and red shades.

One would hardly expect to find rock in ballast that would be worth a polish, but parts of the SP's Salt Lake roadbed are literally ballasted with gem stones. Which puts it in the class with the roadbed over the Sierra—right on top of Mother Lode gold.

But overland trains and freights are in a hurry, and to railroaders'
eyes the real beauty of the Salt Lake Causeway is what Harriman foresaw
there—a level, straight, undeviating line.

When nature selected the site for the city of San Francisco, it ringed
it with ocean, Golden Gate, and bay on three sides and a range of bulky
hills on the fourth. The original rail outlet of the town wound through
these hills on a kind of rabbit course. It was not the sort of a route a
mind like Harriman's would long put up with, and in 1904 the little
stockbroker with the big ideas began to nibble at those hills to southward with shovels and scrapers. Bridges were built, parts of the bay's
edge were filled in, five tunnels were bored for a total of 10,000 feet, and
money was poured at the rate of a million dollars a mile. The 10-mile
Bayshore Cutoff became a reality in 1907.

The restless mind of E. H. Harriman had left few portions of the West
unexplored as fields for rail development; his survey parties were out
everywhere. One of his conceptions was a line across Oregon from
west to east, forking on the east side of the Cascades with a $39,000,000
new main line running south to Klamath Falls, and the eastern prong
intercepting the Union Pacific in the Malheur country west of Snake River.
The scheme was simply a few miles of track, a survey, and some lines on
a map when Harriman died, and the actual railroad is not there yet, but
the cross-state idea appealed powerfully to Oregonians and in course of
time it became a fighting issue that involved, in the end, four big transcontinentals. The way of it was this:

Harriman saw, east of Oregon's Cascade Mountains, an area that constituted about the biggest domain left in the United States that did not
have a railroad. He ordered Union Pacific interests to build from Idaho
westward and be ready to tie in with the Oregon Eastern, an SP affiliate,
that was to come steaming from the vicinity of Eugene. The Oregon
Eastern was formed in 1905. When Harriman died, the government set
its legal axmen to work on the tie-up between UP and SP, and Oregon
Eastern languished. Meanwhile its tracks from Natron to Oakridge were
visible reminders of a line that not only would have sped eastward to
the Malheur and the Snake, but also would have driven one prong south.
The SP's engineers and operating men never could think of that projected
southern prong of the east-of-the-Cascades line without choking with sor-
row, for it would have meant a shorter, faster, less steep, and less curved
route between California and Portland.

That is the way things remained until 1915, when a former Harriman

man, who had been manager of some SP interurban lines out of Portland, tried his hand as a lone-wolf promoter.

Robert E. Strahorn had done considerable promotional work for the Harriman system, though now he was on his own. In "Central Oregon," on the dry side of the evergreen Cascades, he beheld a region 125 miles wide by 165 miles long. Several lines tapped its corners. The Oregon Trunk and the Des Chutes Railway Company, the latter representing Union Pacific interests, had built from the Columbia River southward to Bend, Oregon. The Southern Pacific was at Klamath Falls. The Nevada-California-Oregon narrow gauge connected Reno with Lakeview, Oregon. And the Oregon Short Line branch had advanced from the eastern side of Oregon up Malheur Canyon to Crane. Within those four points was country that had lumber, billions of feet of it, and livestock, and possibilities for dry grain farming.

Strahorn found himself the speaker at mass meetings at various points around the virgin tract. Here was a man, people decided, with rails in his pockets and plans in his head. Portland paid heed. Portland would like to be in on any movement that tapped the promising new region. It resulted in the Oregon, California and Eastern, with Strahorn as its president and personally empowered to lay out his line where he pleased.

After considering the various communities which wanted to be the jumping-off point, Strahorn temporarily settled upon Bend. True, the Des Chutes line and the Oregon Trunk were there, but they had not shown any inclination to go farther—and there was all that timber, 17,000,000,000 board feet by estimate; all that wool, and beef, and potential grain. He announced his intention to build 75 miles southward from Bend at once. Bend was delighted.

But Klamath Falls was not. Klamath Falls was on the opposite, south side of the vacant quadrangle. Klamath Falls had railroad service of sorts from the SP, but it, too, had long been looking north and dreaming of empire. The businessmen of Klamath Falls hitched up and drove the long, winding, bumpy way to Bend, through November weather, laid hold of promoter Strahorn, and started back with him through snowdrifts and driving sleet to show him what a real live town could do.

They got Strahorn through the snows and into the arms of a meeting of 400 citizens, who proved that they meant business by contributing $300,000, a 40-mile right-of-way, and a strip of land for a terminal in the heart of town.

That won Strahorn and his line for Klamath Falls and left Bend desolate. It meant that the produce of the Deschutes, instead of going northward to the Columbia, would go south to California, or east via Ogden. It changed the whole tilt of commerce for that region.

However, a mass meeting and a terminal and even $300,000 are not an operating railroad. Not by many millions. Strahorn ran into all the difficulties to which railroad promoters are heir, and a few variations besides. The always scanty rainfall of the Deschutes country became, for a period of years, almost nonexistent. The SP, which might have helped him, got into a cat-and-dog fight with the Union Pacific over an issue that could have shattered the SP system into a million slivers. And America went into World War I. Still, Strahorn built part of his line. It amounted to about 40 miles and it had 3 locomotives and 75 freight cars. It occupied portions of southeastern Oregon between Klamath Falls and Lakeview.

The violent controversy over the legal right of the SP system to exist came to an end, releasing the energies of that company for new enterprises. Strahorn saw his opportunity. He swiftly sold his meandering line to the SP. That seemed to leave the area between Bend and Klamath Falls to its fate, unless the SP went ahead with Harriman's so-called Natron Cutoff east of the Cascades, construction on which was resumed in September, 1923. Then suddenly the whole Deschutes region broke into the news again, this time at Bend. A ghostly head, with whiskers—the shade of James J. Hill—shoved through the very center of the eastern Oregon map.

The Great Northern–Northern Pacific joint subsidiary known as the Oregon Trunk, which had built from the Columbia southward to Bend sixteen years before, wanted to build still farther. Northern Pacific was not interested, but Great Northern was. Equally to the point, the new transcontinental known as the Western Pacific, which had reached California by the Feather River Canyon and completed trackage to San Francisco Bay, wanted to build northward to meet the Oregon Trunk.

Down in San Francisco, SP officials had chills up and down their neatly tailored spines. If this combination worked, here came Great Northern trains practically right down to Market Street.

SP was at work on the Natron Cutoff when the Great Northern action was taken. Hurriedly SP prepared to rush it through.

But Oregon Trunk got permission to build south from Bend to Klamath Falls and on to a place called Bieber; Western Pacific to build from Keddie, north. It looked as if the Great Northern entry into the bay cities was a certainty. About all the SP could do was yield joint use privileges on its Natron Cutoff tracks to the Great Northern, in order to prevent the construction of a competing line north of Klamath Falls.

In 1926 SP's new $39,000,000 Natron Cutoff, or Cascade Line, was opened to freight and local traffic, and to all through traffic in the following year. It was 25 miles shorter than the old Siskiyou Line and much gentler riding.

So that's the way it is now—if you're people in a hurry or through freight, you go by Cascade Line; if you're pears from Medford, you go by Siskiyou.

As for SP's set-to with the Great Northern–Western Pacific combination, things didn't turn out as badly as they had looked. Great Northern, building south from Klamath Falls, had relatively inexpensive going. But Western Pacific, building from Keddie north, ran into a mess of tunnel-boring and gorge-bridging that cost $15,000,000 to $18,000,000 of borrowed dollars. Western Pacific landed in receivership. To date there never has been regularly scheduled through passenger service via Great Northern and the Western Pacific from the Columbia River to San Francisco Bay.

But the Natron Cutoff, renamed the Cascade Line, is the main track of the SP nowadays from California points to Portland.

Harriman left the Southern Pacific in a notably improved physical state, but—as events soon proved—in a desperate legal morass. For Harriman, when he acquired SP control in behalf of UP, had committed the sin of bigness. Theodore Roosevelt's Department of Justice began to look hard at that UP-SP fusion, and to question its right to exist.

What followed was a suit to force the UP to disgorge its SP stock. The suit was begun in 1908, and five years later the government won a victory. The Supreme Court ordered the UP to sell. Huntington's old holdings, that for a few years had been so snugly lodged in the UP treasury, were sold to the four winds, and SP and UP were back in their old relationship —partners in the central overland route, and bitter contenders for business over their other routes.

17

Kicked Out of Politics

THE SOUTHERN CALIFORNIA land and immigration boom of the eighties, fostered by the SP–Santa Fe rate war, had had its counterpart north of Tehachapi without any railroad rivalry to spur it on, but only the desire of the SP to fill up that vacant valley, develop traffic, and realize on its land. Settlers responded by trainloads. They brought their plows, livestock, household equipment. They detrained at bare little stations that were nothing but sheds and signboards in the wind-swept waste.

The San Joaquin is favored soil, but it has to be farmed by methods that the new arrivals discovered by trial and error. Mainly it needed water through ditches that connected with the short, surging streams descending from the Sierra. These newcomers led hard lives, as do pioneers every-where, but their crops began to be surprising. But the railroad that had prevailed upon them to come, that had hauled them at low rates and put them on the land, turned out to be a relentless muscle man of a partner. There were explosive situations where legal titles to farms were not sup-plied by the railroad as promised, or so the settlers believed, and this after the settlers had put in their improvements. There was revolt, hatred, blood-shed, banditry.

This agrarian anger at the railroad eventually boiled up into the bloody tussle known as the Battle of Mussel Slough. Some 600 settlers, in 1876, had petitioned the government to restore to public entry the portion of the Southern Pacific's land grant lying along the 140 miles between Hol-lister, in San Benito County, and Goshen, in Tulare. They claimed that they had made the land fruitful with 50 miles of irrigation ditches, and that the railroad, which never had laid its tracks there, had announced title to these lands after the developments were made.

In 1878 a mass meeting at Hanford resulted in the organization of a settlers' league. The settlers offered to buy the land from the government at $2.50 an acre, but grimly refused to buy it at the railroads' steeper prices. The railroad company brought suits of ejectment, and won out. But prior to the court decision, masked and armed men of the soil had been patrolling the region like a military force.

In 1880, when a United States marshal attempted to place purchasers of railroad lands in possession, six settlers were wounded and the two railroad purchasers killed. The coroner's jury, a local panel, resolved that "the responsibility of the shedding of innocent blood rests upon the Southern Pacific railroad company," and the uproar that rang through the West did the railroad no good. The five settlers who were convicted of resisting the marshal were greeted, upon their release from prison, by a couple thousand persons at Hanford in public celebration.

The whole disastrous episode had its roots in the uncertain land titles of the time, such uncertainty being due to both the railroad's arbitrary alteration of its proposed route and the settler's determination to break fruitful lands to the plow without waiting wearisome years to find out who owned what.

That was the kind of a struggle the railroad managers thought they understood thoroughly. They fought back, as they had always fought, hurling everything except the drive wheels and the caboose. Nor is there any point in blaming it all on Stanford or Huntington. Every executive was in it; the railroad staff was often just plain overzealous, as well as ornery and stupid. Power blinds its possessors, and power was what they had. At the turn of the century a clever young novelist named Frank Norris wrapped up the whole harsh story of the San Joaquin railroad tyranny in a novel called *The Octopus,* and it made a big impression. To this day, though the novel is seldom read, its title is remembered, and the word itches like a sliver or sticks like an arrow in the more delicate portions of the SP's hide.

This sort of dissatisfaction with the deal they were getting from the railroads was a common quality of farmers all over the Western two-thirds of the nation, and had been so for years. Most of the Western lines had pushed the sale of their lands by wide advertising, public speakers, and excursions. From the Dakotas to Texas, speculative land companies had sprung up, taking over hundreds of thousands of acres and high-pressuring their sale to farmers in Europe and America. Crop failures, depressions, drought, and the plain skullduggery or inefficiency of the railroads helped to inflame the settlers against them because they were the most prominent thing on the landscape, and the easiest to hit.

When the prices of farm products dropped, and railroad rates did not instantly follow suit, the farmers began holding mass meetings. They were land-poor, they had been led to expect too much, nobody had mentioned the vagaries of weather and price cycles, and Populism had raised its head.

A long step forward was taken in 1887, when a Federal Interstate Commerce Act went into effect prohibiting pooling, or rate agreements between railroads; special rates; rebates; discrimination in favor of persons, localities, and particular products; and changes of rates without notice. Though abuses continued, and there was still a route to travel through the courts, a beginning had been made.

In 1879 the wrath of the citizenry of California against the SP took the form of a march to the polls and the adoption of a new state constitution, the chief blessing of which was believed to lie in a Board of Railroad Commissioners whose duty should be to regulate the fares and freight schedules of "all railroads" doing business in California. The three commissioners were cloaked with almost regal powers, and refusal to conform to their legal orders was to cost the offender up to $20,000 fine and two years in the penitentiary.

The new constitution went through with a whoop. But it soon dawned upon the people that a majority of the men elected to fill the responsible office of Railroad Commissioner were invariably put there by the railroads. Parties contended; faces changed; board after board came in and went out; but the regulation of fares and freight rates never seemed to concern the commissioners very much.

In 1891 a British ship sailed into the Golden Gate with a cargo that had been exported from New York to San Francisco via Antwerp in order to keep it out of coastwise classification. The average saving of freight charges on this and the cargoes of fifteen other vessels that tried the device were estimated to be over four dollars a ton. The SP bitterly fought the issue in Federal court, and in the case of "The United States versus 250 Kegs of Nails," the nails, and shippers, won. But Congress promptly amended the law governing intercoastal shipping to make this victory valueless.

Not Southern Pacific only, but the whole Transcontinental Association of Railroads were ranged against any attempt to break the rail rates by recourse to the sea. The Pacific Mail and the Occidental and Oriental Steamship lines continued to be closely controlled by Eastern and Western rail interests.

The answer, it became apparent to the people in the northern part of the state of California, lay in setting up some rail competition.

The upshot, during the hard times following the panic of 1893, was the San Francisco and San Joaquin Valley Railway, sponsored by the sugar king Claus Spreckels and several resoundingly named organizations. Powered by the press, a Traffic Association of California, a League of

Progress, the North American Navigation Company, and a Merchants' Shipping Association set forth to drum up subscriptions. Nothing was too small—a barber put up $1, a bootblack $2.50, a blacksmith $5.

The bill of grievances was a lusty one. Wheat raising, horticulture, and mining were the leading industries, but the men who engaged in these pursuits charged that after a year's hard work they had the labor and the production, but the railroad had the profits. It was claimed that the sections of the state that revolted against the iron rule of the transportation monopoly were punished for their insolence by reprisals in the shape of exorbitant tariffs.

It took a clothbound 200-page book to list the bright prospects and the subscription roll to the "Valley Railroad." And the project accomplished something, too. It built from Stockton to Bakersfield, started a branch on toward Richmond on San Francisco Bay, made money, and knocked rates down. In 1898 it was gulped up by the Santa Fe, which was only too glad to have that entry down the big interior valley and on toward the bay. And there was the SP monopoly in northern California, broken at last.

By the turn of the century, America had renewed its faith in certain virtues which the money-mad business kings of four decades had almost crushed. The 1900s were a decade of revolt. Theodore Roosevelt, in the White House, thundered against "malefactors of great wealth." Effective regulation of transportation companies flowered into the Hepburn Act and the revivified Interstate Commerce Commission.

In California, where the Southern Pacific had its roots and from which it drew so much of its nourishment, the reformers had had a chance to learn something of the art of practical politics in a long running fight with the noisome Ruef-Schmitz machine of San Francisco; a fight that resulted in the commitment of little rat-faced Abe Ruef to the penitentiary, and the steeling of one of his prosecutors, Hiram Johnson, for an attack on bigger game.

Hiram was the son of Grove L. Johnson, from time beyond memory a handyman for the SP's lawyers and political jugglers. But the son of old Grove L. was an astute politician, too. He was an opportunist with long insight into what was good for Hiram Johnson and what was good for the public—and ultimately, for the railroad itself. And he was a great tribune of the people—a sort of poor man's Teddy Roosevelt, in whose mantle he wrapped himself. He correctly adjudged the time ripe for attacking the railroad dictatorship and turned a campaign for the governorship into one of the hottest ever. He won out resoundingly on the slogan of "kicking the Southern Pacific out of politics." The victory was complete. Never was there such an exodus of lobbyists and political termites and teredos from a state capital. Johnson appointed a newly implemented railroad commission, swept every railroad job-holder out of public office, and smashed the old order completely.

It was the end of something that had already died, but had been maintained like a propped-up corpse. Johnson went on to become a United States Senator and, if he had accepted the Republican vice-presidential nomination that was offered, would have become President at Harding's death. Hi missed that one.

But from Johnson's era onward, the Southern Pacific railroad turned to being a railroad—that and nothing more. And, because it was big and strong and able, and had only one thing to think about—running its trains safely and profitably—it proceeded to do a great job. And truly phenomenal was the way public opinion swung around. For the whole populace knew what Huntington, for all his sagacity, never realized: You don't beat folks into loving you, and you don't buy them. You woo them.

The new relationship between railroad and public proved its value a few years later. Union Pacific long complained, when UP and SP were under different managements, that when SP originated any coastal business, it diverted that traffic if possible over the Sunset Route. For by sending it through New Orleans instead of Ogden, SP kept most of the pie. So UP, smarting under the spanking it had taken when forced to sell its Harriman-acquired SP stock, looked over the SP setup and decided that the SP, through its control of Central Pacific, was in exactly the same state of vulnerability UP had been in when it possessed SP.

Ownership and control of the Central Pacific and Southern Pacific by the same men had been in effect since October 12, 1870; from that date onward the two corporated names had been used interchangeably whenever it suited the CP-SP's managers.

And suddenly the government sued to oblige the Southern Pacific Company of Kentucky to sell all its Central Pacific Railway Company stock.

It was a neat twitch to the rug upon which SP stood, and SP was under no doubt as to who was doing the twitching. While SP danced, floundered, and tried to regain its balance, lawyers of both sides got ready.

The SP's legal staff contended that the government was not entering the fray in good faith—that it had been cognizant of the nature of the CP-SP organism from the beginning; that the Sherman Antitrust Law of 1890 had gone into effect five years after the lease of the Central Pacific was made to the Southern Pacific and twenty years after common control had become a matter of public record; that the government, in 1899, had become a willing party to the situation by accepting the SP's guarantee of the

CP's indebtedness, and over the ensuing ten years had set seal to its approval by accepting the SP's checks.

It all was swept aside by the Supreme Court, which in 1917 upset a decision of the United States District Court in SP's favor. On May 29, 1922, a very bleak day for the western road, the nine justices put on their black robes and decreed that the SP must sell its CP stock. The matter was ordered back to the District Court for determination of procedure. And there was the SP, ordered to chop itself, twig by twig and branch by branch, and strew the bits about, with here and there a chunk of trunk. And where would be the West's chief rail transportation system?

Then occurred the most surprising uprising of mass public opinion in favor of a corporation that the West ever has witnessed. Businessmen, travelers, chambers of commerce, public bodies, and private interests of all kinds, rendered aghast at the transportation chaos which threatened the Coast, leaped into the fight. The SP had often had cause to feel that it was something less than loved in the regions which it served. But now it discovered that, in its hour of threatened smashup, it was roundly appreciated.

The public relations people of the railroad, working under President Paul Shoup, had some hand in the creation of this outcry of public indignation against the threatened chopping up of the big outfit into inch-long bits. But it was the shippers who put on the show. They flourished maps which showed that the transportation system of the West, if put under the pruning knife as proposed, would be just a lot of unrelated trackage with its ends hanging in the air. It was pointed out that the proposed dismemberment would break up the gathering system essential to getting the cars into trainload lots preparatory to sending them eastward. That it would break up the system of passenger-train connections. That it would invite the Union Pacific to move in and get a monopolistic grip on the West. That the West's big transportation outfit, which had grown up as an indigenous system adjusted to Western needs, would be turned loose to become tail ends of Eastern systems. That flourishing towns and valleys would lose direct communication lines with each other and with the East. That nothing but chaos, confusion, and upheaval would result. In short, that scrambled eggs just would not go back in the shell.

Congress had already paved the way for the salvation of the SP system. The Transportation Act, passed in 1920 as a general revision of the Act to Regulate Commerce, authorized the Interstate Commerce Commission, among other matters, to approve the acquisition or retention of control of one railroad by another, in the public interest. The enactment of these provisions does not appear to have been directly related to the government's suit involving the Central Pacific ownership. On the contrary, they were enacted as a part of a general policy to vest in the commission a new type of jurisdiction over the financing and control of railroad common carriers, to give the commission a controlling voice with respect to the consolidation of railroads, and to facilitate the creation of a limited number of consolidated railroad systems. But in 1919 and 1920, when this legislation was under consideration by Congress, the tendency of the anti-trust suit was well known to the members of the Congressional committees considering the matter, and the potentialities of the suit undoubtedly had an influence upon the drafting and passage of these provisions of the Transportation Act.

So, following the Supreme Court decision of May 29, 1922, the ICC acted with reasonable speed. On February 6, 1923, it handed down a decision: "Upon the whole record we find that the acquisition of control of the Central Pacific by the Southern Pacific Company, by lease and stock ownership as asked in the application, will be in the public interest."

Dismemberment had been averted. The big, busy, complex, highly integrated transportation system had been saved.

Southern Pacific was ordered, however, to join with UP in maintaining its Ogden Route as one continuous line, with neither SP nor UP discriminating against each other in favor of any other connection, and SP undertaking to solicit business for maximum traffic over the Ogden Route in the whole area between Tehachapi and Oregon.

Shaken by the ordeal, SP put the ten-year battle for existence behind it and went on to other things. It had learned a thumping lesson. It had learned the value of public opinion. The experience of finding itself backed by a phalanx of well-wishers had been stunning and enlightening.

It meant that a brand-new era had opened in Western railroading. Huntington would have been puzzled by this new order. But Huntington had never been stretched on a rack and all but dismembered with UP holding the scalpel. His successors had had that unpleasant experience.

18

South of the Border

THE MAIN FRAMEWORK of Southern Pacific, as it stands today, had been pretty well established by 1887, when the railroad had completed its Overland Route, its Sunset, and its Shasta. But its 5,500 miles of main line were to be tripled in the subsequent years as supplementary lines and spurs were flung out here and there or existing lines acquired. At first there was some narrow gauge to be ripped out and broad gauge substituted. There were heavier rails to be laid as trains increased in length and weight. There were curves to be reduced, bridges rebuilt, tunnels eliminated.

One of the spectacular pieces of new construction was the building of the Southern Pacific line down the West Coast south of Arizona and up to the plateau of central Mexico.

Today the journey over this 1,100-mile line south of Nogales is quite simple—you leave Los Angeles on an evening and are in Guadalajara about seventy-one hours later. En route you have more than a glimpse of the picturesque and colorful.

For this rail trip takes you deep into a foreign land. Geographically the "SP de Mex" stabs below the Tropic of Cancer, putting its terminus on a line with Havana and Honolulu.

It is a wonderful trip, though bumpy. The land of the serape and the burro unfolds itself under the glittering blue sky directly the international customs barrier is passed at Nogales. Some wild rocky country is climbed just south of Nogales, the desert of northern Sonora offers its pipe-organ cacti and its tawny mountains, Hermosillo with its orange orchards is an oasis, and the deep-sea fishermen get their gear ready and detrain at Empalme to take the side trip to Guaymas.

But if you're not bound for the marlin, sailfish, and albacore fishing grounds, or the glittering hotel Playa de Cortes down on Guaymas Beach, you rattle on, with every mile growing increasingly Mexican. You stay with your train into the tropics, and arrive at the station serving Mazatlán, a coastwise city of tiled houses and coco palms and two-wheeled carts, and one of the prettiest bays anywhere. The temperature, however, is apt to send the traveler scurrying back into his air-conditioned train.

Beyond Mazatlán the train continues through steamy jungle, where flowers riot and the air is perfumed. Then, climbing, you pause at Tepic, which is a slumberous little town 3,000 feet up. The houses still have their street balconies the way the conquistadores hung them there. Beyond Tepic your dusty varnish string strains and creaks on rising rails, through tunnels and over roaring streams. Fifteen miles of track hereabouts rested, at one time, on ties of solid mahogany. The sixty miles of barranca construction took thousands of men four years to accomplish and cost the railroad $14,000,000.

At one point the train nudges a cliffside a thousand feet below the barranca rim and fifteen hundred feet above its foamy stream bed. The train puffs out at last upon the uplands at a town named Tequila, and as this is where the powerful white liquor of that name is made, passengers get off—and buy and buy. A squirt of this distillation of the maguey cactus into the boilers of the engine, it is said, would lift the train over Popocatepetl. The SP's line comes to an exhausted end at Guadalajara, which is overnight from Mexico City by the line of the National Railways of Mexico. It is a town of some 383,000 persons, exactly a mile above the sea, distinguished for pottery and glass and arcaded shops and one of the gayest, most fantastic cathedrals ever conceived, and for its Lake Chapala and its dry climate. Many travelers, who find Mexico City a little too much false Paris, consider Guadalajara more Mexican.

Back in 1882, the Mexican International Railroad Company was formed to build a line from Piedras Negras (across the Rio Grande from Eagle Pass, Texas) to the Pacific Coast, with Mazatlán as the projected terminal. Construction began the following year, and Torreon was reached five years later. During this time, SP acquired most of the stock then outstanding, and C. P. Huntington became president. Durango was as far as the line went—540 miles—toward Mazatlán, and from that time on (1892) construction was limited to a connection to Monterrey and various branches, bringing the total mileage to some 900 miles when the stock was sold to the National Railways of Mexico in 1910.

Going back to the West Coast: the Sonora Railway, previously operated by the Santa Fe, was taken over by Southern Pacific in 1897. Construction lapsed until the Harriman regime. It got under way south from Empalme Junction near Guaymas in 1905, and also north from Mazatlán in 1907. The engineering drive was provided by Col. Epes Randolph.

Five years later trains were running over the 669 miles of new track from Empalme to Tepic.

The warlike decade 1910–1920, when Mexico seethed with revolution, halted further construction and made operation of the completed section difficult. In a nine-year period the 105-mile section north of Tepic could be operated for a total of only five months.

There remained a gap of 102 miles from Tepic to La Quemada to be built before trains could be operated from Los Angeles all the way through.

One of the Yaqui uprisings against the government lasted for months, and a number of railroad men, mostly linemen, were killed. That was in 1926. Recalled J. A. Small, who later went on to become president of "SP de Mex," "On one occasion I was on top of a pole, repairing the telephone line, when I spotted three Indians in the brush with rifles. They were watching me, but as they made no move I finished repairing the line and left. When I arrived at the next station I found that the line had again been cut. That night I received a note from the Yaqui chief which read: 'Do not climb poles and fix lines again; if we did not recognize you it might be dangerous.' "

As lineman or as president, Small had winning ways, for he became friends with the Yaqui general Pluma Blanca, and was permitted to travel through that general's territory without molestation, a privilege granted to no other person but Indians.

Small managed to maintain contacts with every president of Mexico from 1910 to 1949, besides enjoying the favor of such revolutionists as Villa, Orozco, and Maytorena. During the revolution of 1911–1912 Small and his co-workers were ambushed but escaped injury. Many times they were captured by one faction or the other. In a sixty-day period, 200 bridges were burned. In the tough years up to 1928, trains were wrecked, crews and passengers killed, and road gangs annihilated. However, for the past twenty-three years all has been tranquil along the line of "SP de Mex."

Completion of the 102 miles between Tepic and La Quemada involved some of the heaviest railroad construction ever undertaken. The tough going was in the upland barranca or gorge country, a lava region which rails had to penetrate before they could break out upon the plateau that contains Mexico's large cities. Thirty-two tunnels had to be driven through the volcanic debris. In 1927 the "bullfighters'" job was done, and the first trains operated over the 1,103-mile through line from Nogales to Guadalajara.

The line makes Southern Pacific an international railroad, and once you pass Nogales there is not a doubt of it. Even the porters are "bullfighters." But the whiskbroom is still there.

19

Down the Radiant Shore Line

WHILE HIGHBALLING across the Southwest, we left the Coast Line stymied at two points south and east of Monterey Bay. Those points were Tres Pinos, a hamlet in the San Benito Valley of the Coast Range, and Soledad, a mission town 142 miles below San Francisco.

"Don't spend a cent if you can help it!" had been the spirit of Huntington's orders in those lean days of national panic. Tools had been laid down at Tres Pinos in 1873.

The original route planned for the SP was to have carried it over the Coast Range from Tres Pinos to Goshen Junction in the San Joaquin Valley, 140 miles southeast. In anticipation of this meet-up, 40 miles of track were laid from Goshen Junction westward to a point called Huron. But any hopes Tres Pinos, Goshen, and Huron had of becoming places of earth-shaking importance were laid aside when Stanford made a quick inspection.

"Where's the local business to come from?" he asked.

"There isn't any," he was informed.

"What's on the other side of these steep hills?"

"The *llano verde,* green plain. It's quite empty."

"Run the line somewhere else."

Man's eyesight had not yet penetrated through the crust of dry earth on the east side of the Coast Range to show the wonderful oil deposits of Coalinga and Kettleman Hills, which such a line would have traversed.

The railroad builders moved on and eventually did drive the other, or Soledad, prong through to Southern California. But by the end of the seventies, the coastal SP still only ran from San Francisco to Soledad where a daily line of stages connected for Santa Barbara, 200 miles off to the south.

When rails did reach Santa Barbara seven years later, they came from the opposite direction. During 1887 an extension was built from Saugus, north of Los Angeles, westward through Santa Paula and Ventura and up the shore line. The whole population of Santa Barbara turned out one August day to view the arrival of the iron horse at the brand-new station. "Here it comes!" shouted someone, and hats of many kinds—sombreros, straws, and derbies—were flung in the air.

While Santa Barbara celebrated the opening of its connection with Los Angeles and points east, the line southward from Soledad continued with truly Spanish leisureliness. King City was reached, and oak-studded Paso Robles. Then there interposed the rugged grades of the Santa Lucia Mountains, a spur of the Coast Range that brought the civil engineers together in some serious huddles, for those grades were steep. To this day, helper locomotives are required to lift the trains, and there is a tunnel that for years, before air conditioning, was guaranteed to gas the most earnest sleeper.

When the civil engineers tackled the Santa Lucias, they promptly ran into a shoal of problems. The 150-mile section north of Santa Barbara required the construction of several tunnels and a horseshoe curve, and a scenic route along the shore, where the iron crossed the outlets of numerous arroyos and gorges, called for high bridges. South of Santa Barbara stood the Santa Susana Mountains trying to push the railroad into the sea.

Santa Barbara, Los Angeles, and San Diego did not get their complete coastal route to San Francisco Bay until 1901. The link through Oxnard and Burbank came in 1904. Like the mule-riding Franciscan padres who had preceded them on this long trail through the hills and fields of poppies, the construction engineers took their time.

When the Coast Line finally was finished all the way to Los Angeles, the passenger trains that rumbled over it were not notable for comfort or new-fangled ideas generally. For there was no serious competition, just some coastwise steamers that poked along lazily out there on the Pacific. There were no automobiles to speak of, only the most uncomfortable of buses, and of course no planes.

But it is all changed now. Daylights and Starlights and Larks, streamlined and comfortable, clip right along. The trains slither past crumbling adobe missions strewn by the Spanish friars of a hundred and fifty years ago. They pass ranches whose Spanish names tinkle like mission bells. They sweep past fields where sweet peas and other flowers grow in broad acreages, like so much hay; and through many modern towns, ringed with orchards. In Spanish days all this was Arcadia. Here and there a barrel-trunked grapevine, an olive tree, or a pear tree still grows that was planted in those far-gone times.

The line runs close to the shore for many miles, and out there is the show that Americans had pressed toward for so many decades—the sun going down into the Western ocean. It does so with satisfying regularity, nicely visible from the train windows. As railroad men would put it, precisely on the "advertised."

20

Gandy Dancers and Bridge Monkeys

AFTER THE DEVIL'S RIVER of southwest Texas washed out the tracks and disrupted traffic with two Texas-size floods in 1948, the railroad decided upon a drastic engineering and construction measure. This was the raising of the big bridge and its supporting piers 15 feet. Hoisting a seven-span, six-pier railroad bridge would be regarded as something of a bar-bell exercise even if there were no traffic to consider. But this bridge was ordered raised while the transcontinental trains continued to thunder back and forth across it.

"Can you do it?" the executive vice-president asked H. J. McKenzie, then chief engineer, in Houston.

"Yep," said McKenzie.

Two gangs of 40 men each went at the job. With 100-ton jacks, the bridge was raised 1 foot at a time, starting from the No. 6 or westernmost pier and continuing pier by pier until the whole bridge was up 3 feet. Then concrete was poured in under the jacked-up steel. When it had set, seven days later, the jacks went into operation again and a few more feet were gained. More concreting; and when the task was done, there was the bridge, 3 feet higher than any flood mark of El Rio de Diablo's recorded history. The chief engineer of the Texas and New Orleans lines agreed that he had had a busy summer.

When the pioneer builders threw their Central Pacific across the Sierra and over Nevada-Utah, they did it with a single track of light iron. That served for some time, but when the little wood-burning engines and wooden trains began to be replaced by more modern equipment, rails grew heavier and bridges stronger—but the line was still single-track. But in 1906 the SP began to do something about double-tracking a part of this route. About two hundred miles of second track had been completed at various spots along Sacramento and Ogden's 693-mile route when the work was suspended in 1914. But in 1923 it was taken up again. The biggest item was the double-tracking of the summit tunnel, 10,326 feet, longest on the SP lines, exceeded in America at that time only by Hoosac's 23,175 and Cascade's 13,413. While the longest railroad tunnel in the world is the Simplon in the Swiss Alps, 12½ miles, the summit tunnel of the SP atop the Sierra Nevada as holed through in 1925 was quite a job. Nine hundred thousand pounds of dynamite went into Tunnel No. 41 at the summit, and 220,000 cubic yards of granite came out.

The tunnel enjoys natural ventilation, as generally it is used only by eastbound trains on a descending grade. It is a single-track tunnel. Westbound trains use the old tunnel 132.6 feet higher. With four more new Sierra tunnels and the double-tracking, SP poured $12,000,000 into the improvement of its Sacramento Hill—half as much as the whole Central Pacific had cost, by present guess, half a century earlier.

By 1925, the Western Pacific had its line paralleling SP across portions of Nevada, so a sensible agreement was made between the two companies to use each others' tracks for a 178-mile stretch.

At Yuma, back in the days of battle between C. P. Huntington and Tom Scott, the Colorado River had been bridged in a hurry-up fashion, and that bridge had stood, bolstered one way and another, for many years. But in 1923 the railroad got around to throwing a steel bridge across the surly brown river. A spot about a quarter mile upstream was chosen, and over the new span went, 400 feet of it in the clear.

Six years later, one of the mightiest of SP's bridges was begun. This was the $10,000,000, mile-long double-track bridge across Suisun Bay, 35 miles from San Francisco. Ever since the seventies, overland trains had been ferried across that mile of water between Benicia and Port Costa. Finished in 1930, and constituting the longest, heaviest, double-track road bridge west of the Mississippi, the Martinez-Benicia Bridge put the behemoth ferries *Solano* and *Contra Costa* out of business and ended a phase of Western railroading that had been as characteristic as the Sierra snowsheds.

When the Coast Line was driven through and over the Santa Lucia Mountains in the 1890s, some exceedingly dangerous rock was encountered. The mountains had been formed by the uplifting of volcanic masses grinding and crushing each other. Sometimes serpentine and sometimes crumbling, but always treacherous, the rock would have been tough to handle with modern electric mules and compressed-air tools. With hand tools it was extremely difficult and dangerous, yet the drillers made it. They drove seven tunnels and took out 1,100,000 cubic yards of material in seventeen months. Years later the railroad set about widening those ratholes, and had frequent occasion to marvel at the achievements of their predecessors with their hand tools.

But in spite of the courage and the industry that went into the digging of those tunnels, they never were things of pleasure for the traveler. Passengers gagged and choked.

Tunnel No. 6, the famous Santa Margarita, was a particularly venomous rathole. Climbing southward from the town of that name, its 3,610-foot length ascended at the rate of 116 feet to the mile and reached a summit in the middle of the hole. From that point, trains descended toward San Luis Obispo. A train traveling north would plunge into the vapors just left at the top of the rise by the train rushing south. It was a perfect pocket for gas, which collected until it was solid enough to chew.

"How will you lick this?" the railroad asked its chief engineer of the time, W. H. Kirkbride.

"I'll run another tunnel on top of it, like a horizontal chimney," said Kirkbride, who was a man's man and an engineer's engineer.

So his gangs started in. Because of the heavy movement of trains through the tunnels while work was under way, digging crews spent a lot of their time coming and going, or wiping their eyes and waiting for smoke to clear. The new, upper tunnel is scarcely big enough for a man to stand in; it is really an attic to the old tunnel, separated from it by a floor of spaced timbers. The smoke curls up into the attic, and as far as the trains below are concerned, that is the end of it. And, of course, with diesels the end of the smoke is complete.

With a going railroad, the work of the gandy dancers and the dirt stiffs, the bridge hogs and the stake artists, the mud chickens and the benders, never stops—the last spike is never driven. It won't be driven until the last steam or diesel locomotive, the last Pullman, freight car, and caboose sprout wings and take to the air, and that won't be for quite a while. The earthbound railroads are still the nation's champion load haulers.

21

Getting Out the Big Hooks

SO YOU'VE BUILT your railroad—690 miles of it at first, then 5,000 miles, then 15,000. Well, what have you now? Trouble, any railroader will tell you. Trouble and plenty of it. The headache of keeping the railroad operating. Storms, and floods and snows that bury the rails many feet deep, and heat that twists them like snakes, and trestle fires that whirl up out of nowhere, and tunnel fires and sabotage and earthquakes.

Since trouble is a continuous part of the business, railroads are equipped for it. The relief trains with their derricks, or big hooks, are ready night and day, and if you value your hide you don't get in the way of the fierce breath of a boss wrecker when he has work to do.

Sometimes the disaster is just a plain smashup, caused by failure of equipment or lapse in judgment—episodes that, per ton-mile or passenger mile, are now pretty nearly nonexistent. More often, the trouble is caused by nature and Old Man Weather.

An example of nature in a wrong mood was provided one day along Devil's River, the spring-fed stream that flows through the rocky hills of west Texas.

It's a short river—hardly a hundred miles from its Sutton County source down to its merger point with the Rio Grande 15 miles west of Del Rio. It meanders through a semiarid thin-soil country underlaid by rock and heavily grazed by sheep—a situation ideal for creating flash floods of tidal-wave fury. It is normally 3 to 6 feet deep where the SP crosses it.

On June 24, 1948, heavy clouds gathered, and the cloudbursts came. Twenty-four inches of rain sprayed and spouted down in 14 hours. The Devil's River basin acted like a tin roof and funneled it all into the wide but usually dry channel. Pinto Creek, Sycamore Creek, and Mud Creek to the east of Del Rio also rose. More torrents fell on the country east of Devil's River, over Sycamore way. Flash floods tumbled one after another upon the SP tracks and swept away culverts and embankments.

Division and general headquarters at San Antonio and Houston hummed with activity. Out on the line, the repair gangs moved swiftly. Reports came in as from a battlefield—Pinto Creek Bridge badly struck; 125 feet of a 20-foot embankment at Mud Creek gone; half the 1,000-foot approach to Sycamore Creek wiped away.

Then the real news broke. Devil's River Bridge, one of the biggest bridges in west Texas, had taken the impact of the angry river's onslaught of water and tree trunks. Three 150-foot steel spans, one 200-foot span, and part of the 126-foot I-beam trestle approach from the east had been demolished. Waters raged 8 feet above the rail and continued eastward for miles. And the waters, rolling on down Devil's River channel, swelled the Rio Grande and took out half of the 805-foot east trestle approach to the International Bridge between Eagle Pass and Piedras Negras.

Chief Engineer H. J. McKenzie of the T&NO lines (now president of the "Cotton Belt"), the SP east of El Paso, wading to his waist in Devil's River's water, found himself with a helper who had been through that sort of thing before and had come hurrying like a fire horse to a fire. It was A. T. Mercier, then president of the SP when back at his desk in San Francisco, but out here just a man in rubber boots who wanted to see what was going on and didn't mind how often he slipped in up to his neck. T&NO's boss, Executive Vice-president E. A. Craft from Houston, was there slipping and sliding in the Devil's River beside him, watching the way those gangs worked.

It was worth watching. The repair crews had come from everywhere— from the Dallas-Austin Division, the Houston, the Victoria. There was a bridge and building gang from the Pacific system. Within six days, the railroad had been repaired to a point where work trains could get to Devil's River and start reestablishing that great bridge. Ten days after the flood occurred, the gangs had performed the feat of repairing the 126-foot approach trestle and building 650 feet of new trestling to replace the steel truss spans that had been swept away. During the course of it all, a Mexican laborer carrying a bag of sand slipped and shot through a flooded culvert, coming out at the other end. "Where the hell is the sandbag?" yelled the foreman.

And then, on the morning of July 4, down came the floods again. Within a single hour, despite 15 loaded cars of gravel that had been placed on it to weigh it down, 500 feet of the new work vanished.

The second rise was nothing like the first. But it put 35 feet of swirling water in the river bed and hurled 12 of those steel-sided gondola cars downriver to join the smashed and submerged steel spans that had once been the bridge. New rain after rain continued falling, causing the river to play a hundred tricks, while the repair gangs toiled to get something hammered down and bolted home. Often they had to dive deep under the water to set anchor bolts in the solid rock bottom of the stream. But by July 9, the 500 feet of trestling had been restored. Trains were soon running again.

It is when trouble hits that the spirit of a railroad gets its testing. Sometimes the crisis calls for on-the-spot ingenuity and resourcefulness.

There used to be a girl telegrapher up at Truckee, along about the year 1900, who typified all that is best in chips-down railroading. Her name was Miss Woods. That is the only name she is remembered by—her first name has passed into limbo. She was tall, dark-haired, pleasant-looking, with healthful coloring in her cheeks from living at a mile-high altitude, and about thirty-two years old. Nobody ever called her anything but "Miss Woods," because she was full of womanly dignity. But when high-mountain blizzards knocked out her telegraph wires and those sissies down in Sacramento couldn't tell her what orders to give the trains chugging up and down the single track that crossed the Sierra, Miss Woods simply hopped in and put the trains on a train sheet of her own making, dispatching the long strings over the mighty "Hill" in both directions; and if necessary she pulled on her boots and mittens, wrapped a shawl about her ears, grabbed up a lantern, and went out in the snow and managed matters according to her own notion of how a railroad ought to run. She held a freight here and she sent an Overland there. Maybe none of it was in the book, but tradition says she got the trains through.

Ironhearted Miss Woods has been gone from the railroad scene for many a decade, and there is a lot of double tracking that has gone into service, and important advances like signal interlocking plants and electrically operated train-dispatching circuits. But when the winds are wild in the high mountains and the great trees are crashing, maybe her ghost is still around.

Probably the worst winter that ever hit the Pacific lines of the company was that of 1889–1890. But it is not necessary to go back sixty years for weather records on that scale. Early in 1938 a combination of snow, rain, and wind hit the California lines of the company in a way that railroaders still talk about wherever dolly flappers and car whackers, pig maulers and tallow pots, bull snakes and old rails gather. For nineteen days the rains fell, and in the higher regions that meant snow—and heavy.

First hit was the section of the lines north of Sacramento. Snow, floods, rock and dirt slides in the Sacramento River Canyon and wind damage all over kept the repair crews going as if they were full of Mexican jumping beans. A fall of 343 inches of snow, the heaviest ever recorded in any month at the Sierra Summit (the total for the winter was 805 inches),

FOOTSTEPS OF THE PADRES

First train into Santa Barbara, August 19, 1887

ALONG THE PACIFIC

The Coast Daylight steps northward, Los Angeles to San Francisco, close above the ocean surf

created a situation up there on the "Hill" that called out every piece of snow-fighting equipment and kept it out.

The snow battle went on along 312 miles of track. And then, after thirteen days of it, a hurricane swept in from the Pacific. Over went pole lines and trees in the rain-soaked earth from San Luis Obispo to Gerber, smashing communications and blocking the trains for hours. For the first time since the San Francisco earthquake thirty-two years before, SP's general office at San Francisco was without wire contact with other system points, and five minutes of that sort of thing is enough to bust a general office staff wide open at the seams. This period of suspense for 65 Market Street lasted eight agonizing hours.

And no sooner had the section gangs cleared the northern California tracks, than Southern California joined the party with one of the most violent rains and floods since Noah launched his ark. The rain started February 27 and by March 2 everything loose in that end of the state was afloat, together with a good deal that had been thought bolted down. Streams that a child could usually jump across became deep torrents. The Santa Clara, Los Angeles, Santa Ana, and San Gabriel rivers and all their tributary gulches and creeks ran wild. Los Angeles was cut off. All railroad and highway service halted.

For two days there was no wire communication. In Soledad Canyon the Santa Clara River ripped out 4 miles of main line and five steel bridges, buried three more bridges under sand and debris, and clogged two tunnels. In the Colton area the Santa Ana River and Lytle Creek joined forces to make a shambles of the SP and Pacific Fruit Express yards, silted up the tracks to a foot in depth, and took out 450 feet of track and trestle along the main line of the Sunset Route. In Los Angeles a 300-foot double-track bridge buckled under, and river embankments were washed away from under the main line. Two days and nights of struggle saved a 35-span steel bridge at Montalvo. That piece of work by the big hooks and the wrecking gangs made it possible to reopen the Coast Line when the waters receded. On the morning of March 5 the Coast Line trains steamed into Los Angeles. Sunset route was operating again on March 7, and the San Joaquin Valley line through Soledad Canyon on March 15.

When the waters receded and the mud was pushed aside, SP counted up the cost of the squall and found it $2,323,000. That would have built one-tenth of the whole original Central Pacific.

Those 1938 troubles? Well, ask the veterans about the floods of 1940: how rains of cloudburst size hit on February 26 at Pollock in the rugged mountain canyon of the Sacramento River 15 miles above the then-building Shasta Dam.

The first thing that happened was the derailing of five cars of a freight. Then the water, with an all-time crest of 35 feet 7 inches at Kennet, roared down the canyon and left an alarming picture of violence and destruction.

Thousands of feet of embankment were torn away. Near Castella and Delta, hundreds of feet of track were left suspended in air. Miles of pole lines and highway went out. The waters rushed out over the Sacramento Valley plain and put out of service both the east-side and west-side main lines.

Even the big hooks could not get through from the south. So they came from the north. Service north from Oakland was managed by detouring freight and passengers clear to Fernley, Nevada, and then over the Alturas Cutoff to Klamath Falls and Portland. The town of Dunsmuir in the mountains had been partly evacuated and part of its railroad yard washed out to a depth of 5 feet, but between February 26 and March 4 the bull wreckers and their big hooks got the trouble in hand and on the latter date had the trains running over the Siskiyou again. But there had been men at work!

In 1942 the Pacific Northwest had a silver thaw that is remembered. Silver thaws are lovely to look at—if you're not a railroader or a lineman. Atmospheric conditions were such that rain and sleet froze immediately upon contact with steel. Thin strands of wire took on disastrous weights of ice. Communications lines snapped, and there went the signals. That silver thaw in the Willamette Valley took a hundred men, 150,000 feet of twisted duplex cord, and 7 miles of emergency cable to repair the SP's communications alone. It called for initiative and ingenuity all up and down the line to keep the trains moving safely while the eyes and ears of the system were momentarily numbed.

And there was the night of July 17, 1944, when two ships loaded with ammunition exploded at Port Chicago on one of the upper reaches of San Francisco Bay. The explosion, which killed 300 persons and injured hundreds, occurred just as a section of the Challenger was leaving the nearby Martinez-Benicia Bridge. Windows in 9 coaches were broken and a passenger was injured by flying glass. There were also injuries to railroad personnel in and about the station. While the railroad miraculously escaped without loss of life, the big hooks came from Oakland in a hurry and found plenty to do—192 freight cars in various states of shamble, 16 totally destroyed. The draw of the big bridge was raised and lowered a number of times and found to have gone through the catastrophe undamaged, as was the track. The railroad had built well. Even in the Port Chicago yard, where vast quantities of munitions were stored and handled, the closest investigation discovered only one broken rail.

But the granddaddy of all jobs for the big hooks, although it is now more than forty years back in the book of history, was the fight between the SP and the Colorado River when that mustang of a stream broke loose on its wildest rampage of recorded history. That was such a struggle that it moved out of the chronicles of technical railroading and became a drama of national interest. It will be told in a chapter of its own.

The big hooks of a big railroad seldom rest for long. The battle with the Colorado River lasted through 1905–1906 and into 1907. While it was at its height, citizens in San Francisco, at 5:13 on the morning of April 18, 1906, were tumbled out of bed by an earthquake. Streets cracked. Water mains burst. Persons who dashed out of doors saw what they thought were dimes floating in the air. Those were manhole covers, rocketed skyward by exploding gas. For the next three days fires raged. In the doomed Palace Hotel, the bartenders offered everybody free champagne. When it was over, the city counted its losses: 425 dead, 15,000 injured, property damage estimated at $350,000,000, several square miles completely gutted.

The Southern Pacific regarded the relief task as a job that was particularly its own. On the second day of the fire, 1,073 carloads of refugees were transported. In 35 days the passengers removed to safety numbered over 224,000. Many of them were taken only across the bay, but many were taken long distances, and it was all with the compliments of the railroad. In that thirty-five-day period the SP moved 1,600 carloads of relief supplies, besides giving handsomely to the relief funds. When the worst of the emergency was over, the big hooks started repairs. Temporary tracks were laid on city streets to remove debris and to bring in rebuilding supplies.

Down at Fourth and Townsend streets the unlovely building that had been the general offices was a mass of rubble, with most of the company's records mingled with the ashes. In time the bricks were removed, but for many years the lot stood idle, with its scorched vaults standing like watchtowers over the desolation, and a flight of granite steps leading from the sidewalk up to a portal which no longer existed.

An example of what the crisis did to one railroader was shown in the case of Jack Brennan, later the superintendent of the San Joaquin Division. The so-called "San Francisco" earthquake had wreaked havoc over much of the SP's Coast Line, and among other things it derailed a merchandise train just north of Pajaro, now Watsonville Junction. Brennan arrived in charge of a work train, and for the next two months he operated what was nearest to a one-man railroad in the SP's history. He was in an isolated spot. Nobody had time to bother him. That was just about heaven for a railroader. He supervised construction of a "shoo-fly"

—a temporary track to by-pass an obstacle—around the derailed cars, directed the repairing of the Pajaro River Bridge, managed the sale and distribution of supplies from the wrecked train to relieve a food shortage, and did just about everything but pull the trains through by his own man power—at which his beefy frame would probably have done its share if called upon. When it was over, the company awarded him overtime pay at the well-earned rate of twenty-four hours a day.

22

Grabbing the Wild Mustang's Tail

JOHN TANGNEY, 6-foot-2 and solid-muscled, was roadmaster at the turn of the century over a stretch of main track that ran between Cabozon to the west of San Gorgonio Pass, and Yuma on the Colorado River, together with such iron as served Imperial Valley off southward. This was the Colorado Desert, a country where a man showed judgment if he dashed a bucket of water over his wrenches before picking them up, the sun was so hot down there, and even the copper rivets in a pair of overalls could sear like a branding iron.

One morning John Tangney was returning from Yuma by train when something ominous struck his eye. The great sink off there below Old Beach station (now Niland) had turned into a billowy lake, and this was no desert mirage, for sheets of water were being driven up against the train windows.

Though the day was a Fourth of July, John felt a shiver. He got off four wires in succession to his boss in Los Angeles. The Colorado River was up to tricks. But nobody at Los Angeles seemed to be particularly excited about it. The river, where that spilled-over water came from, was presumed to be contained behind adequate works.

"Help me, or I'll stop the trains!" roared John.

To help him the railroad sent him some cars of oil.

John tried to subdue those wind-whipped waters with oil, but he might as well have tried to hold back the Colorado River with a spoon.

What did those rising waters signify, out there in Salton Sink? The nation soon learned, and watched the ensuing struggle.

The Colorado River is 1,700 miles long. It drains about one-thirteenth of the United States. It rises in the Rockies and finds its way in two branches down to a meeting in southeastern Utah, from which point it rushes across northwestern Arizona, dips south, and dies in the Gulf of California.

It is a weird, lonely river. For hundreds of miles it lies at profound depths in a series of canyons. Down those vertical side walls rains and cloudbursts carry enormous loads of sand from the deserts behind the rims.

It is a variable river. Sometimes it dwindles to a flow of only 20,000 to 30,000 cubic feet a second. Sometimes, when the Rockies are letting their snows melt in flood, the river rises to 200,000, 300,000, even 500,000 cubic feet a second. In recent years Hoover Dam and Lake Mead and other works have been created to detain the runoff, but for long ages the river had been accustomed to roaring out of its gorges unrestrained until it met the more level reaches of the Colorado Desert.

Here, today as well as in pre-Hoover times, the river alters its pace to a walk. The silt, which it bore easily while leaping down foamy rapids at an average of 10 feet to the mile, now begins to drop. There is enough of that sediment to cover, every year, a square mile of the Colorado Desert with solid earth to a depth of 53 feet. With this silt the river builds up its side banks and its delta. Through this self-imposed course it flows sedately, disarmingly, with its banks rising higher, century by century.

Those river-built banks pass alongside a depression which once constituted the head of the Gulf of California. It is called Salton Sink.

At Yuma, 80 miles from the present-day Gulf, the river is still 142 feet above sea level. But due northwest of Yuma, about 100 miles distant, there is a point out in Salton Sink that is 287 feet *below* sea level. The invitation to the river is obvious. If it were to break through its self-imposed right-hand bank, it would have a place to go that is lower than its sea outlet.

And the main transcontinental tracks of Roadmaster John Tangney's railroad dipped right down into and across one side of that sink.

Such was the situation that the railroad's builders had found when, in 1877, they took the risk and aimed their line straight from San Gorgonio Pass down across the desert for the Colorado's juncture with the Gila at Fort Yuma.

But since the engineers took their calculated risk, another ingredient had been added to the ever-present danger of a river leaving its overhead channel. Settlers had moved in, calling that region of agricultural promise the Imperial Valley. Seeing in the fertile sand, 100-degree heat, and convenient water the makings of a second Nile Valley, they had been entering the region and staking out farms since the early 1890s. In 1896 the California Development Company was organized by S. W. Ferguson, J. H. Beatty, H. Heber, and C. R. Rockwood to conduct water from the Colorado River a few miles below Yuma to a point 14 miles

away where an old channel, called the Alamo, seemed to point the way
for a natural canal.

The point at which the river was tapped happened to be slightly south
of the United States–Mexican border—a matter that was to have complica-
tions. The land to be irrigated lay for the most part north of the boundary,
and was to be reached by distributing canals after the natural course of
the Alamo, through Mexican territory, had served its purpose.

Construction of the 14-mile canal that tapped the river was started in
1900 about 100 yards south of the border, and was carried through to
Calexico in 1901, when irrigation was begun. Grain, alfalfa, and cotton-
wood trees changed the face of the land. Villages, citrus groves, vegetable
farms, and date groves appeared where, for ages past, this had been the
land of the lizard and the saltbush.

But the Colorado River was playing with the Imperial Valley settlers.
It had its fun first by plugging up the canal intake. The development
company, hearing yells for water from its colonists, put a dredge to work
and sliced a by-pass around the head gate to serve until the head gate
could be freed of its sandy plug. (Recall the volume of silt that the river
was bearing.) In October, 1904, the lowest intake, known as No. 3, was
cut in order to hush up the clamoring settlers.

Daily readings at Yuma for twenty-seven years had recorded only three
winter floods, and never two in a single winter. The summer floods were
of clocklike regularity, and the development company engineers were
sure they would close those cuts before high-water season arrived. And
the crops went on growing in the sun. But No. 3 was still open when,
early in 1905, the river took its fun in another way.

Far away in the high reaches of the Rockies, the snows of the previous
winter suddenly melted, and the Colorado rose. It rushed down its
familiar channel and, a few miles below Yuma, found that set of side
cuts open. It did exactly as a herd of mustangs would do if they came to
an open gate. It poured through.

The development company threw in all the men and machinery it
had, trying to shut the gate. The river played with these attempts. It
tossed at the frantic settlers not one or two floods, but six. Each flood
tore the opening wider. Each gouged the old Alamo channel deeper.
Each drove the colonists' engineers crazier. And the sink, which lay between the point of break-through and the SP's main tracks, accepted more
and more of the truant water until, some 66 miles from Yuma and
52 miles from the break-through, the water was up to the SP's tracks.

That is what Roadmaster Tangney tried to tell his bosses, and for the
relief of whatever ailed him they sent him those cars of oil.

When, soon after, the Golden State Limited came plowing through with water flying, the railroad decided to take more drastic emergency measures, and get its tracks out of there.

While the railroad fought to keep its trains running, the cause of all this—the big break-through where the river had left its channel below Yuma—was going uncorrected. When the local developers found they couldn't seal off the break, they turned, wild with worry, to the railroad. Farms were dropping into two new rushing rivers that had been formed by the break, and the Salton Sea that had replaced Salton dry sink threatened to submerge all that corner of California and bury it like Atlantis.

The development company officers appealed to Julius Kruttschnitt, who was the practical railroad man then in charge of all operations on the Harriman lines. Kruttschnitt retorted that the break-through was their problem. So they took it up with Harriman. That little man, whose vision penetrated mountains and spanned continents, promptly authorized a loan of $200,000 to the development company.

The railroad also hustled an engineer to the scene with orders to clap a bridle on the wild mustang of a river, and do it fast. He was F. S. Edinger, a man of experience, who had built the SP bridge at Yuma. At the moment he was a private contractor. He was sure he could handle the river. He threw works around and about the break, including a brush and piling dam. By that time the late autumn of 1905 had arrived, and with it the time for a slowing up of the river's force and volume. Edinger thought he had won a victory. Mountain-born rivers generally sleep when ice and snow grip their sources.

But the Colorado was only playing possum. Came November 30, close to the customary time of very lowest water, and a sudden flash flood, merging with another pouring down from the tributary Gila, swept away Edinger's dam and a good piece of his reputation. An attempt was made to extend a dam from an island opposite the intake to the west bank of the river. More high water, and once more no dam. This was getting to be monotonous.

It was also turning into tragedy. The year 1905 had been bad enough. With the spring of 1906, would there be more rises? The river soon answered the question. Yes, there would be more rises.

When it was fully realized what had broken loose on the Colorado Desert, Harriman lifted the responsibility for repairing the break from hands that had failed and put it in the arms of Epes Randolph. That was a real compliment to the unruly river.

Randolph was one of the foremost engineers of his time. He has left his mark all over the West; he built, among many other works, the SP de Mexico. A slender man, Randolph always wore a Southern tie and a boiled shirt. He looked like a Methodist minister, but he could play poker for $1,000 a chip. He also could use the American language with its most effective nuances.

At the time he was summoned to come and grab and subdue the Colorado River, Randolph was sick with t.b. He lived mainly in Tucson, occasionally venturing toward Los Angeles if the weather was right. But when the call came, he had his private car, the Pocahontas—he was a descendant of the Virginia Indian princess—taken right to the job and left there. Nothing but rising waters induced him to move his car, and then not very far.

The job that confronted Randolph was threefold. He had to close the break, he had to get the railroad to higher ground, and he had to keep communications open from Old Beach clear down into and across Imperial Valley. To help him, he brought in H. T. Cory, another resourceful engineer. Cory was a very polished gentleman. He, in turn, had a subordinate named Tom Hind. Hind was a very polished roughneck. "Goddam him, he can't think!" he would yell of some co-worker. "He doesn't know whether the brick holds the mortar or the mortar holds the brick!" One of Tom Hind's jobs was to move the railroad station at Old Beach up to safer ground. He broke every rope in the country doing it, but he got the building out of reach.

Moving that railroad was a saga in itself. At no time did anybody know just how high the waters would rise. At first a single shoo-fly was built. When the water kept rising, another shoo-fly was laid, and then another, until, in all, there were ten.

While driving piles near the break-through, it was feared that workmen would fall in the water, so skiffs were kept handy with Indians at the cars. The Indians found the warm sun conducive to rest and there was some doubt whether the copper-colored lifesavers would be of much use in a pinch. But when Frank Ditmar, a bridge builder, fell into Tangney's Lake, the Indian below yelled, "I no sleep! I ketch um!" and soon had Frank by the lovelock with a swoop that suggested a long line of scalp-grabbing ancestors.

The rising water created eighty-six washouts while the new line was being successively built, removed, and rebuilt in the stretch of some 44 miles between Mecca and Old Beach. As fast as the waters rose in the gullies that scalloped the lake, rails were relaid, and when the stock of rails ran short, men waded out into the flood and dug the old rails up from 2 feet under. John meanwhile walked ahead of his trains, often wading with his pants rolled up high, and his legs were literally boiled by the combination of water and sunburn under that searing sky so hot that even horses got sunstroke beneath it. But the trains were kept running and not one was derailed. In the end the railroad was building long sections on ground far above the old level. Today the road is on comparatively "high" ground, although between Niland and Indio, 63 miles of it is below sea level, and at Salton station it is 202 feet below sea level.

But by April of 1907, when the surface of Salton Sea was at minus 198 feet, it stood 74 feet higher than the site of the abandoned line. The railroad had pulled out of there just in time.

But that was only part of the story. The real scrap was with the river. (Remember, this was the river whose awful power and drive had hewn the Grand Canyon.) Working under Epes Randolph of the boiled shirt, courtly manner, and explosive vocabulary, Engineer Cory had set up living quarters near the break-through. He saw to it that adequate railway trackage was provided, got ready a big quarry at Pilot Knob just across the river from Yuma, and prepared to grapple with the river when its voice should once more drop to the drowsy ripple of a midwinter flow of twenty or thirty thousand second feet. For here was going to be one of the biggest rock-dumping operations the railroad had ever tackled. Cory little realized that it was to be only a curtain raiser to one still bigger.

The half-mile river channel first was narrowed to what was deemed manageable size, 600 feet, by jetties. Then a mattress of wire rope and brush was woven and sunk across this channel, where Cory proposed to build a dam. Summer floods hit him, but he held his position, and by September had in place a pile trestle carrying a railroad spur. Brush was sunk under the trestle and weighted down by rock. Steam shovels and trains of dump cars moved from quarry and clay pit out upon the trestle, and the work of plugging started.

Cory, looking at his work, felt good. But with the first trainload of rock, the trestle caved and the train leaped the track. So the track had to be built over again.

Elsewhere, strong supporting levees were run. A massive concrete head gate was built into the new dam. Cory was just beginning to congratulate himself a second time when, on October 11, 1906, the river gave one more of its characteristic playful upheavings, and two-thirds of the head gate lifted and departed for points downstream.

Cory began to feel like Edinger. But he had his eloquent and persuasive assistant, Tom Hind. Tom was sure he could close the river below the gate and force the water back into the main channel, provided they would furnish him with enough rock—and fast. Cory told him he would have his rock.

Then occurred one of the epics of Southwestern history. From Nogales on the Arizona-Mexico border clear to the city of Los Angeles, which was smaller in area in those days, every quarry that could provide a pebble was drawn upon. Fifty-cubic-yard dump cars, known as "battleships" and originally built for the Salt Lake fill job, trundled gravel across the deserts and heaved it into the breach. Trains were so handled that for several days one car was dumped every five minutes, day and night.

On November 6, 1906, Hind and Cory, almost exhausted, announced victory. The Hind Dam was completed and the river was back in its channel.

Whereupon, after waiting exactly a month, the river gave another heave as a result of a kick from the Gila, and within thirty-six hours, Tom's dam was a memory.

It was this disaster that woke the national government to a realization that calamity impended. And the government did what the colonists had done—it appealed to the SP to carry on the fight with every resource at its command, and curb that river.

The circumstances were politically difficult—the break was in Mexican territory, and the national administration had neither time nor authority to ask Congress for an appropriation. President Theodore Roosevelt asked Harriman to go ahead anyhow, and save the Imperial Valley and send in the bill. For Teddy, it was a "bully" battle. For Harriman it was the same. What resulted was, in Harriman's expressed belief, the high spot in his spectacular railroading career.

Upon Harriman's orders, everything on the SP lines gave precedence to the fight with the rampaging river. This time the big hooks were really trotted out. Traffic for 1,200 miles was disrupted. Practically the entire Los Angeles and Tucson divisions were closed except to the 3,000 rock-loaded flatcars and cars rushing timbers.

Two trestles were built out over the 100-foot fissure. Special trains loaded with timbers were hauled from as far away as New Orleans. Rock was rushed from distances as great as 480 miles. In many cases it was necessary to use 10- and 15-ton rock, for smaller stuff rolled away. And into the mighty contest waded thousands of men. There were Indians, Mexicans, Greeks, Negroes, Italians—a cross section of America. Oddly, though, there were few Chinese. The toilers who had built the railroad in the first place had all gone back to China, and exclusion laws had kept their descendants out.

That was the showdown battle. Eighty thousand cubic yards were dumped in fifteen days. Never before had rock been handled in such speed and volume. But still the rock-lugging battleships rumbled. Still the sleek passenger trains waited at sidings while cobbles and boulders rolled by. Still the extra-fare passenger yielded precedence to the dirty-faced men in overalls and sweaty shirts. On February 11, 1907, Cory reported to Epes Randolph that the break was sealed. For good? Everybody wondered. Yes, it turned out—for good. By a hair's breadth, and the indomitable will of a railroad and the expenditure of $4,000,000, Imperial Valley had been saved.

The railroad, remembering Roosevelt's promise, presented a bill to the Federal government for its labors in yanking a valuable slice of the United State back from a watery grave. The bill kicked around Congress for years, and was finally settled in 1930 with a check for $1,012,700. It was but a fraction of the cost, and did not include a quarter century's interest.

Today, close to the SP tracks, there shimmers an inland sea of a quarter million acres. Tangney's Lake, otherwise the Salton Sea, is a visible and permanent reminder of the narrow escape of the great sunken garden of the Imperial Valley.

John Tangney, as a young fellow in his eighties, living in Oakland in later days, often crossed the bay to San Francisco to talk with a friend who was a section hand, instrument man, and all-round handyman, at Old Beach in the days of the battle with the river.

"Remember when you walked ahead of the trains, John, to test the footing?" this friend would ask.

"Yes, and it's many a mile you walked in front of the locomotives, too, because I told you to roll up your pants and get out there and do it. Little did I know, or care, that the man I was giving orders to would someday be president of the railroad."

"You didn't care about man or the devil, or anything on earth except the welfare of the road. You even used your fists to carry a point when occasion called for it."

"That I did, which is sad to remember, for I am a man of peace. Just the same, there were some high-spirited lads working for the railroad those days and you were one of them. I mind you kicked a Yaqui Indian in the teeth once—"

"He came at me with a knife. I'd run out of pay vouchers. Let's say no more about the kick in the Yaqui's teeth. What else do you remember, John?"

"I mind how you forged my name to a requisition and sent to Los Angeles for some very fancy provisions, not once but several times—"

"Must you bring that up?"

"Well, then, Mr. Mercier, I mind that when we were relocating the line on higher ground, and you were the instrument man, you couldn't find a reference point to tie the center of the grade to, so you guessed at one—"

"Speak lower, John. Somebody might hear. There's a tangent of track out there in the desert to this day that's about four feet out of line, but only you and I know about it. After all, we were fighting a lot of water, weren't we, John?"

"Too dom much of it!"

23

Snow–Still Fighting It

MENTION OF SNOW has been made in this book. It is betraying
no confidence to state that every year, between fall and spring, the
stuff is still there. In the beginning it was a builders' headache; it has
been a maintenance and operational problem ever since. In the Sierra it
was early decided to fend the stuff off with sheds. In the Siskiyous and
Cascades the decision was to just leave the railroad outdoors and let
the blizzards swirl.

The early snowsheds were constructed after the manner of a house,
with steep peaked roof. Logs for posts and braces were felled on the
spot amid the surrounding forests of pines, firs, and cedars. Sawmills
close to the job ripped out the planks. Many expert woodsmen were
employed to ax out the braces which fitted around the supporting posts.
Roof planks were largely of sugar pine, laid longitudinally, without bat-
tens.

Engineer Sam Montague made a report in 1873 on the construction of
those snowsheds, which he called "galleries," describing them as follows:

> A novel and important feature of the work on the Sierra Nevada
> has been the construction of galleries for the protection of the track
> from the heavy snowstorms incident to that region. The experiment
> was first made of covering the track in the cuts only, depending upon
> snow plows for clearing the embankments, but experience soon proved
> that where snow was liable to accumulate to a great depth, its re-
> moval even from the high embankments would incur great expense,
> and often delay the movement of trains. It was therefore deemed best
> to make the covering through the deep snow-belt continuous. More than
> thirty miles of these galleries were built, consuming 44,639,552 feet,
> board measure, of sawed timber, and 1,316,312 lineal feet of round
> timber . . . and 721 tons of iron and spikes.

Snow, pushed down by thaws and torrents, would pack behind the slopes of the roof and force the sheds out of line. That called for a large force of men to keep shoveling the roof snow from one side to the other, thus transferring the weight and forcing the sheds back into line again. Then an experiment with semiflat roofs was tried, the 3-inch planks being handed the job without supporting rafters. Sag due to heavy snow loads and the factor of drip onto the roadbed below showed that another answer was needed.

Present-day snowsheds are a sturdier development of the early flat-roof sheds, with a multitude of refinements developed through years of experience.

Single-track sheds, where they exist, have overhead clearances of 22 to 22½ feet, and side clearances of 8 to 8½ feet. Double-track sheds are of two types. Where the tracks are on 17-foot centers, a row of posts between the two pairs of tracks is provided. Where tracks are on 13-foot centers, the ceiling span over the two pairs of tracks is trussed. There are openings like unglazed windows in the boards of the sheds between the wall posts. These ventilate the sheds in summer and give the passengers occasional charming, if tantalizing, views. In winter, plank shutters go up.

The sheds are coming down now wherever the track is on fill or in a slight cut where the rotaries can keep things clear. The remaining 6 miles of sheds have been retained in through cuts, sidehill cuts where slides are possible, and over sidings and switches.

The original railroad track, forerunner of the present-day westward track, was first put into service to Summit in November of 1867. The first snowsheds were erected shortly after. The second present-day main track, or eastward track, was placed in service in 1925. At this time, snowsheds for its protection and that of its connections were installed. This called for a revamping and renewal of essentially all the snowsheds on the westward track at Norden, which is the summit station now and the point where helper engines turn around. Norden's elevation is 6,880 feet.

The snowsheds at Norden are of many types: single-track, two-, three-, and four-track, and for turnouts. The posts are big sawed timbers. Sidings and roof boards are not laid tight; the air that filters in through the cracks gives welcome ventilation, as do the window openings on the downhill side.

What, besides building sheds and galleries to protect its trains, did the railroad do about those snows?

Prior to 1889 snow-fighting outside the sheds was done with bucker plows, flangers, and the strong arms of many shovelers. Tom Ahern, who became superintendent of the Sacramento Division, describes it this way:

"With the bucker plow and six to twelve engines, we would back away some distance from a drift and take a run at it, with every engine 'down in the corner' [heavy foot on the gas, to the modern reader]. When we hit the drift, snow literally spurted aside until stopped by the pressure, when back we went for another run. So it went until we bucked through —that is, unless plows were derailed."

As the banks were built up with snow on each side, they became too high for the plow to get rid of the accumulation. It was necessary to excavate chambers in the snowbanks so that the next trip of the plow would find a place to put the stuff. This called for an army of men with long-handled, square-nosed shovels. At one camp it took ten oversize ranges to prepare enough food for the diggers, who developed tremendous mountain appetites.

The flanger was, and still is, used to clean out the ice and snow packed between the rails. The operator rode on an open flat car, raising and lowering the plows. It was a high-speed ride and took steady nerve and hands. Later a shelter was provided for the operator, and an air lift for the plows, with its valve operated by the engineer.

The first rotary, which made everything so different, was received in 1889. From then on the snows began to take a licking.

The graybeards of the SP listen to present-day winter and snow stories with a yawn and a smile. They remember the winter of 1889–1890. *That* was a stem-winder! The record bears the graybeards out. So does a yellowing diary once kept by a woman telegraph operator with the pleasant and springlike name of Miss May Southern, who used to be stationed at Sims on the Shasta Division and really knew her winters.

The Shasta region, while geographically north of and distinct from the Sierra, shoves its knobs and passes up into the same smashing storms that the Sierra draws upon itself, and pulls down the same sort of blizzards. Miss Southern's sharp eye caught and noted the following details, which she put down in her diary:

Winter set in October 20th, with heavy rains. October 30th, train service irregular, landslides numerous, large forces clearing track. . . .

January 15, 1890, bumper crop of snow began arriving—snowing furiously, like twilight, two feet on ground this A.M. Train 15 crept northward in the teeth of the fiercest snow storm that ever roared down the Sacramento Canyon; stalled at Tunnel 11, mile and half north of Sims. 116 passengers on board, Vice President C. F. Crocker's private car, Mishawauka, attached to rear. Snowed incessantly for over sixty

Top. Heavy snows in Sierra made necessary the erection of 60 miles of barnlike snowsheds. This type, built in the sixties, had peaked roof

HAND SAWS AND HORSE CARTS

Bottom. Filling in the high trestle at Secrettown, just east of Gold Run on the west flank of the Sierra, in 1877. Wheelbarrows and two-wheeled dump carts were still used to build the roadbed

Rammer-type snowplow of the Central Pacific at Cisco, high in the Sierra winterland, in 1867

FIGHTING THE WHITE DEMON

Rotary snowplow pauses for a picture-taking in 1890

hours, fell so fast and furious [that] river [was] covered over; reached a depth of eight feet on level, much deeper in drifts.

Food in diner and Crocker car soon exhausted. Pullman porters carried food on their backs from Sims to feed women and children. My mother and sisters baked bread day and night as long as flour lasted. Brakeman in Crocker car with pneumonia.

Problem of heat serious, wood water-logged and buried under snow, coal oil and candles soon exhausted, darkness made more dismal by howling of panthers, coyotes and other night animals driven by the snow to seek food lower down. Deer often seen bounding into river pursued by a panther.

Food becoming scarce, my father slaughtering stock and killing off chickens; complaints of passengers loud and long, cursing the country, the company, and Mr. J. Pluvius. Wires dead, cut off from the world. Linemen coming in speechless and half frozen.

Depot only hot spot, men in overalls crowding in, drying their garments, smoking strong tobacco and expectorating copiously on red hot stove. An attempt made from Dunsmuir to rescue train, relief party snowed in at Castle Crag. Relief train on way from Sacramento encountered two feet snow at Redding, bumped into work train north of there, and commissary car badly wrecked, did not expect to meet anything coming down the line except snow; scooped out slides all way to Delta, where snow four feet deep. Way cleared with pick and shovel to Sims. Arrived January 20th with 300 men, who had been without food for thirty hours; they struck, stormed depot and threatened violence.

Assistant Superintendent Pratt and other officials barricaded the doors.

I was just a young girl and badly frightened by the sight of the starving men who surrounded us; through a crack in the door negotiations opened with leaders resulting in my father butchering his milk cows; men tore off hunks of meat with their hands and ate it raw, like animals. Took whole day's work to exhume buried train, which left Sims January 22nd, southbound, and packed high with snow, attracting much attention on its way down the valley. Passengers sent to Portland by water.

In answer to the call for snow shovelers had come ex-convicts, bums and toughs of every description, nearly every nation on earth is represented, some in low cut shoes and shirt sleeves. For lack of rubber boots, men bind their legs with gunnysacks held in place by bale rope or wire, this soon caked with mud and snow, to the weight of already over-developed feet, so the toilers soon played out.

Their complaint was not so much of the scarcity of food as the lack of whiskey and the money to buy it.

At Dunsmuir twelve feet of snow, freight shed crashed in, burying the bodies of William Whiting and a brakeman, killed on the road. Building total loss. Every man engaged in shoveling snow off buildings; church fell in, number of houses collapsed and families had to move out. Citizens let nature take its course in clearing premises. Town short of provisions.

Just north of Upper Soda Springs [not the Soda Springs of the Sierra] avalanche slid down mountain, carrying everything before it; section crossed the Sacramento dammed the river so completely that no water went through or over the dam for twenty minutes. Snowplow and engine buried, out of sight. Took a day's excavating to uncover them.

Of that mighty storm, the Sisson *Herald* of January, 1890, reported:

Inventory of losses by storm—Three large two-story buildings crushed, porches and awnings strewn in ruins on sidewalk. Town looks like it had been bombarded by hostile army and badly wrecked by exploding shells. Snow packed on sidewalks to second story, every man pressed into service to save cracking roofs; several horses killed; people going in and out of windows. Horses fitted with snowshoes.

[January 26.] We are here, well blockaded, situation worse, provisions to last three weeks, not many cattle, will kill fat horses if necessary. [The newspaper was printed on cloth and old posters.]

Eighteen hundred men went to work to free the trains snowbound in the Siskiyous. Avalanches had buried snowsheds in some places from 50 to 250 feet deep. In the Sierra, where conditions were similar, 2,500 men were flung into the conflict. The reports continued to come in as from a battlefield:

Seventeen days' blockade lifted in the Sierra; Emigrant Gap out of food, great suffering, 500 loaded freight cars snowed in on sidings, great damage, buildings crushed, lives lost; still snowing.

Sacramento Valley flooded. Coast towns under water. People suffering for food, death rate high from pneumonia and la grippe. Business at complete standstill.

At Tunnel 9, between Sims and Delta, probably biggest slide that ever swooped down mountain side filled tunnel and river; north end of tunnel buried 100 feet.

February 11th—Railroad situation going from bad to worse. Slide in Cow Creek Canyon, Oregon, formed a lake three miles long and seventy-five feet deep, besides filling a tunnel. Estimated loss to railroad $1,500,000. All hopes given up for clearing track, Ashland to Portland, for many weeks. Oregon towns under water; great loss of livestock; terrific rains all through Northern California.

Central Pacific blockaded again, snow sheds toppling over with snow. Sacramento River at Red Bluff twenty-five feet above high water mark; still rising. Fills on Siskiyou sinking, banks and hillsides caving, cuts filled.

The road finally was opened in the middle of April after fifteen miles of new track was laid.

The graybeards are right. The winter of 1889–1890 was a ripsnorter!

In 1908 the inventive minds of the railroad developed the use of the spreader. This smoothed the accumulated snow to a width of 20 feet from the track, leaving it level with the tops of the rails. Best suited to snows only 4 or 5 feet deep, it did not hesitate to sail into snowbanks twice that high when emergency called for it. V-shaped plows also went on the pilots of a number of locomotives. During light snowstorms, the line is now kept open with pilot plows and flangers, followed by the spreaders. When winter clamps down—as it still does—the big rotaries go forth. Year by year they become larger, more powerful. There is no more impressive sight anywhere than a view of one of these whirling snow-chewers coming hell-bent out of a tunnel on a wintry day, sending half the landscape into a spiral ahead of it—a man-made cyclone that tears into the shining white "beautiful" and chucks it high and far. When the long trains follow, they dive between banks that loom higher than the car roofs. But the road ahead is clear.

The storms of January, 1935, gave the rotaries a decisive chance to prove their worth. When 186 inches of snow on the ground was reported on the summit, Superintendent W. L. Hack of the Sacramento Division and Merle Jennings, trainmaster, started out from Roseville with a wide-wing rotary, cab-ahead locomotives, 16 freight cars, and a full crew of snow fighters. Hack announced that this winter was going to settle the controversy of modern equipment versus snowsheds. If the snow should fill the cuts faster than the rotaries could handle it, the ramming method would be reverted to; but that snow was going to be moved out of there. Ahead of Hack on the Hill were three more rotaries, six flangers, and a spreader.

With huge fan wheels revolving at high speed, the rotaries were pushed ahead by 6,000-horsepower locomotives. Some of the rotaries had fans 11 and 12 feet in diameter. The fans, housed in hoods reaching down to about 3 inches from the rails, tore and bit and gouged and whirled and spewed. Wings gathered the snow in, feeding it to the spinning choppers. Up and out flew the snow 20 feet on each side.

Down from Norden at the summit, three months later, came a message: "New winter snowfall record in Sierra. Total at Norden this year (April 5) 801 inches. Previous record, established in 1880, at Norden, 783 inches." But trains had been going through. Hack and the rotaries had won. Snow would continue to be a problem in the High Sierra as long as trains should run. But the weapon for its control had been found. And the snowsheds, miles and miles of them, could continue to come down.

Whipping Sierra and Siskiyou snows is only part of SP's eternal struggle. Sometimes the snowfall in the Cascades of southern Oregon is greater than even in the other winter-bound regions. Battalions of rotary plows (including wide-winged ones), flangers, and spreaders are maintained in that region also.

The 9,000 miles of the railroad's lines in six Western states are vulnerable in many localities. And what snow does not get, flood or fire may. Every day is an emergency day in railroading. The normal thing is crisis somewhere. Especially when operations take place over landscape of infinite variety and every degree of altitude, depression, temperature, and weather.

24

Boom, Bust, and Bang

DURING THE CAREFREE TWENTIES, the big brass of SP were as follows: Julius Kruttschnitt, chairman of the executive committee, and William Sproule, president. Paul Shoup, a man of imaginative mind, followed Sproule into the presidency in 1929.

The years 1928 and 1929 fattened the SP's coffers with the largest operating revenues in company history. Then the road, along with industry in general, suddenly leaped through the open drawbridge of depression. In 1930 revenues plummeted to the lowest in ten years. In 1932 revenue ton-miles were about half what they were in 1929. Locomotives were laid up in droves. They stood on the storage tracks, growing moss and whiskers.

In the following year, revenue passenger miles were 63 per cent under the peak year, which had been 1920. Dividends were skipped for the first time in over a quarter century. The number of employees was cut in half.

These were times for drastic top-brass adjustments. A. D. McDonald, whose training had included the comptrollership, waded in as president.

Despite lack of revenues, the company was too deep into some undertakings to draw out of them. Three railroads were added to the system, including the 1,800-mile St. Louis–Southwestern (Cotton Belt) and full control of the 200-mile San Diego and Arizona.

To simplify accounting detail, the twelve corporations comprising SP's lines in Texas and Louisiana were bundled up into one, the Texas and New Orleans Railroad Company.

The decade which started with financial panic and ended with the drums of war saw some epochal advances in the art of moving goods over SP lines. Freight trains moved faster. Some skipped along at a clip 75

per cent faster. The ton-miles rolled off per freight train per hour had
increased 37 per cent.

This was good railroading. How was it accomplished? In particular,
by better locomotives. In one year, 28 of the mighty 6,000-horsepower
cab-ahead steam locomotives had been put on the lines for snaking great
trains over the mountains. When war struck, more than 150 of these mon-
sters were in use. There were 54 of the husky "general service" locomotives,
the type which, in fancy red and yellow pants, pulled the Daylights along
the California coast.

Official headquarters of the Southern Pacific Company were moved from
New York to San Francisco in 1939, and the board of directors was
reorganized with an all-Western executive committee. That definitely
brought the SP back to the West where it had started.

If the SP and other American railroads were even partly ready for
World War II, it was because of the hard-won experience gained in
World War I. Railroaders with good memories had no trouble recalling
the congestion of 1918. They recalled those freight cars, loaded with
high priority government freight, jammed into immovable masses.

In that bumbling if valiant period, SP had played its valiant if bumbling
part. At the end of 1917 the government had taken over all the nation's
important lines. Facilities were consolidated, railroads used each other's
tracks, and the freight was somehow rammed through. Government control of United States railroads had lasted twenty-six months.

In that massive and stumbling experiment, one lesson that the railroads
learned was to keep out of government management if possible.

So, when SP thought it saw World War II shaping up, it caught a
glimpse of the strategic part it would have to play and it began making
ready. Before Japanese fliers swarmed over Pearl Harbor on that Sunday
in December, 1941, the railroad laid 1,400 miles of 113- or 132-pound rail
in place of lighter rail; provided miles of new sidings, extensions, and
yard trackage; eliminated tunnels, replaced bridges, and expanded shops.
There were large purchases of locomotives, cars, and other equipment.

And then, suddenly, Uncle Sam became the railroads' largest customer.

SP's first big test in mass transportation since World War I came during August, 1940, when peacetime movement of soldiers sent 119 special
trains over the company's Pacific and T&NO lines. The lines passed the
test on precision schedules.

Three weeks before Pearl Harbor, death took Angus McDonald. The
hard-hitting Scot had taken his railroad through the debacle of the thirties
and brought it out intact. SP's record of never having gone into receivership and never defaulting on a bond issue remained unbroken.

Into the breach stepped A. T. Mercier, who had been next in command. Bald, round-faced, high-domed, quiet, penetrating, salty-tongued, and accessible, he was a railroad man's railroad man.

On the Sunday when the war bombs fell, the SP's new president hunted up the West Coast's commanding general.

"What will you do if bombs fall on your bridges and roundhouses?" Gen. John L. DeWitt asked him.

"Do as we always do when trouble hits," answered Mercier. "Build them up again."

An army of SP railroaders swiftly reported to their posts. Hooded lights for signals, locomotives, and trains made their American debut. The SP trains moved through the blackout over guarded bridges throughout the Pacific Coast zone for 150 miles inland.

Then the railroad dug in its heels and really went to work. The men and women of the American armed forces turned out to be a traveling lot. On the average, every one of the many millions made five train trips during the training that preceded embarkation, and the trips averaged 1,159 miles. When an infantry division moved, it took 65 trains. An armored division, with its 3,000 vehicles, required 75 trains. Being a land-grant railroad, the SP was under obligation to carry military traffic at a reduced rate, and its line over the Sierra Nevada drew an impressive share of this transportation. In any average twenty-four-hour period of the war, little Norden on top of the hump saw more "wheelage" go by than normally arrived daily in Seattle over four transcontinentals.

Seven weeks after the fleet's bombing at Hawaii, the railroad had moved 670 extra military trains over its lines. And for the next five years in succession, all past freight traffic records toppled on SP lines. When the Japanese surrendered in 1945, the company's freight traffic was running nearly three times that of 1939. Passenger traffic in 1944 had been five times that of 1939. Through the years of hostilities the system's lines handled 28,349 special government passenger and mixed trains, comprising 437,567 cars exclusive of freight cars. These were in addition to 86,359 special military cars handled on regular passenger trains.

The figures of this period tend to become dizzying. For SP was strategically situated on the front lines of supply serving ports of the Pacific and the Gulf. There were more military establishments on its lines than on any other railroad in the country. With mounting production from hundreds of huge aircraft, shipyard, and other war industries continuously swelling its traffic load, equipment took a beating around the clock. But the old-timers and emergency helpers who manned the system managed to squeeze more hours of service out of every locomotive and car than ever had been done before.

Thousands upon thousands of SP men and women, meanwhile, left their jobs and fanned out upon the fighting fronts. Besides carrying rifles and flying planes, they formed whole railway and shop-operating battalions. They ran military trains from Alaska, where temperatures dropped to 68 below, to Iran, where the mercury tried to pop from the glass.

Of the strange predicaments in which 19,980 SP men and women found themselves, whether highballing trains under fire along the war fronts, nursing, or hauling material at the rear, as unique as any was that in which Pete Matson landed. In civilian life Pete had been chief train dispatcher for the subsidiary Northwestern Pacific, his office on the quiet north shore of San Francisco Bay. War's assignments thrust him into the job of running a military railroad in North Africa. It was a line considerably larger than the whole NWP. But that was not what bothered Pete. What had him excited was that he was quartered in a scared-out sultan's palace, where he occupied the state bedroom with the biggest, whitest bear rug that anyone ever stepped on. The floor was teakwood, laid in beautiful patterns, and there were tapestries, gold-encrusted coats-of-arms, and paintings for his enjoyment. Everything had been left in the adjoining harem but the girls.

However, it wasn't life in a sultan's palace for most. And as SP's man power left throttle and crowbar for the armed services, the railroad was put to it for personnel to handle the vast mechanism that simply had to be kept running. Many an old-timer, who thought his railroading days were done, heard the yell of the call boy again and got up in the early hours of dawn to shuffle off to roundhouse and shop.

Like all industries, SP also went into the kitchens and schoolrooms and recruited help. With 100-pound women handling 30-ton electric cranes, housewives and girls ruling mighty steam hammers, and others performing in a thousand shop, store, roundhouse, and operating jobs, the wheels were kept turning. Four thousand women tackled nonclerical jobs. "I'll be late getting home to cook dinner tonight," phoned many a housewife. "I'm down at the roundhouse, greasing an engine." White-collar workers from every walk of life filled in on the dirty-shirt jobs on weekends.

The search for mechanical power that could be reconditioned and put into service was far-reaching. Many locomotives, some of them dating back before 1901, were recalled from the lines in Mexico and from affiliated companies. From yards and sidings and roundhouses came venerable museum pieces to be set up as stationary boilers, or to yield their parts to the rebuilding of other mechanical antiques.

A special war problem of SP's lines was the fact that a large portion of them were single-track. Expensive installations of Centralized Traffic Control, as explained in Appendix A of this book, increased the capacity of that track by 50 to 75 per cent.

The test on the single-track system was particularly severe in SP's western territory where the company's 1,400 miles of north-south lines through Oregon and California connected with transcontinental rail arteries. On this strip of seaboard were located the aircraft plants that produced 60 per cent by weight of all the fighting planes built during the war. Here were the shipyards that produced 44 per cent of the nation's new tonnage cargo. In this area of the company's Pacific Lines were located 290 military and naval establishments, where 15 installations had stood before the war.

A good example of what was happening took place out on the Nevada desert on Mina branch of the Salt Lake Division. The branch, once called the Carson and Colorado, dated back to Nevada's boom days in silver. It had been incorporated in 1880 by William Sharon, Virginia City magnate, and D. O. Mills of San Francisco. In 1881 the line had been placed in operation down along the west line of Nevada and the eastern boundary of California.

"This railroad is either three hundred miles too long or it was built three hundred years too soon," exclaimed banker Mills, after making an inspection trip.

But the line managed to flourish, to his surprise, for about ten years. Then the price of silver hit the skids and the mines served by the Carson and Colorado closed one by one. Wags remarked of the forlorn little road, "It's the first railroad that begins nowhere, ends nowhere, and stops all night to think it over."

But Tonopah and Goldfield came into being; the C&C, part of its narrow-gauge track replaced with standard gauge, hauled big quantities of ore. It was taken over by the SP in 1900. Thorne, Nevada, was one of its one-man stations until 1929, when the government began constructing a naval ammunition depot at Hawthorne, not far away.

When World War II came along, Hawthorne, for which Thorne was the rail receiving and delivery point, became one of the largest munitions storehouses in the nation. Enlarged station, freight sheds, baggage rooms sprang up all over the landscape. From nothing at all, the station's monthly handle of freight jumped to 380 carloads, to 2,200, to 5,000. Business increased from $60,000 during all of 1938 to $11,500,000 in a single month of 1944. And there were the nineteen persons employed to help Agent Tomlin, who had been sweeping his own platform and watching the snails whiz by ever since 1919.

In that martial period the SP's dining service likewise underwent a strain that will live in memory as long as brown arms handle skillets and cleavers in swaying diners over singing rails. Twenty-five million meals and varied food items were served in a single year. That's a volume never before approached by SP or any other railroad. Twelve million complete meals were served on trains or in railroad restaurants. Enough sandwiches were served daily to pile 1,750 feet high.

And then, almost as suddenly as it had come, the war was over.

The immediate problem was to return the millions of men and women of the forces, and the hundreds of thousands of war plant workers, to their homes. For a time it seemed as if every man, woman, and child in the United States was riding the trains.

But back to their former jobs of running a railroad returned thousands of SP people, relieving the amateurs and the graybeards who had batted for them.

"I'll be home to cook dinner tonight," phoned many a housewife. "I've greased my last locomotive."

What a job all hands had done!

25

Softer Riding – and Faster

THE DEPRESSION, which hit the SP a body blow that it felt from the swamps at Bayou Teche to the banks of foamy Clackamas, was perhaps one of those blessings in disguise which nobody likes at the time but appreciates afterward. The giant went to his knees and came up revitalized. Nothing so drastic had happened to the system since California belted it out of politics, enabling it to go about the special business of being a transportation system and nothing else.

The disheartening experience in the early 1930s of having lots of cars but no freight or passengers shook down the ashes of old thinking. Maybe the point was not just to run the trains. Maybe it was to sell the trains.

With business at a standstill, management was seeking new ideas.

One of the ideas, which surely must have spun Collis P. and Uncle Mark in their well-earned graves, was "Dollar Days." For designated dates, fares for round trips were slashed to 60 per cent of what they usually were one way. Such excursions, the ads whooping "100 miles of travel for $1," really brought the people out. From red cap to stationmaster, everybody was all smiles again while it lasted. The company also discovered that the human hide loves to tan itself, and ran specials to the beaches. And up into the mountains went the snowball specials. This on a railroad that ten years before had forbidden its advertising department to show pictures of mountains with a trace of snow on them, lest Easterners think all was not roses in January in California.

But it was apparent that the public would have to be wooed back by something more dependable than one-day bargains. Days of "take it or leave it" service on the railroads were gone. What did the public want? Well, among other things it wanted air conditioning, body-fitting seats that a traveler could sit in comfortably for hours, decent lavatories, real speed, and some good meals at square prices. ("Look at Fred Harvey." "To hell with Fred Harvey." "Just the same, look at Fred Harvey.")

The depression was a time for long-range thinking—and mighty sudden acting. So some of the things that had been simmering on the back of the stove for years were brought to the front and the gas turned up. The first air-conditioned equipment, 14 dining cars, went into service in 1932. They were the product of the big Sacramento shops.

"How are we doing?" asked the shops.

"Fine! Keep going!"

From that date onward, air conditioning, greatest of boons to passengers in a region that is half desert, became a must. Conversion was done both on SP's initiative and in conjunction with the Pullman Company. SP's Houston and Sacramento shops rang with this activity. Within four years, the customers of SP's "lace-curtain department" had air conditioning on all its principal transcontinental and local trains.

The forerunner of the present-day Daylights, Hustlers, and Sunbeams had gone on the run in 1922. A Friday and Saturday special on a summer daytime schedule of 13 hours had been tried out between San Francisco and Los Angeles. In a couple years it had become an accepted institution and was painted a snappy gray to deflect sun rays—quite a change from the hot drab trains that had hoisted dust for so long. The "summer special" went on a year-round basis, doing the 470 miles in 12 hours—nothing to excite speed cops. In 1936 came the first Daylight. It made the run in 11 hours.

These were improvements, but the big surprise was still in store.

Early in 1937, the citizens of Los Angeles and San Francisco were invited to come down to their respective stations and take a stroll through the first of some true streamliners which SP had dreamed up for the daylight passenger run between the two cities. The public stared at the flashy red, orange, and black trim of the brand-new trains and at the steam locomotives which had fantastically acquired skirts and aprons.

"What have you got here, George?" visitors asked of the grinning porters.

"Step inside. You ain't seen anything yet," retorted George at every opened vestibule.

Foam rubber cushions—since when had the railroad given that much concern for the posterior comfort of its riders? Reclining backs that really fitted the human spine. Five-foot windows giving an unbroken view of the scenery. Radio equipment. Tavern cars with semicircular bars, venetian blinds, and slightly sinful colored lights. Parlor observation cars with pastel decorations, fluorescent ceiling lights, and chairs that rotated. Snappy diners with specially designed napery and silverware and distinctive modern furniture. Coffee-shop cars with some more of those sun parlor windows. Separate kitchen cars. And baggage elevators through which luggage was loaded and unloaded through sliding panels on the outside of the cars, so that passengers who were getting off did not have to stand and wait. About the only thing that looked familiar was the porter's whisk broom. The whole stainless-steel and plate-glass job represented an investment of about a million dollars a train. Was this the SP?

Well, it was; and the public took the new equipment to its heart. The schedule dropped to 9¾ hours, and inside of five months the pair of trains had carried 100,000 passengers—within nine years, 9,000,000. Today the Daylight is the most profitable train on any American railroad. It has been the inspiration for Sunbeams and Hustlers down in Texas and for the Shasta Daylights—several notches onward in luxury and beauty—on the Portland run. Also, a pair takes the Inland or San Joaquin Route, between San Francisco and Los Angeles; and Starlights, of same type equipment, make the Coast Line night run.

History wasn't through being made on the Coast Line. For years the Lark and the Owl, coastal and inland trains between San Francisco Bay and Los Angeles, had been ordinary Pullman trains of the green curtain, smoky lavatory variety; but one evening the Lark showed up all dressed in silver and smart gray. Perhaps there are more beautiful trains in America than the two Larks that now run by night along the California shore line, but it takes hunting to find them.

The overnight sleeper trains are equipped with private room accommodations only. Roomettes are for single travelers, with wall bed, toilet, full-length mirror, and individual ventilation. The bed swings down all ready to sleep in. The passenger can lower it at a finger-touch, without hollering for George. There's a clothes locker, too. Compartments have all that privacy, together with convertible sofa bed and upper bed and a writing desk of sorts. The drawing rooms readily accommodate three persons and are said to be capable of enfolding five. (It would take some managing.) The "Lark Club" is a dining and lounge unit two cars long with no door or partition between the cars; and a separate kitchen car is articulated into the scheme. This three-car unit of diner, kitchen, and full lounge turned out to be a big hit.

The business upturn of 1936 brought more advances. For the first time since 1929, large-scale buying of new equipment was possible. The streamlined City of San Francisco began clipping the breeze over Chicago and North Western, Union Pacific, and Southern Pacific tracks. This was an 11-car diesel-electric speedster, making five trips a month. The initial investment was Union Pacific's. (Its successors are owned jointly by the three connecting roads.) The cars were diminutive on the first City of San Francisco, and the lady who couldn't get her girdle more than half on or off in the cramped sleeping quarters and had to waddle the length of the aisle to the women's room was not an unknown sight. It all added to the gaiety of travel.

The year 1937 brought a couple of "economy" trains into East-West travel. The Californian appeared on the Golden State run between Los Angeles and Chicago. The Challenger, complete with cheap meals and baby-sitting stewardesses, began stepping along on the Overland Route. (The stewardesses disappeared during the war and haven't returned. It was a transplanted idea from the air liners anyhow.) Another San Francisco–Chicago streamliner, the Forty-niner; new Coast Line Daylights; and two trains of the same design between Houston and Dallas, called Sunbeams, took their places on the rails. In 1938 the vest pocket City of San Francisco became a grown-up, 17-car train. A twin was added on the run in 1941.

The better trains had individual toilet facilities that banished forever the close-packed mens' or ladies' lavatory where, as the jokesters had it, every time the train went around a curve the washer washed the wrong face. The delicate perceptions of the traveler were catered to by cocktail lounges with circular bars, attentive barkeeps, soft lights, and good liquor. And, nowadays, the dining cars are done in pastel shades. Our rugged and departed ancestors were glad to pound off the train and grab a bear steak at the first eating place. But who wants to be a rugged and departed ancestor?

The bear steak concept—that is, the idea of using local foods—lasted a whole lot longer around SP commissary circles than the bears did. The idea was strong with thrifty Allan Pollok when he was in charge of dining service back in the twenties, and fancy foods from far places just didn't appeal to him. ("But Fred Harvey serves Maryland terrapin and Canadian reindeer in New Mexico." "This is prune country. Eat prunes!") There were long-suffering ones who vowed that the railroad could turn good roasted coffee (Pollok bought the best) into coffee in the cup that tasted as if it had been made in the steam chest of a switch engine.

Pollok carried all the figures of a truly staggering business in a notebook of 2 by 4 inches. That saved time and saved paper.

The era of new thinking brought economy meals—big ones—and various low-priced specialties.

One blessing the SP and its passengers had enjoyed for many years. The steam locomotives burned oil. In the beginning, the Central Pacific burned wood, and the woodmaster's job was to see that plenty of 4-foot cordwood was always on hand at the station. There were times when the fireman ran out of the needful and had to scrounge what he could find off the countryside, and there are even stories of passengers turning out and helping, even to pulling sagebrush.

Coal followed wood. But what soon was keeping steam-driven wheels churning over the miles was petroleum. More than 3,000,000 gallons a day began going under the boilers. That kept clinkers out of a lot of eyes, and played its part before the days of air conditioning in making the dusty desert miles endurable.

But the real story of comfort improvement, after the deserved bow has been made to air conditioning, belongs to the fine new modern trains. So, in 1949, the Oakland-Portland run also got an all-coach Daylight. The 444-passenger Shasta Daylights were announced as a pair of "million-dollar trains." This was an understatement. Their actual cost was just too sensitive a subject to be hollered about. Actually, the figure for the pair came closer to $5,000,000.

The consist of each of these fast-stepping beauties was: diesel locomotive, baggage-postal, 9 chair cars, triple dining–coffee shop–kitchen assemblage, tavern car, and parlor observation.

There was pressurized air conditioning, "feather-touch" doors, sky-view windows especially ventilated to keep from fogging, piped music, and seats as form-fitting and relaxing as an old overstuffed chair at home. Lakes, forest, and sky had been photographed in Kodachrome and their hues reproduced inside—pine needles and sky reappearing in the drapery designs, Lake Odell's blues getting into the décor of one car, Shasta's volcanic browns, yellows, and lava reds in another. The bartenders took pleasure in showing that a Martini could be placed on the bar while the train was going around mountain curves, and did not spill. The test was at the customer's risk.

A hundred and thirty passengers at a time could be served in the restaurant cars. The waiters were full of flourish. Food was good, service fast, prices—especially in the coffee shop—reasonable. The SP, which digs into the red three to four million dollars a year on its dining service, was sick of hearing about meals on Santa Fe and henceforth intended to lose money on its meals in style.

Whipping along in the valleys at 75 miles per hour, Shasta Daylight makes the 718 miles between Portland and San Francisco in 15½ hours. It gives all this glitter, glamour, and comfort for $13, including reserved seat charge, plus tax, or about 1.81 cents per mile. The Shasta Daylight is out to lick the buses, which charge $9.95, plus tax, for the same journey.

The growth of modern chair-car business is an SP phenomenon. Chair cars, not sleepers, provide 85 per cent of the company's passenger revenues. SP's riders cover long distances, but they like foam rubber and coach rates.

In August, 1950, Vice-president Claude Peterson's lace-curtain department trotted out another of its streamliners—the Cascade. Powered by

6,000-horsepower diesels, the 13-car twin streamliners cut 2 hours off the old Cascade's overnight time between San Francisco and Portland, making it 16½ hours. Eight of the eleven passenger cars on each train are sleepers, with five different types of room accommodations, and one specialty proved to be the separate toilet and washroom for each of the 46 larger rooms—replacing the chummy exposed toilet and washstand of yore. Full-length closets, individually controlled heating and ventilation, full-view windows, 130 feet of dining and lounging space in a three-car club unit, and feather-touch car-end doors were further additions to the grace of travel. Paul Bunyan no longer has to go ahead of people to get them through the train.

With the addition of the new Sunset later in the year, the plan of expansion of luxury facilities on the SP's main lines was pretty well rounded out—with daylight streamliners and nighttime streamliners running the length of the system's lines on the Coast, and eastward via the Union Pacific, the Rock Island, and the all-SP route to New Orleans.

Passenger facilities are what the traveling public sees, feels, sits on, eats, looks out from, and is bounced by. The era of the fast, pleasant train ride has arrived.

26

But Freight's the Thing

JORGE JIMINEZ of El Centro, who picks cotton, tomatoes, and cantaloupes for a living, never heard of Collis P. Huntington, Col. Tom Peirce,
Col. Tom Scott, or E. H. Harriman. Nor, except in a hazy way, does Ed
Parker of El Centro recall those gentlemen. Ed is the foreman of a railroad icing plant down Imperial Valley way. What counts with him at the
moment is that this is cantaloupe-picking time, and the crop is coming on
fast, and the packing plants are furiously busy, and the fruit trains are
rolling, and he has tons of ice to move.

So Jorge and Ed are up early this morning, as are hundreds of other
pickers, foremen, farmers, truckers, packing-plant bosses and workers,
icers, and railroaders. It looks like a 2,000,000-crate year for Imperial
Valley's cantaloupe growers. That means 60 or so solid trains, pulling out
of El Centro, Calexico, and Brawley, one after the other, and moving over
the hot sands to Yuma and thence eastward to the breakfast tables of
America.

By now Jorge has been in the fields an hour or more. Jorge and his
fellow pickers, stocky, strong-backed Mexicans in cotton clothing and
straw sombreros, pluck the melons and drop them carefully into trap
sacks slung against their backs. Trucks move the melons to the sheds. D. A.
Harrigan, an agricultural commissioner, tests the sugar content of the
arriving loads with an instrument called a refractometer. Fast-working
graders select and pack the cantaloupes into their little pine crates, and
Ed Parker is a busy man, in spite of the 100-degree heat. He is seeing that
the "reefers," or refrigerator cars of the Pacific Fruit Express, are ready
for their loads. Air blown through the ice bunkers of the cars, precooling
the melons to 40 degrees, halts maturing, prevents overripening, and
readies the produce for its long journey. Each reefer under Ed's jurisdiction takes 5 to 6 tons of ice initially, and 3 tons more after the precooling.

The solid trainload of melons is loaded. The shipper, who has taken charge of the melons from this shed and arranged for their railroad transportation, does not know where they are going. They will end up in Kansas City, Memphis, Chicago, Dayton, or almost anywhere. He won't know until the market's status at each of scores of distribution points becomes clearer, and that won't be until tomorrow or the next day, or the next. All he knows now is that he has the melons, he has turned them over to the Pacific Fruit Express, and they are in the hands of the Southern Pacific Railroad. The PFE office in El Centro will keep track of each car's location throughout its journey and teletype the shipper's orders for its diversion.

The train moves out, with an articulated cab-in-front locomotive snorting along at its head. It rumbles across the All-American Canal at Araz Junction and makes for Yuma. Back in the caboose, Conductor Mark Mullins of Tucson checks over his sheaf of waybills. Temperature outside the iced cars climbs to 112 degrees, to 115. At Yuma a big diesel road engine takes over. There the cars' bunkers are re-iced; again at Tucson; and then at El Paso, where the T&NO takes charge.

The train continues. The teletype has been clicking. Not Tucumcari, the Rock Island, and Chicago for this shipment; the Chicago market has plenty of cantaloupes just now. So continue east. . . .

The train rolls over the hump at Paisano, Texas, just about an exact mile above the sea and a couple of hundred feet more than a mile above El Centro, where it started. It drops down to Marathon, Texas. At Dryden, its fireman picks up train orders giving its perishables the right-of-way over one more westbound freight, which presently is encountered waiting on a siding, as so many others have been. It is re-iced at Del Rio. It glides into San Antonio; more decisions have been made by teletype.

Houston and New Orleans have enough melons. The long train is diverted northward, via Flatonia, for Corsicana and the Cotton Belt; the shipper is now debating between Memphis and St. Louis. The train is re-iced at Hearne. At Corsicana, the interchange from T&NO to Cotton Belt is done in fifteen minutes. No. 805, a big 4-8-4 fast freight locomotive with 70-inch drivers, takes hold. And at Texarkana, Engineer Sam Brooks is waiting, his locomotive oiled and ready to take over. Near Brinkley, Arkansas, Imperial Valley's melons slide past the Blue Streak, Cotton Belt's fast merchandise train that is coming the other way.

The teletype has been clicking again. The shipper has detected that St. Louis wants those melons at the rate of a fractional cent a pound more than Memphis does. So the "fruiter" makes for a many-piered bridge across the Mississippi into Thebes, Illinois, and thence into the East St. Louis yards. Five mornings ago the melons were growing under the hot California desert sun. Today, cold and firm, they move from the refrigerator cars into consignees' trucks, and as fast as modern local distribution can whisk them they are on sale in the St. Louis fruit stores and stands—and next morning on St. Louis tables.

A sixtieth portion of a great 6,000-carload crop has been carried speedily and in perfect condition by a great rail network, for the benefit of a great and well-fed country. It will happen again tomorrow, and tomorrow beyond tomorrow. Melons and oranges and berries and tomatoes, lettuce and peaches and asparagus and cherries—the whole cornucopia of the West and Southwest, forever being replenished and emptied out upon the American table.

Huntington and Peirce and Stanford and Scott may have foreseen something like that. But only something. There was no Imperial Valley in their day; no Coachella; no Salt River; there was only the interminable sand. But still they foresaw a dim vague outline of it all—and how they scuffled and battled to bring it about!

A railroad system is far vaster and longer lived than the men who create it, who do the original imagining of it, who dream it and launch it. A modern railroad system is one of the biggest things conceived by engineers and construction men and the desk men who have to direct the finished line and make it pay. And Southern Pacific, or any one of its separate routes, or even the affiliates of those routes, is big. Big in usefulness.

On the seventh floor at 65 Market Street, San Francisco, sits W. W. Hale, vice-president, system freight traffic. Bill Hale is big and genial and he finds his job—which is sizable, as will be explained—lots of fun. He looks out over a stretch of territory which he has to imagine after the first few miles, for it soon dips down behind the hills and the curve of earth— a territory consisting of eight states, which his freight cars serve directly, and forty more states which they serve indirectly. Freight is the biggest revenue producer on the SP lines, accounting for seven-eighths of its income. Along the 15,039 miles of SP road, main, and branch, originates one quarter of all the rail-borne perishable food products of America—and Bill's job, in which he has plenty of assistance, is to see that it reaches the American table fresh and on time.

Along those lines, too, is carried a great variety of other stuff; but the figures on perishable foods are startling. "Let's make a salad," said Bill one day, "out of a year's haul on this little old system." He took a memo up and looked it over, grinning. "Lettuce. Sixty-nine thousand carloads on the Pacific lines alone, in '50. That's a hell of a lot of lettuce. What kind of a salad do you want? Tomato salad? All right, 10,000 cars. Fruit salad? Well, here's 3,100 cars of peaches, 7,800 of pears, 6,000 of bananas, 14,000 of grapes, 30,000 of citrus fruits—to name a few. Want a side dish of celery? How'll 8,800 cars of it do?"

Tossing in 16,500 cars of fresh root vegetables, 2,800 of watermelons and a few other comestibles, Vice-president Hale summed up: "Total of 251,000 cars of fresh vegetables and fruits picked up west of El Paso in a year and hauled around. That's a lot of eating."

Through Pacific Fruit Express, equally owned by SP and Union Pacific, the heavy and fast movement of fresh fruit and vegetable crops from producing sections of the West to consuming centers all over the nation has been developed into one of the remarkable achievements of commerce. The outfit was organized by SP-UP in 1906. At that time a relatively small tonnage of perishables moved from the vast Western garden-ranches. Refrigerator cars had proved their worth, but they were few in quantity and were owned by private interests.

PFE started its operations with 6,600 cars. This made a fair-sized pool which various sections of the West could draw upon as their perishable crops ripened. At the present time PFE owns or leases about 38,000 "reefers," and they operate over practically all railroad lines in the United States, Canada, and Mexico, even by ship into Cuba. The largest refrigerator-car line, both in cars owned and distances traveled, PFE's annual traffic totals 500,000 carloads. At Roseville, just under the Sierra Nevada, it has the world's largest railroad ice-manufacturing plant.

Perishables are 12 per cent of SP's gross freight revenue, making SP the heaviest perishable carrier in the nation. Animals and animal products are 2 per cent of the whole—the inroads of trucks are visible there. By and large, it might be said that SP hauls cauliflower and grapefruit, and thinks cauliflower and grapefruit, where many big Eastern lines haul and think coal. But the eight Western states are so varied in their produce that even this mountain of fruit and green stuff is only about one-eighth of the freight that SP hauls. Out of the pine and fir forests of the Northwest and the redwood forests of California SP loads 26 per cent of all the lumber shipped by rail in the United States; out of Louisiana, Texas, Arizona, and the San Joaquin Valley of California, 17 per cent of the cotton; out of Utah, Nevada, and Arizona, 85 per cent of the nation's rail-hauled copper ore and concentrates.

"A freeze in the south," says Bill Hale, "may cut the orange crop off at the knees, but the same winter weather and a jump in the market may produce freight of another kind somewhere else. The territory's so varied that I plumb forget to worry."

Another factor also helps to iron the wrinkles in a freight executive's brow. The Western and Southwestern states have been growing fast, and are swinging away from a purely agricultural economy into a manufacturing. So the railroad hauls increasing quantities of manufactured goods, both ways. Filling the freight cars both ways is a railroad man's dream. It can't be done with the reefers, the iced cars that tote the fruit and the lettuce. But the other cars, the boxcars, and the flats now carry manufactured goods eastward as well as westward. Quantities of steel pipe, for instance. Thousands of cars of it. Steel pipe from the East, for the oil and gas fields and pipelines of Texas and California. And returning, steel pipe fabricated around Los Angeles, for the pipelines and oil fields of the mid-continent and beyond.

"It's great stuff," says Bill. "No claims, no kicks about missed connections. Nice business to have."

For 1950 the empties coming home along the SP represent 34.1 per cent of the total freight mileage, which is the same as the all-railroad average.

Rates? People call every day to protest about rates. The book of tariffs, they say, is too big. Too complicated. Nobody but a freight man can understand it.

Once upon a time freight tariffs were very simple. Let's see what they looked like when all the freight tariffs in Texas, for example, could be printed on one sheet. Let's unfold a bit of paper 11 inches by 8¼. Some familiar railroads are signed to it—Houston and Texas Central, Texas and New Orleans, Buffalo Bayou Brazos and Colorado, Houston Tap and Brazoria, and Galveston, Houston and Henderson. The date is April 20, 1864.

In those uncomplicated times, a barrel of ale cost 40 cents to move a mile by rail. Coffee, per 100 pounds, cost 25 cents a mile—at which rate, to haul a bag of coffee across the continent would cost $7.50 per pound. Fodder, per bale, cost 12 cents a mile. Lumber by the car cost $4.50 per mile, and a car carried only 4,000 board feet. Anything above 4,000 took double rates. There was also a neat little item for demurrage. It really paid a consignee to get his car unloaded in a hurry, for the charge beyond the first 24 hours was $80 a day.

In these times of overgrown tariff books, the average charge on a ton of freight hauled a mile by the SP is around 1.375 cents.

To fill in the picture, it may be stated that SP freight amounted to 37,000,000,000 ton-miles in the more or less "normal" year 1950, putting the line third to Pennsylvania's 50,000,000,000 and New York Central's 39,000,000,000. The SP had crept up from fourth place which it held in 1929, passing Baltimore and Ohio in the process. In the forty years since 1910, SP freight business has tripled. In comparison with the ton-mileage of mighty "Pennsy," that great four-track hauler of coal and steel, SP in four decades has moved from 26 per cent up to 75 per cent. And by far the most of SP is still single-track. That calls for real railroading.

A side light is that although SP has a rail monopoly in two of the great perishable-producing sections, Imperial and Salinas, and the requirements of perishables-moving are exacting in the extreme, those two valleys have the finest service the railroad can give.

But the West is full of valleys, little and big, that are important exporters of produce to the tables of the nation. Here and there are some so isolated that even rails do not reach them. Lake County, in California, is an example. Perched on top of sizable mountains so close to San Francisco that flying boats sometimes land on its lakes when the bay is fogbound, Lake County nevertheless does not have a mile of rail. Natural obstacles have discouraged the capital investment that would be necessary.

Yet Lake County ships close to 1,000 carloads of pears every year—and by rail, as will be explained. The pears are great golden Bartletts, of premium quality, and if properly handled fetch a premium price. Handling pears carefully, keeping them cold, and landing them in the markets unbruised is a job for shipper, packer, the Pacific Fruit Express, and the trainmen who snake the long "reefer blocks" east.

When a grower sees that his pears are approaching picking condition, he phones to his fruit growers' exchange, which pools his order with others and notifies the Northwestern Pacific, a subsidiary of SP. The railroad man swings into action. He arranges to have that grower's pears picked up by Pacific Motor Trucking, an SP affiliate, and moved down by truck to the town of Ukiah, which lies at a lower level in the adjoining county. Ukiah is served by Northwestern Pacific's rails. The pears are transferred to a precooling plant or into precooled cars. That sounds easy, but to have the precooled cars at the right place on the right date calls for careful timing and expediting in several directions. The NWP has picked up the necessary refrigerator cars from the SP at a junction called Schellville and moved them to Santa Rosa, where there is an icing plant. This was handled by PFE, which has a district manager at Santa Rosa to supervise the refrigerator-car situation. When iced, the reefers are moved to Ukiah and placed ready for loading at 7 A.M.

At 3:30 P.M. all loads ready to move are switched into reefer trains and started on their way and by 3:30 the following morning are turned over to SP at Schellville for the long trip, over mountains and plains, to the marketing centers. A second train leaves the shipping territory at 10 P.M. with the cars that were not loaded in time for the earlier departure.

By now, four outfits—Pacific Motor Trucking, Northwestern Pacific, Pacific Fruit Express, and Southern Pacific (the first two subsidiaries of SP and the third equally owned by SP and Union Pacific)—have pooled their equipment and meshed their arrangements to get the succulent Bartlett pears down out of the mountain county and onward. But here enters that other interesting feature of the program. Neither shipper nor the SP knows where those refrigerator cars are going. That, as with lettuce and other perishables, depends upon market requirements that change from day to day and hour to hour. But growers back in Lake County, the county without a railroad, know that the right market will be found for the crop that represents a year's labor. And the sturdy reefer, after finding that market, will start back to the Coast for more fruit, this time oranges, perhaps, from Visalia.

But all the important freight doesn't move in solid trains, or in solid cars either. An important item is the less-than-carload lot of package freight that is wanted somewhere fast.

The railroad has developed an overnight merchandise freight service between a number of points such as Houston and Dallas, Los Angeles and Phoenix, and elsewhere. Here is the way it works between two typical points:

Late in the afternoon, a wholesale paper house in San Francisco receives a phone call from a Los Angeles paper distributor for a hurry-up order of two reams of paper of substance 80, color mauve, needed by a Los Angeles printer the next morning to finish a job that is already on his presses.

The San Francisco paper house phones SP. In San Francisco a pickup truck (SP's trucking equipment is painted the red and orange of the streamlined Daylight trains and are labeled PMT) rolls up before the warehouse doors close and takes the two packages of paper, 500 sheets each. The little shipment is yanked to the railroad freight yard at Fourth and Berry streets and hoisted aboard a specially equipped merchandise train, strictly a hot-shot, called the "Overnight."

Other lots of merchandise, small and big, arrive by similar pickup at the assembly point. All go into the waiting Overnight, otherwise No. 374, or Coast Merchandise East. (It is actually headed south, but since Los Angeles and San Francisco are on the east-west New Orleans-to-the-Pacific route, every train between the two cities operates east or west, in railroad language.)

The time passes. 7:00 P.M. Trainmaster Wayne Mace gives No. 374 a last once-over. Tonight it has 36 cars. At 7:15 the car doors slam shut. The last seal is placed. A white triangle painted on the door of each car tells that it is regularly assigned to this hot-shot service. Jimmy Jordan, superintendent of the Coast Division, ranges an eagle eye over everything. Car whackers poke their bugs, or torches, under and about for a final check of cars and couplings. Up ahead, a burly 4300 Mountain-type or a 4400-type locomotive—the combination "general service" steam racehorse and draft horse that is used to haul those fast passenger trains, the Daylights—backs down from the "barn," or Mission Bay roundhouse, and gently nudges into the shafts. Engineer and fireman swing down for their own last-minute checkup. They're going to rattle the hocks off her tonight. Back in the bouncer, Brakeman Charlie Hodgins receives several hundred waybills from Charlie Ward, waybill clerk. Waybills which could not be made out fast enough to travel on this train with the goods will be shot ahead by wire. Hodgins strikes a fusee to give the highball. No. 374 is out at 7:40 P.M. It's an hour and twenty minutes ahead of that famous high-liner, the Lark, and it will stay ahead, putting into Los Angeles still out in front.

Out she clumps, over switches and crossings. Engineer Harry Watson lifts his hand in signal to ashcat Clarence Whitcomb that he's opening her up.

The brakeman, perched in the caboose cupola, calls "all green" as 374 speeds past Bayshore tower. San Francisco Bay tosses back the dark rippling shadows of the San Bruno Hills. Burlingame, Redwood, Palo Alto, and it's 8:55 P.M. and San Jose. Here 18 more cars, with merchandise from San Jose and Oakland, are picked up. At 9:30 the train of 54 cars, loaded with 1,605 tons, is moving again. The prune and apricot orchards of the Santa Clara Valley flit by. At Coyote, a hamlet, a red order board notifies Engineer Watson that Telegrapher Jacobs has some orders for him, and Head Brakeman Dick Stewart steps to the gangway to scoop them up. Slow order—cut speed for a few miles. Harry does so, knowing that he will pick it up again.

And he does. He's clipping her off at the stacks now. Madrone, Morgan Hill, Gilroy. Little towns with their red neon lights laid out like rubies along the highway that parallels the track. Chittenden Pass. The winding road down to Pajaro River. Betabel curve. The whistle and the light trail of smoke in the moonlight tell the countryside that Harry's calliope is on time. Watsonville Junction at 10:45, where 14 cars for Coastside points are cut out. Another train, the Monterey Merchandise, is waiting; Pacific Grove, Salinas, Santa Cruz, Monterey, and Watsonville will have their merchandise parcels in the morning. Twenty minutes, a new crew, and on for San Luis Obispo.

Conductor Chet Dennen has been checking the waybills since 374 cleared the Watsonville yard and headed down the main line.

"We'll have to go like a scared rabbit," he remarks, "to keep ahead of the Lark—but we'll do it. Leonard Spangler is at the throttle and his ashcat is Bob Munn."

San Miguel, whose little white mission sleeps beside the tracks. Paso Robles. Santa Margarita, about a thousand feet up, and the Santa Lucia Mountains ahead. A helper engine is added to the string. Over the Santa Lucias, which offer 2½ miles of 2.2 grade going south and 10½ miles returning, are flipped behind. The San Francisco–bound Overnight, or No. 373, that left Los Angeles on an identical errand, screams by. Nos. 374 and

373 are strictly on time at the meeting point, which was managed by Centralized Traffic Control. At San Luis Obispo it is 2:38 on the train-men's watches, exactly as on the "advertised."

More cars and the helper engine are cut out at San Luis and there is another change of crew. Hugh Taff takes the throttle. Daylight breaks. No. 374 larrups into Santa Barbara, 120 miles below San Luis Obispo. Two cars are cut out. At 5:45 the train is on its way again. It has its fourth engineer of the night, A. D. Olin.

On she clips. Still-sleeping Ventura, Oxnard, the Santa Susana Mountains, waking Burbank, Glendale. The concreted banks of the Los Angeles River. The Los Angeles freight station, where the PMT trucks are lined up. It is 8:15 A.M. and the printer who is waiting for his paper will have it in a few minutes, strictly on time.

A highway truck—and there are plenty of them operating—could have handled the shipment handily. And except for a highly efficient service devised by the SP to meet that sort of competition, a highway truck would probably have had the business.

But the highway trucks didn't get it. To an SP mind, the store-door pickup, the overnight fast merchandise train, and the store-door delivery are the finest and most satisfying things that have come along since payday. The coordinated rail-truck idea was introduced to railroaddom via the Coast Route of the SP out in California, or so SP believes, though it is commonplace now in regions all over the country.

What happened was this: Back in 1929 SP grew alarmed about the competition of the trucks, and organized a motor-truck service of its own for the store-door pickup and delivery of less-than-carload freight. For a testing ground of this revolutionary theory in a railroad's handling of merchandise freight, the SP's electric line between Los Angeles and some twenty Southern California stations, the Pacific Electric Railway, was used. For the purpose, Pacific Electric Motor Transport Company was set up. In 1930, the service was extended to points on the Southern Pacific itself. Pacific Electric Motor Transport Company became Pacific Motor Transport Company. In 1933, SP created Pacific Motor Trucking Company for the purpose of operating trucks over the highway between points on its rails, as distinguished from the pickup and delivery service in cities and towns that had been performed by Pacific Motor Transport.

It proved to be a good idea. The scheme was being put to work out of San Francisco and many other California and Oregon points. Next was the establishment of coordinated train-truck service to give metropolitan centers overnight delivery of merchandise freight to outlying territory.

And so, in 1933, a natural evolution put a fast express-type service between San Francisco and Southern California points, linking train operations with PMT to give merchandise freight overnight service, with store-door pickup and delivery. The service zoomed, and reached to most communities served by SP in California, Oregon, Nevada, and Arizona.

The main purpose in expediting merchandise freight by the truck-train method was to use trucks as supplements to the mass movement of freight which trains, on rails, can do so economically. It resulted in more trains, not fewer.

Next stage was the development of specialized trains, the fast Overnights such as No. 374, to give these shipments the speed of passenger trains. That came in 1935. The sensational Overnight, the first exclusive merchandise train, a solid freight operated on fast schedule, made its bow over the run we have just taken, between San Francisco and Los Angeles. Similar fast merchandise trains began appearing all over the system within the trade areas of the important distributing centers. Freight cars were specially built and equipped. "Break-bulk" points were established at certain stations, where the cars disgorged their contents and the waiting trucks whisked them away. Mails became too slow for the waybills—the goods got there first. So teletyping of waybills was introduced.

Almost daily, fresh applications were found for the scheme. Construction materials, in carload lots, began to go from rail points to project sites, trains being met by railroad operated trucks. Fruit crops began moving from farming centers to the rails in the same single-management manner. All this activity certainly did not seem to stop the West's prodigious independent trucking industry; the big 60-foot diesel outfits with their twenty-two tires went on pounding the highways in ever-increasing numbers. But the SP was holding a lot of freight to its rails that otherwise would have been lost. SP's operations in Texas and Louisiana plunged deep in the newfangled way of expediting merchandise freight in the early thirties. By 1944 the railroad's system-wide trucking routes covered 12,491 miles of regular going.

The Overnights between Los Angeles and San Francisco, and elsewhere, had to come off during the war; the nation had other uses for the equipment. But store-door pickup and delivery of less-than-carload lots continued to function, and the Army, Navy, and wartime industrial establishments made huge use of the railroad's highway truck routes. And after the war, some of the first things to come back were the Overnights.

For freight's the thing.

The railroad, while eager to handle all the overnight merchandise freight it can get, and all the perishables, welcomes the steel pipe and other non-expedited freight that constitute the West's growing manufacturing industry. But they, too, can give a freight department some grief, as in the case of a gondola loaded with ore that was shipped by Bethlehem Steel from

San Francisco. It was no ordinary ore. A special brand of rock for a special alloy of steel, the dab of stuff in the big gondola was heavier than it looked, and worth a neat $15,000.

The gondola started north. En route, the shipment disappeared. If the ore had been highly volatile wine from sunny Napa Valley it could not have taken off into thin air more completely. Bethlehem, failing to get its shipment to destination, burned the telephone wires to the SP in a desperate treasure hunt. The car was located all right, but its ore was gone. A section foreman at Toledo, Oregon, had thought the car to be an empty, and the extra-heavy rock in the bottom of it just a lot of litter. Always glad to ballast his tracks, he had shoveled the stuff out and tamped it between the ties. The railroad went after the $15,000 worth of track ballast with spoons and sieves and everything that would scrape and lift.

Yes, it's fun being a freight man. Nothing to worry about at all—never anything.

27

Certain Gents in Masks

ONE OF THE STRANGEST smashups in American railroad history, because every shred of evidence showed it to be premeditated but nobody made even a snatch for a traveler's wallet, occurred on August 12, 1939. The brilliant streamliner City of San Francisco was the victim.

At the controls was Edward F. Hecox, a sixty-five-year-old engineer who had come up through all the chairs, including that of one-time stage driver. A steadier man never piloted a diesel.

The long, sparkling train was bowling down Humboldt Canyon in Nevada at a 50- to 60-mile clip. All was going smoothly. The last train had passed that way three hours earlier. Automatic block signals displayed the "proceed." The hour was 9:30 P.M. and the train was 5 or 10 minutes late. It shot around a curve and Hecox saw a bit of tumbleweed lying against a rail. Perhaps a moment's thought would have told him that tumbleweed does not blow when it's green, and this clump was green; but a man may be forgiven for not calling on such botanical knowledge on the instant— nor could he have stopped the train if he had thought of it.

There was a roar, a shriek of steel on ties, the dousing of lights, a grating and a bumping and the shock of cars going over, and Hecox and his pulling unit had plowed through a torn-up rail and rammed across a bridge and 997 feet beyond it before stopping.

Hecox dragged himself out of the wreckage, made a quick appraisal, and started down the track at a run. At the first emergency telephone he called Carlin, and the message he uttered brought every doctor and nurse in that part of Nevada and sent President A. D. McDonald, Vice-president Joe Dyer, and General Manager L. B. McDonald hustling from San Francisco, together with a corps of detectives and newsmen.

The sight that met their eyes was appalling. Eleven cars had been derailed and four sent spinning off the embankment into the Humboldt River. The diner had gone through the bridge. Twenty-four persons were killed, 108 injured. The Elko General Hospital absorbed all it could of the injured, and the rest were hurried down to California points. Fortunately the rival Western Pacific's track was not far distant, SP and WP having a "pair track" agreement in that territory, and trains could be routed over the parallel line.

Detectives swarmed. They found some queer things. Nuts, bolts, and angle bars had been removed from a rail joint, apparently with a wrench. The inside spikes had been pulled up from nine crossties. The rail had been forced inward 45⁄8 inches, probably with a jack. The rail had been spiked down in its new position, and the end of the rail had been daubed with brown paint. This, and the tumbleweed, had prevented the end of the rail from showing up in Engineer Hecox's headlight. The misaligned rail had not been forced inward far enough to break the electric bond wires connecting the signals.

The FBI and other sleuths, after dragging the Humboldt River for 900 feet, brought up an iron claw bar, an iron bar recognized as the handle of a journal jack, a small roll of wire, a blue cloth zipper jacket weighted with a rock, a spike maul, and a 37-inch track wrench wrapped in a canvas jacket. The evidence indicated that these tools and others found near the scene were stolen from the railroad and used in displacing the rail. Chief Engineer W. H. Kirkbride had also picked up a can of mahogany-colored paint near the scene of the wreck. The paint had been used to camouflage the displaced rail from the vision of the train engineer. Spectrographic analysis showed that kind of paint on the canvas jacket pulled from the river. It all added up to clear evidence of vandalism, and the SP posted $10,000 reward for the criminals.

There were enough evidences of intentional malice to satisfy a judge, and the road was held blameless.

But why? But why?

Did someone plan to loot the broken train, but lose his nerve? Or was the fiend a lunatic, or a deliberate killer? Handsome enough rewards were posted to turn up the malefactor, if anyone had information of him, but no one turned him in. The rewards have gone unclaimed, and the perpetrator of the wreck of the City of San Francisco, whether motivated by revenge or malice or some insane conceptions of fun, still remains unmasked.

Not far from where the City of San Francisco was derailed, the West had had its first masked robber train holdup. That was sixty-nine years before, or eighteen months after the Central Pacific first started running.

The train to so distinguish itself was No. 1, the Atlantic Express, which pulled out of Oakland on the morning of November 4, 1870. Its consist amounted to a shiny red wood-burning locomotive, a combination baggage and express car, a day coach, and a round-ended sleeper.

As the train teakettled its way up the Sierra, a jolly group of characters from Virginia City and the California mountains loitered in an abandoned mine in Nevada's Peavine Mountains, 3 miles beyond Reno and 385 miles east of the starting point. They had cards, bottles, grub, blankets, and a fire. Their leader was Big Jack Davis, a pious-appearing fellow, who looked as if he could turn his collar around backward and walk up to the pulpit of any church. This disarming mien had cost a lot of poker players of the Comstock region a lot of money for their evening's entertainment. Jack had surrounded himself with a staunch gang of cutthroats. A telegram from a confederate down at the bay had told them that No. 1 had $60,000 in its express car.

Number 1 tooled up the mountainside, dipped over the crest, and ran into a two-hour delay at Truckee. A couple of freights had collided ahead. A bright moon shone when the train tootled out of Truckee and slid down toward the desert.

At Verdi, a lumber siding, things happened. Engineer Small found a gun in his ribs. Men in masks had climbed over his woodpile and dropped in upon him. Under orders and some hard, steely nudging, he yanked the whistle cord. That sent the trainmen leaping for the hand brakes and Conductor Mitchell jumping to the ground to sprint ahead and see what was what. He soon found out. Seven masked men were what. "Unhook the baggage car from the coaches!" their leader yelled. The cars were unhooked and, while the amazed conductor stared, down the grade and out of sight sped the engine and baggage express.

Conductor Mitchell was a man of enterprise. He had no engine, but he had a downgrade and a schedule to maintain.

"Release the brakes!" Mitchell yelled to his trainmen, and the two passenger coaches set off in pursuit.

When he caught up with the engine and express, Mitchell found that the express had been robbed, and the express messenger, engineer, and fireman had been herded into the express car and told to stay there. Somewhat more than $40,000 in gold and specie had been carried off, but a good many thousand dollars' worth of bar silver had been left behind—too heavy to carry.

And that was the Coast's first train robbery.

The second was not long in coming. Within twenty-four hours, in fact, and to the same train. It happened at Independence, Nevada. Another gang jumped the engine and express car, threatened the new engineer and fireman with rifles and carbines, kicked all trainmen but the engineer off the train, had themselves hauled a few miles farther, and leaped off with about all the money and silver that the first gang had spurned. There were four of them, and they clattered southward on four waiting horses.

The first gang was soon rounded up. Three had made for a little inn north of Verdi and excited the curiosity of the innkeeper's wife, who watched them through a knothole, saw the loot, and sent for peace officers. Eleven thousand six hundred dollars in twenty-dollar gold pieces do make a pretty sight. The captured men squealed on Big Jack Davis; the chief of police at Virginia City broke up a good card game by collaring the pious man; Big Jack took the chief back to Verdi and showed him the rest of the money in a culvert; and that was that. Nineteen thousand seven hundred dollars came out of the culvert. Davis talked the judge into letting him off with ten years, talked the governor into pardoning him in three, and died a few years later in a gun battle with a stagecoach messenger.

The second band of brigands who robbed No. 1 proved to be cavalry deserters from a Utah garrison. They were trailed by a dropped glove.

But that single journey of a single train opened up a whole new Western industry. It flourished long and lustily and, on the whole, with singularly little novelty or innovation. Sometimes the occasion was excitement, sometimes hatred of the railroad, but most of the time—as in all other industry —just the old-fashioned profit motive.

Jim Symington, an affable fellow, had punched with his railroad conductor's "pliers" the tickets of No. 17's passengers, and he spotted a friend named Ed Bentley and sat down to chat with him.

Ed was a deputy sheriff of Modesto, in the San Joaquin Valley, and he was bound for Goshen Junction.

The landscape was obscured with the darkness of a cloudy February evening. Far away, a light burned in a settler's cabin. This was the era of great agrarian hatred for the railroad, back in the 1880s.

"The country is growing plumb crowded," said Jim. He stretched his legs and relaxed. Hen Gebert, the brakeman, sat down too in the murky smoker. The southbound rattler picked up speed.

The brakes ground. The cars lurched. "What—" sputtered Jim Symington.

The train stopped in the prairie, that evening of February 22, 1889, and Jim got off to investigate. Ed and Hank followed.

As Conductor Symington neared the head end of the train, there was a burst of blue and pink light and a roar, and the express car rose from its tracks and settled back. Jim Symington and another trainman who had joined him on the west side of the train were knocked to the ground. When

Jim found his feet again, or became aware of them, they were already in rapid motion away from there. They continued in high speed until the hamlet of Pixley was reached, 2 miles north.

"We're being robbed," he gasped.

The few citizens of Pixley heard the news but were only mildly moved by it. Apparently somebody hated the railroad even more than they did. Before Jim Symington could stir them to action, the train itself rolled in. It had backed the 2 miles and it bore the body of Hank Gabert, who had stopped a load of buckshot as he stooped, lantern in hand, to peer under the train from its west side.

Engineer Pete Boelger told his story. A few moments after the train had left Pixley in the first place, and just as it had settled into a nice comfortable jog of 20 miles per hour, something hard had been shoved into his ribs. He had turned to find a masked man behind him. "Stop at the next crossing a quarter mile down the track and you won't be hurt."

That was when Pete had slammed on his brakes.

There were two bandits, said Pete. Five, said J. R. Kelly, the express messenger, whose car had been blown when he refused to throw out the treasure box. Nine, swore the passengers, or fifteen. But Kelly had been inside his locked car and the passengers were pretty much flat between the seats or on the aisle floors, so Pete Boelger's description stood. Two men in masks.

What Pete was not able to add at the time was that their names were Chris Evans and John Sontag, that they were a pair of disgruntled settlers who believed themselves done out of their land by the high-handed railroad, that they had declared war on the road, and that the Pixley robbery was the opener in a campaign that was going to last four years, cost another ten lives, result in one of the most sensational manhunts ever mounted in the West, and all but wreck one of California's two penitentiaries.

Eleven months passed. Deputy Sheriff Ed Bentley had made quite a story of what he would have done if he had got up to the head end of that train in time; Conductor Jim Symington had covered himself with laudations for the way he raced for help; Engineer Pete Boelger had more or less got over the feel of that cold revolver on a cold, foggy February night, when the railroad got it again.

This time it was No. 19, also southbound, and once more it was in winter darkness. The string of cars had pulled out of Goshen Junction, 23 miles north of Pixley, when Engineer S. R. De Pue and his ashcat, W. G. Lovejoy, felt the prickly caress of guns against their spines. The details of the Pixley affair were still fresh in their minds. They were off the engine and leading the way to the express car before the cars stopped

"Goat," the first yard engine operated on Portland Division, 1884

OLD AND NEW IN OREGON

The diesel-electric Shasta Daylight at Odell Lake in 1951

Top. Pioneer locomotive "C. P. Huntington" compared with a 2-10-2

THE GREAT DAYS OF STEAM

Bottom. The "C. P. Huntington" tries itself for size alongside one of the Daylight locomotives

bucking. At their urging, the express messenger tossed his box out. A tramp who was riding the rods took occasion to poke his head out, and was shot and killed. The two robbers made off. Headlines, company detectives, posses, nothing definite discoverable. There had been $20,000 in the box. Sontag and Evans, who had made for the Sierra wilds, were well fixed for bacon and beans. Peace on the San Joaquin Valley route lasted for another year.

Southbound No. 17 got it again in February, 1891.

It was a routine job. The masked pair slipped aboard the tender at a place called Alila and took Engineer Thorne and Fireman Radcliffe in tow. At the door of the express car, things went a little awry for the desperadoes. C. C. Haswell, the Wells Fargo messenger, declined to open the door.

"Open up!"

"Go to hell!"

"Open up or we'll blast you open!"

Haswell got the shape of a man in his sights and was ready to let go when a shotgun roared. A burst of buckshot creased his scalp. He got one shot out through his loophole in return. Passengers on the train also put up a fusillade. The robbers hastily departed. Fireman Radcliffe was badly wounded. The train went on to Delano.

Sheriffs, posses, detectives, more headlines. There was a wild chase after nothing at all in a westerly direction toward the Coast Range. There were reports that the desperadoes were surrounded—that their surrender and capture were imminent—that the surrender had been postponed—that the quarry had slipped away or never had been there. Messenger Haswell, lionized at first, was subsequently tried for accidentally plugging Fireman Radcliffe. He was acquitted.

The railroad detectives and the sheriffs of Kern and Tulare counties had a stroke of luck. They discovered that the four Dalton brothers, badmen from the Missouri country, were wintering in California. A couple of them had been quietly building a store on a mountain road at La Honda, near the Coast. Grat Dalton was grabbed and convicted of the shooting, Bill Dalton was held as an accessory, and Bob and Emmet Dalton dusted fast. Grat Dalton walked out of the Visalia jail in an easy escape soon after.

With at least one of the three jobs pinned on Grat Dalton, the railroad breathed easier—for a few months. And then a train holdup on the valley line shook that theory to pieces. Southbound No. 19 pulled out of Modesto on the evening of September 3, 1891. A mile from the station, two men dropped off the coal into the cab, bagged the engine crew, and used them for cover to advance on the express car.

No. 17, No. 19, No. 17, No. 19. The same pair of trains, always in the evening, always southbound, always attacked from the coal tender, always the move to the express car.

However, the script was altered a little from that point onward. There were some men of fighting heart aboard the train. Two of them, Messenger W. V. Reed and a helper, whipped out revolvers and prepared to hold the fort in spite of the dynamite which soon was hurled. The first charge blasted a hole in the wooden express car big enough to drive a horse through. The robbers then handed the captured fireman a candle and told him to climb in through the hole. Messenger Reed, who had been at the far end of the car when it was blasted, advised otherwise.

"Don't shoot," pleaded the fireman, starting to clamber in.

"Drop that candle or I'll shoot it out," informed Reed.

"Go on in, or this second stick of dynamite will go off under you," stated one of the bandits.

The unhappy fireman decided Reed was the most dangerous, and backed out just as another dynamite stick skittered across the car floor. Its fuse fell off.

A couple of railroad detectives named Harris and Lawson, who had been riding the cushions, were approaching meanwhile along a fence line. Len Harris saw some legs under the express car and took a shot at them. The legs moved rapidly aside and a shot sang in return. There was more shooting both ways and Harris got a bullet in the neck. The robbers, disgusted with their luck, adjourned to a couple of saddle horses tied nearby and rode away.

Sheriffs and posses of Stanislaus, San Joaquin, and Tulare counties, posters and rewards of $3,000, the arrests of numerous pairs of men who happened to be "one tall and one short," a wild hunt for the rest of the Dalton brothers—and again, nothing. The hunt continued until, thirteen months later, the Dalton gang was liquidated in far away Coffeyville, Kansas, during a bank robbery.

But just before the famous battle in Coffeyville, and at a time when the Daltons were soon known to be far away, desperadoes struck the SP again in the San Joaquin. It was once more train No. 17's turn. The site was near a spot called Collis, another of the dreary tank-station-and-siding hamlets of that long, lonely valley of dust and wheat. The name has since been changed to Kerman.

On an August night in 1892 a couple of threshing-crew bosses, Jack Kennedy and John Arnold, rode toward their camp in the wheat field after an evening of poker at Collis.

"What's that thing down there? That black thing?" asked Arnold as they neared the railroad track.

"Looks like a buggy," decided Kennedy.

"Funny place for a buggy," commented Arnold.

A distant chugging—No. 17, southbound, leaving Collis station—told them that the hour was midnight.

"I'm going to have a look at that buggy," remarked Kennedy.

Arnold yawned. "Not me. I'm hitting the blankets."

No. 17 chuffed and clanked, then unaccountably ground to a halt.

"Now what—" exclaimed Kennedy. "Trains don't stop around here unless they have to." He reined his horse and sat listening. There were voices on the night air. One said, "Have a cigar." Then, "Put this dynamite under your engine wheel and light it."

"What with?"

"With the cigar I gave you, of course."

Kennedy swung from his horse and darted toward his tent. The rest of the threshing crew were asleep. He came out with a shotgun.

He hurried over the stubble and neared a ditch alongside the tracks just as the night was lit by a lurid flare, and the dusty air was split by a loud clap. Against the flare of light he saw the silhouettes of several men.

Kennedy crawled along the ditch and found himself within shotgun range. The night was starlit; there were several figures moving. There were voices, some of command, some of protest. He weighed the weapon in his hands. Some of those shapes might be trainmen. Best to go easy. Wait and be sure.

Another blast.

It filled the night with red and purple and green and yellow pyrotechnics. For a bare instant the express car was seen heaving and shuddering. The succeeding blackness was intense. A shotgun, not Kennedy's, whanged a bucketful of shot along the train to keep passengers and train crew ducking.

Kennedy found other persons beside him. Arnold was one. Two of them were train passengers. The threshing crew were there, too. Kennedy was still unable to make out which silhouette near the express car was innocent victim and which was villain. Gun cocked, he held his fire.

The conversation was easy to hear. "Open those safes!"

"I can't. They're time-locked."

There was a thump of something hard, probably on a man's head. "Now open them."

"Kill me if it will do you any good, but I tell you I can't. They're for Chicago, New York, and Kansas City."

"All right, load up with what's loose and climb out."

Events later showed that Wells Fargo express messenger George D.

Roberts, a man of indomitable stamp, had been seated on his stool thumbing waybills when the first blast came under his car. It knocked his light out, tore the untied shoes from his feet, and hurled him into a corner of the car. He had crawled to his revolver and crouched with it in a corner. The second blast knocked him in a heap, but was not toward his end of the car and failed to knock the fight out of him. A couple more blasts, with the same result, though the car was beginning to look like shredded hay. Another stick of dynamite rolled in. Roberts tried to kick it out with his stockinged foot. The stick didn't go straight; it remained in the car. Roberts flung himself flat. Again the car humped and jumped. While he was dazed, the assailants bounded in and covered him with pistols, and one snatched his keys.

There was enough left of the indestructible Roberts to make a porter for one of the sacks of loot. The fireman, at the point of a gun, was made to carry the other. Kennedy, the armed observer of it all, was unable to get in a shot because the messenger, the fireman, and the pair of robbers were closely bunched. The quartet marched off, and presently the buggy was heard clattering away into the night. Spectators rose with a yell and made for the badly shaken Roberts and the groggy fireman, Will Lewis.

Passengers came up from the car floors and out of car lavatories. Gun-toter Kennedy realized sadly that he had lost the chance of a lifetime to get in a well-aimed hatful of slugs. The partially disabled engine clanked off with its string for Fresno, the nearest town of size. It arrived there at 1:30 A.M. Some reports had $5,000 stolen, some had $50,000. The only certainties were that the SP's valley line had been stuck up for a fifth time in four years, by a technique that varied each time only in the quantities of dynamite used; that the successive holdups had carried with them a dramatic quality of rising excitement and suspense, coupled with rising rewards; that this fifth blow had produced an authentic hero who, unlike Messenger Haswell, was not in any way chargeable with shooting the wrong man; and that there were two or three fellows abroad in the San Joaquin who really had it in for the railroad.

Who were they? Some sleuths and railroad brass were still sure they were the Daltons. But the Daltons were given to ranging far and free, whereas these five blows had all been struck in a concentrated area. It seemed more probable that local settlers were conducting a bit of private and lucrative feuding against the hated corporation. That narrowed the field; San Joaquin's population still had certain numerical limits. Detectives combed over the names of all who had been heard making threats or nursing grudges against the railroad, and one way and another they reduced the possibles to two or three men, known to be associates, who lived near each robbery at the time of its happening and then moved to another point in the valley soon afterward. When they discovered that two of the suspects, Chris Evans and John Sontag, filled all the requirements and had not been home on the night of the Collis party, the search abruptly narrowed.

From the moment it was determined that Chris Evans and John Sontag, dispossessed and disgruntled settlers, had not been home on the night of the Collis robbery but had been off somewhere with a hired livery rig, the case began to "break." The railroad detectives moved cautiously at first. They had arrested the wrong man too often and were cagey. Will Smith, a cinder dick assigned to the railroad's No. 1 sleuthing job of the nineties, met Chris Evans on the street of Visalia a morning or so after the Collis party.

"Howdy, Chris," said Smith to the stocky, stooped man with the farm-chore hands.

"Morning, Will," said Chris.

"Seen John Sontag and his brother George lately?"

"They're up at my house."

Smith drifted around that way. He picked up George Sontag, against whom there was no particular evidence, and with another officer went back for John, or for Chris if he could get him. Chris had returned. The sight of the officer meant only one thing. He grabbed a gun. That, to the detective, was the tip-off; innocent men don't grab guns when they see guests on the threshold. Evans turned and ran. Smith fired a shot. John Sontag, who was on hand, fired another. It missed Smith, but fatally wounded the second officer. And the chase was on. Flight, a second bloody battle, escape into the rough foothill country, and a terrific fight in a mountain cabin where two possemen died; arrest; escape from prison, further gun battles in which John Sontag was mortally wounded and Evans had an arm shattered and an eye shot out; rearrests, new jailbreaks, violence of a hundred kinds, including an effort to carry Folsom prison by assault and spring its famous prisoners—it all came to an end with John Sontag dead and prison gates clanging on Evans.

During the long manhunt, settlers had given frequent help to the desperadoes and newspaper reporters had even ferreted them out and interviewed them. The portion of the public which had shielded the fugitives hated the railroad more than it hated crime.

And then there were the De Autrements, many years later.

With a revolver pressed against his head, Engineer Bates brought No. 13 to a sudden stop, the locomotive just outside the mouth of Tunnel No. 13 in the Siskiyou Mountains, near the California-Oregon border. The long train stalled in the dark and smoky tunnel.

Across the cab young Marvin Seng, the fireman, looked uneasily into the muzzle of a sawed-off shotgun in the hands of one of the two swarthy young bandits.

"Get down on the ground and keep your hands up or you'll be dead ones," commanded the bandit with the shotgun. (The conversation will again have to be imagined.)

Old Sid Bates set the brakes to prevent a runaway, and followed the fireman to the ground. He and Seng stood by the engine with their hands up while the younger desperado covered them with his automatic.

The second holdup man joined a third, who was waiting at the tunnel mouth with a suitcase. The two of them walked into the tunnel, carrying the heavy bag. They returned shortly, stretching two long wires along the ground.

Daugherty, the mail clerk, opened the door of his car to see why the delay. A bandit fired just as Daugherty slammed it tight again.

"Come out of there or we'll blow you out," called the man with the gun.

Daugherty ignored him.

A bandit touched the ends of the wires together. A terrific explosion in the tunnel followed. Smoke and steam poured from the entrance. One of the holdup men tried to enter the wrecked mail car, peering about with a flashlight. The smoke and steam drove him out.

"I'll go back and uncouple her," he said. "Then we'll run her up the track a piece. Come on, you, and help."

Young Seng followed, as ordered. The smoke suffocated him and he returned. The bandit pushed into the tunnel alone.

In a few minutes a man, bearing a red lantern, came groping toward the mouth of the tunnel. He was Johnson, the brakeman.

Two shots rang out.

Johnson faltered, stumbled on, and fell at the feet of the robbers.

"Wait a minute," he gasped, "that fellow in there wants you to pull ahead."

Then he lost consciousness.

The younger bandit ordered Old Bates into the cab again.

"Pull her ahead," he instructed.

Bates gave the locomotive the steam. The wheels spun. The train did not budge. Old Bates explained that the brakes were locked by the explosion.

"You can't fool with me," threatened the younger man, "I'll give you one more chance to pull ahead or I'll blow your brains out."

Bates opened the throttle wide. The engine snorted. Again the wheels spun on the tracks. The train did not budge.

The third bandit came running from the tunnel. "It's all up," he yelled. "We can't get into the mail car for half an hour with all that smoke and steam, and we can't pull her out with the brakes jammed."

He looked at young Seng, standing by the locomotive, his hands above his head, the muzzle of a gun threatening him.

"Two's dead already," said the bandit to his accomplice. "If we kill these two there won't be any witnesses."

Two shots. The fireman crumpled.

"Bump off the old man and beat it quick," the leader called to the younger desperado in the cab with Old Bates.

One more shot. Bates toppled from his seat by the throttle.

After a while Marrett, the conductor, came stumbling from the tunnel. The smoke and steam that had balked the bandits still stifled him. He looked around and saw only disaster and dead men. He examined Old Bates and saw that he was dead. Marrett turned off the engine valves. Then he found Seng lying on the ground, dead, a pool of blood by his head.

Marrett turned to Johnson, the brakeman, unconscious but still breathing. A passenger came up, and together they gave Johnson first aid, thinking he had been gassed by the smoke in the tunnel. Then they opened his shirt and found four gun shot wounds in the pit of his stomach. He died in their hands without uttering a sound.

How was he killed? Who were his assailants?

"The mail clerk's dead," the passenger told Marrett. "He was blown to bits."

Marrett looked around him. He saw the long wires running from the mail car. He saw two knapsacks and three pair of foot pads, hastily dropped. He found a pair of overalls. He examined the locomotive and could find no sign of an explosion.

"It wasn't an explosion," Marrett concluded; "it's a holdup."

He hurried down the tracks to sound the alarm and to get a relief crew for his train, filled with excited passengers and stalled in the dark, reeking tunnel.

Dan O'Connell, the chief detective, arrived that afternoon to look for clues and to trail the murderers. There was not much to work on. No living man had seen the bandits. A roadbed worker thought he had seen two men swing aboard No. 13, about one o'clock, as she pulled into Siskiyou Tunnel near the California-Oregon border.

The meager evidence included the wires and the remains of the detonator which set off the dynamite at the end of the mail car.

There were the two knapsacks. Where were they bought? If the merchant that sold them had put a trade mark on them, it was destroyed by the bandits.

And the foot pads! They were carefully creosoted. That made it impossible for the dogs to get a scent from which to follow the trail of the desperadoes.

It was a planned job, but criminals always leave their cards somewhere.

The overalls contained the "card." From them, hounds rushed from Portland caught the scent and followed the trail through the woods for a way, then suddenly lost it. Black pepper, plentifully sprinkled behind them as the bandits ran, had defeated the dogs.

But the overalls were carefully packed and sent to San Francisco. A professor of criminology at Berkeley, E. O. Heinrichs, became interested in them. He pored over the dirty garments. He measured them and estimated the height of the bandit who had worn them. He found tiny chips in the pockets. Examining these under a microscope, he concluded that the wearer of the overalls had been working in a logging camp. The chips were newly hewn.

Then the professor made a ten-strike. Crumpled deep in the pencil pocket he found a tiny piece of paper. It was a money order receipt. He found a number, a date, and the post office from which the money order was sent. It was from Eugene, Oregon.

The postmaster at Eugene traced the money order. It was sent by Ray De Autrement in Eugene to Verne, a brother, in Lakewood, New Mexico. From Ray's father it was learned that Ray had been working in a lumber camp with his brothers Roy and Hugh.

About this time the two knapsacks found at the scene of the crime were identified by a merchant in Eugene as two of three he had sold a short time before to Hugh De Autrement.

The evidence pointed at Ray and Roy, twins, twenty-three years of age, and Hugh, nineteen, just graduated from high school in Lakewood, New Mexico. Of the three, only Ray had a criminal record. He had served a year for criminal syndicalism in the state of Washington. The hunt for the three was long, but it was successful. The end for the trio was the state penitentiary at Salem, Oregon.

The De Autrements, tripped by a pair of overalls, were responsible for the most sensational of SP train holdups, the possibly bandit-directed sabotaging of the City of San Francisco excepted.

28

Ferryboat Days

SAN FRANCISCO—BOUND TRAVELERS on the Overland, Shasta, and San Joaquin Valley routes reach the end of rail at Oakland Pier, a great wooden train house with the stain of years hanging from its cavernous ceiling and the sign "Central Pacific" still visible here and there. The brown and yellow building was erected back in the days when ladies wore bustles and businessmen wore stovepipe hats. This dark shed is an authentic part of the overland scene; as much so as the waddling ferryboats which await the trains; as the often fogbound bay itself.

But a visitor to Oakland Pier whose mind runs back a decade or two finds something missing. The hordes of commuters rushing for the big red electric trains are gone.

The Overland or Cascade arrivals move with their hand luggage past veteran ticket choppers, over a time-worn ferry apron, and onto the clean canvased deck of one of three remaining ferries, white and glistening and shipshape as of yore. But here again something has changed. The whole trainload of passengers is gulped by the boat with the facility of an old-time commuter gulping a cup of coffee, and there is room for more. Many more. The passengers are lost on the big *Berkeley,* which used to be crowded to the gunwales.

"Where are they all?" he asks. The great San Francisco–Oakland Bay Bridge is the answer.

A gong bongs in the engine room below, the boat pulls out, a few sea gulls curve and plane in pursuit . . . there used to be flocks of them, too, for the stewards would toss over a lot of half-nibbled food. Which reminds the passenger—how about a thick china cupful of that ferryboat coffee? He hunts out the dining room that used to be in the cellar of the ship and finds it a dark hole, the lights and smells and animation gone, the stair roped off. In the cabin on the upper deck, under the Victorian art glass transoms, there is a sort of soda fountain instead, where coffee and pop are dispensed.

He goes out on the forward deck.

Here at least is something familiar. The wind whips in through the Golden Gate, under the long orange-red bridge of that name. A brisk trade wind from the Pacific, it buffets between Alcatraz Island and Telegraph Hill and caroms off Goat Island. The traveler braces his feet and holds his hat. Today there is no fog. Yonder spreads San Francisco with towers, hills, Ferry Building, wharves, and—yes, on three or four streets —the cable cars.

But something else has got into the picture a great east-west silver swipe across the sky. A bridge that takes off from the east shore on stilts, hangs by cantilever principle till it tires of that, dives through Yerba Buena Island by tunnel, and emerges to spring for the San Francisco shore in two festoons of cable held up by steel towers and anchored in the middle by an islandlike chunk of concrete. It is a double-decked 8¼-mile bridge with autos skipping along on the upper deck, commuter trains and trucks and buses on the lower.

Because the San Francisco–Oakland Bay Bridge was not built to handle overland trains, through passengers still take the twenty-minute ride by ferry, and carry on a picturesque and satisfying tradition.

It began in gold-rush days with sailboats and rowboats. In the budding days of San Francisco before the 1850s, crossing the bay was a matter of difficulty and some peril. The first regular steam ferry service was established in 1850 by the *Kangaroo,* making the trip twice weekly. It was joined by a small iron "propeller" not considered worthy of a name, and a couple of Sunday excursion boats. The *Hector,* which succeeded the *Kangaroo,* was a small side-wheeler operated by a set of cogs and an engine designed for a sawmill. A boat named the *Red Jacket,* commanded by Capt. John R. Fouratt, introduced a notable family of ferryboat skippers; eighty years later, when the era of ferryboating entered the shadows of the two transbay bridges, there were still two Fouratts skippering the double-enders.

Until Central Pacific took over in the 1860s, systematic ferrying between Oakland and San Francisco was done by a pair of slugging business rivals named Charles Minturn and James B. Larue. They charged a dollar at first, but soon fell to trading punches, and the rate slipped to a dime, but finally stabilized at a quarter. In 1865 Larue sold his vessels to the Central Pacific and in 1866 Minturn took his activities to the north shore and established a transportation line which became the genesis of the SP's present-day Northwestern Pacific.

Minturn's service between San Francisco and the East Bay had operated under the name San Francisco and Oakland Railroad Company. His little ferry, the *Contra Costa* (not the big car ferry of Benicia fame), started running on September 1, 1863, from a point long since obliterated, about where Oakland Pier juts out. Another pioneer local ferrying outfit, the San Francisco and Alameda, in 1864 put on a craft called the *Sophie McLean*. When the first overland train arrived on the east shore of the bay on September 6, 1869, the *Sophie* took its passengers over the waters. The Central Pacific group had acquired both ferry lines, and moved the *Sophie* and its successors to the new Oakland Wharf in November.

This pier, also called Long Wharf (later succeeded by another of the same name), extended out into the bay 6,900 feet. The ferryboat *El Capitan* shuttled back and forth over the bay from this land terminus. In 1871 came the new Long Wharf, a 2-mile finger with three ferry slips, one of them for a freight-car ferry. During that year the line on the two sides of the "creek" dividing Oakland from Alameda carried 1,867,000 passengers. A short while afterward, the first of the San Francisco foot-of-Market-Street ferry buildings was erected. It did duty until the 1890s, when the present building was erected—a structure which engulfed and disgorged millions of local and through travelers a year for the ensuing forty years, and then suddenly became silent as a mausoleum.

The pride of the bay in the 1860s was the slim, speedy steamer *Chrysopolis,* which was operated by the California Steam Navigation Company from San Francisco to the foot of K Street, Sacramento. Once she made the 90-mile run in 5 hours 19 minutes. Her tall twin stacks and ornamented side-wheel housings gave her a jaunty air.

The *Chrysopolis* was launched in 1860 at Steamboat Point, foot of Fourth Street, San Francisco—length of wooden hull 245 feet, beam 40, capacity 1,000 passengers, fittings the last word in plush and beveled-mirror luxury. After fifteen years of river life she was sold to the Central Pacific and considerably transformed. She became 16 feet longer, 72 feet wide at the guards, and a double-ender—in other words, a ferry. She was twice rebuilt after that, the last time in 1920, but she kept going with the same old engines until the great bridge put the ferry out of operation in 1939. Seventy-six years her vertical-beam single-cylinder engine had been chugging. When sold to the wreckers she went out like a Viking. She was put to the torch. Her name, as a ferry, was *Oakland.*

In 1887 the SP acquired the South Pacific Coast Railroad, a short line with large original ambitions projected by Jim Fair of Comstock mining fame. Jim's line started from the south end of San Francisco Bay and ran as a narrow-gauge to the big redwood tree region of Felton, near Santa

Cruz and Monterey Bay, with an eastern terminus at Centerville south of Oakland—the last few miles being managed with freight and passenger cars drawn on rails by a horse. Originally the South Pacific Coast had been intended to span the state and join with the Denver and Rio Grande, but its ambitions remained on paper. Among other properties it also had a ferry line, Alameda to San Francisco. This started operating in 1878 with the ferryboat *Newark*. The *Newark* passed under the SP house flag and continued ferrying passengers for an all-told service of some six decades, though she took on a new look from time to time.

Another history-maker was our friend the *Berkeley*, a steel-hulled propeller-driven double-ender when launched in 1897. She was bigger than anything that had trundled the bay before, and quite a house-moving job it was to get her across, through winds and tide rips, and into her slip without taking out half the piles. The time arrived when the *Alameda* and the *Santa Clara* made the *Berkeley* no longer look like a circus tent for size, but hers was the last quiet chuckle: she was still to be doing business on the bay when those waddling queens were gone, and she is doing business yet.

After Jim Fair launched his ambitious railroad which never became a transcontinental, SP ran ferries from a long fill on the Alameda shore, where they connected with the ex–Jim Fair trains for Santa Cruz and also suburban trains for Alameda and Oakland. For decades, long after this line had been widened to standard gauge, the route was known as the "narrow-gauge." The alternate route, or "broad-gauge," started by boat from the same ferry building in San Francisco and met the trains, over-land and local, at Oakland Pier on the other side of the Oakland-Alameda "creek" (San Antonio Creek).

A third line, chiefly for vehicles, ran up the estuary between the two fills and was called the "Creek Route." It gave a 45-minute ride, and a good one, for the amazing sum of five cents, and its restaurant was especially popular, because on the long, leisurely ride there was plenty of time for a three-course meal, including pie.

With the Central Pacific in control, when the subject of a commutation rate came up for the San Francisco–Oakland ferries, Leland Stanford fixed it at three dollars a month. A. N. Towne, the CP's general superin-tendent, and F. H. Goodman, general passenger agent, protested that this was below cost. Stanford held to his project. "I want to make it easy for people to live in the roomy Eastbay, where they can get land for homes cheaper than in constricted San Francisco," he let it be known. "One way to do this is to make transportation charges as nearly like carfare as possible."

The cheap rates had a decisive effect in building up Oakland, Alameda, and Berkeley. More boats were put on, and there they went, solemnly and methodically picking their way across the bay like careful old ladies crossing a wet street—the *Oakland,* the *Newark,* and in time the *Encinal,* the *Piedmont,* the *Berkeley,* and their sisters.

Passengers could look through plate glass into the warm, snug engine room, where polished steel rose up and down, up and down, steel "wipers" yawned and lifted the valve rods, and up through the highest deck the walking beam rocked sedately to the rhythm of engines turning at a calm, leisurely 19 revolutions a minute.

Over the years the plate-glass windows became a kind of register of brides and fiancées and other travelers who tried their diamond rings on the surfaces. The earliest among them must have had many grand-children, who in turn tried their diamond rings before the stately *Ukiah, Encinal, Piedmont, Garden City, Newark* and their like went to the scrap heap.

Down in the engine room a man in blue serge pants and a vest—never a coat—and stiff-visored cap sat in an armchair between twenty-minute trips, but listened alertly and went into solemn action at the bell. Grasp-ing a 6-foot steel bar, he turned a shaft level with the floor and this did mysterious things (specifically, it opened an intake valve and its opposite exhaust number). There was a hiss of steam and a sense of mighty hap-penings. When the big piston, for that is what moved, reached the end of its stroke he threw the bar the other way.

Aloft, out in the weather, the walking beam up-tilted. Down went the engineer's hand lever, and down came the walking beam. And the boat was off. After he had hand-cranked her on her way he composed himself again to wait for more bells, and a great series they were, detonating through the boat and informing all knowing passengers that the vessel was entering her slip, that she was in mortal fear of pushing the whole Ferry Building halfway up Market Street, that she wanted her paddles reversed—*fast*—and that if she were allowed to come in safely this time, she would never, never barge it so recklessly again. And the white water really went crazy. But the boat always bumped. Then after she had been made fast, a deck hand threw aside the light rope which held the passengers back, and fled for his life to the side of the traffic. In the morning those hundreds were apparently always late for work, in the evening late for dinner.

Once in a blue moon the engineer would let his engine get on dead center. Then he would have to crawl into the paddle box with a long pole and turn the great wheel over by hand—no small feat. The paddle boxes barely held in the explosive language he used. Anybody who ever hand-cranked a Model-T Ford will appreciate the feat of hand-cranking a steamboat a couple of hundred feet long.

For years the regular fare on the transbay ferry remained at ten cents, with monthly commutation tickets three dollars. The ten-cent-a-day commuting customer had reason to rejoice at his bargain. He got a twenty-minute ferry ride and a train ride of fifteen to twenty minutes more. During those steam-train years, in the town of Alameda the company did not bother to provide fare collectors until passengers stepped onto the San Francisco–bound ferry. Consequently, residents of the island town used to travel the length of their 5-mile community several times a day if they wished, all with the compliments of the railroad. But there were those who breathed hard, even in this halcyon period, at the greed of the so-called "Octopus."

One of the spectacular features of transbay ferrying was the operation on the upper bay, between Benicia and Port Costa, where the overland trains were broken up and ferried across. Before adoption of this route, when Central Pacific had to reach Oakland from San Francisco by way of Niles Canyon, the whole Coast Range had to be surmounted.

This did not appeal as a permanent arrangement, and a better route was sought. Nature provided one, but also had thrown in some obstacles. The Coast Range is slashed cleanly by the Sacramento and San Joaquin rivers at the point of their juncture and emergence into the waters of Suisun Bay, an eastern bulge of San Francisco Bay. In 1878 a line was swung from Tracy, southwest of Stockton, around on the south shore of this water-level route. A way was found to cross the bay's narrow arm, Port Costa to Benicia. Here a rail line awaited, and had already been brought into the developing SP system. It was the California Pacific's railroad from South Vallejo to Sacramento. To join the two rail lines across the turbid channel with a bridge was a matter requiring Federal approval and a huge investment. Since neither permission nor funds were available, a ferryboat big enough to carry entire trains was constructed. On December 28, 1879, the car-transfer ferry *Solano,* easily the largest ferryboat ever built up to that time, began lugging trains across Carquinez Strait. With the even bigger *Contra Costa,* built in later years, it continued in service until recent times, when the strait at last was spanned with a mighty railroad bridge.

The SP's white ferries had competition for bay traffic. This was provided on the Eastbay run by the Key Route's trim orange-colored propeller boats. The Key boats were smaller and faster, their east-shore connecting trains tapping some residential areas not served by the SP.

During their happy era the ferries of the two lines were more than a part of the life of San Francisco Bay. They *were* the life of the bay. People had a unique trust in them, not only for their safety record, but for their all-around beneficence. The lost and found department of the SP ferries helped to earn this faith and returned mislaid articles in quantity, including mateless gloves at the rate of two or three hundred a month, misplaced baby buggies, diamond rings, and cash.

On rainy days anywhere from a dozen to thirty umbrellas were left on the boats. If the lost articles bore a name and address, the owners were phoned. An infant child was left on the ferryboat one morning by an absent-minded mother. Baby made the round trip in the care of the stewardess and was reclaimed forty minutes later. Deckhand Jose Cepo found a handbag containing upward of $50,000 worth of jewelry on the steamer *Santa Clara*. Its owner reclaimed it with far less excitement than did an entomologist who got back a ten-years' collection of bugs and beetles he had walked away from.

The breezes of the bay stimulated appetites to a grotesque degree. In the course of a month in 1927 the company's ferryboat commissary put before its patrons by count 1,460,000 cups of coffee, 235,500 snails, 312,000 coffee cakes, 40,000 dishes of oatmeal, 115,000 platters of ham and eggs, 40,000 loaves of raisin bread, and 3,600,000 doughnuts. The doughnuts were things of wonder, and customers had an often-voiced opinion that they came from the foundry of the Sacramento shops, or were links from old ships' chains. But they went down fast. Two or three persons were often served at a single stool in a single boat ride.

There was fun on the ferries, too. Golfers of the twenties who commuted between Alameda and San Francisco on the 7:50 A.M. ferryboat *Piedmont* utilized a Tom Thumb putting course of imitation grass and an inclined plane to practice their short game, with an occasional hole-in-one into San Francisco Bay. On all boats there were daily card tournaments that lasted for years. There were gala Christmas parties. On New Year's Eves the boats ran all night and the trainmen were understanding hosts, shoving the passengers aboard if they could walk, or carrying them if they couldn't.

The end of it all could not quite be foreseen.

In January, 1927, the company launched a fine new electric auto ferry, the *Fresno*, to the cheers of a hundred visiting citizens of the San Joaquin Valley's raisin metropolis. Largest auto ferry on the bay, the *Fresno* was the forerunner of a total of three, each 265 feet long, with capacity for 100 cars. Each cost more than half a million, and according to the longevity tables should have been doing business on the bay for the next fifty or sixty years.

For a time the SP's ferry business continued to flourish like the green bay tree. It had taken over the Northwestern Pacific, which had boats to the north shore; it took in as a partner a rival outfit handling automobiles across the Golden Gate and to Berkeley. In its heyday it had 43 double-enders crossing the bay. It was the biggest ferryboat operation in the world. In the peak year 1930 the auto-carrying affiliate transported 6,117,000 cars and nearly 15,000,000 passengers. In all, SP carried 40,211,000 ferry passengers that year.

But six years later the two bridges, that across the Golden Gate with its 4,200-foot span and that 8¼-mile structure using Goat Island as a stepping stone, consigned the ferries to where the Central Pacific–Southern Pacific had once sent the stagecoaches and prairie schooners. But there were those who looked back on the long record of safety—one life lost in half a century, during which period upward of a billion and a half passengers had been carried—and at the picturesqueness and the homely comfort of it all, and felt a twinge of regret.

In 1936, SP's Interurban Electric Railway Company was set up to take over the interurban service via the San Francisco–Oakland Bridge. Ferry-boats in connection with interurban service made their last runs to Oakland and Alameda piers on the night of January 14, 1939. It was an occasion for typical ferryboat high jinks and some considerable pathos.

For a time SP's bridge trains carried on. But as tolls for autos on the bridge steadily lowered, traffic on bridge trains also fell off. Early in 1940 Interurban Electric asked authority to discontinue service. In July, 1941, it left that branch of business to the Key Route and faded into history.

And so, one Sunday in February, 1941, a train composed of old North-western Pacific locomotives Nos. 23 and 109 attached to 7 wooden coaches of ancient vintage drew out of Sausalito over the interurban system and headed for Sonoma, birthplace of the Bear Flag Republic. The trip was sponsored by the San Francisco branch of the Railroadians of America, and was a nostalgic dip into the past. A few nights later 500 members of the Sierra Club, an organization of outdoor enthusiasts, staged a party on the ferryboat *Tamalpais* in commemoration of the half century of week-end hiking in which the ferries had played their part. On the same day's regular 5:15 commuter trip, old-timers provided the passengers with crying towels. As midnight of February 28 approached, the ferry *Eureka,* making the last trip of the line to the Marin shore, paused under the Golden Gate Bridge in hail and farewell to the steel structure that had put it out of business.

The next day, which was a Saturday, Capt. Victor Verdellet, Senior Engineer E. A. Creighton, and the entire crew donating their services, the *Eureka* made a final circuit of the bay for all who cared to ride. Seventeen hundred persons did. And with that friendly farewell, seventy-three years of continuous steamer service to north shore, begun by the little steamer *Princess* in 1868, had ended.

What became of the famous old bay ferries? Three—the *Russian River, Klamath,* and *El Paso*—are still running, carrying automobiles between San Rafael and Richmond. There are three more—*Eureka, Berkeley,* and *Sacramento*—doing service for the SP between the foot of Market Street and Oakland Pier. That is all. The rest have put to sea, to serve other harbors, or have retired to sheltered nooks to serve as fish-reduction factories and night clubs and boathouses, or have yielded to the wrecker's torches. The *Stockton* and the *Fresno,* which were launched so proudly in the 1920s, are cruising now out of Seattle as the *Willapa* and the *Klickatat.* The largest ferryboat ever built, the 433-foot, 5,373-gross-ton *Contra Costa* (that used to share, with the *Solano,* the burden of carrying whole overland trains across Carquinez Strait) is a disintegrating hulk near the scene of her one-time labors. The original *Thoroughfare,* which ran for four decades from San Francisco to Oakland on the Creek Route, and saw the whole evolution of vehicle transportation shift from horse-drawn drays and buggies to automobiles, was cut in half and part of her given, as a last voyage, the task of lugging a section of Dumbarton Bridge down to the south end of the bay. After that, the ferryboat section was buried under the bridge member as casing for a pier.

But it was the *Yosemite* which did the most Ulysseslike voyaging, after the bay bridges scattered the fleet. Never before out of the bay, the boat, after seventeen years' service on the various auto-carrying routes, set out through the Golden Gate on a 9,000-mile trip. Rechristened the *Argentine,* she was headed south to spend the rest of her life plying a 30-mile course across the Rio Plata between Buenos Aires and Colonia, Uruguay, connecting with a highway leading to Montevideo. Lower deck boarded up, one propeller and shaft removed, extra oil and water tanks installed, and a large flag of her new country painted on her sides, off she went, with a farewell toot to the Golden Gate Bridge as she passed under its mighty span. And there went about the last of the white fleet.

Until August, 1950, the little stern-wheel steamer *Petaluma* chugged nightly between San Francisco and Petaluma town. The trip of 35 miles had more twists and turns to it than a voyage to China.

The *Petaluma* was the last stern-wheeler on regular run in California waters. Its engine was built in 1872, its hull in 1914. The SP owned the craft, with two subsidiary corporations in between. Capt. Jack Urton and copilot Antone Gloss, with engineer John Leach, had a freight run that long defied competition by truck, as it defied wind and fog and collision and mud bank and 16-foot tides. They were not allowed to carry passengers—all they carried was freight and tradition. So Captain Jack scowled at the fog and, by compass and chronometer and the feel in the seat of his broad-gauge pants, made his eighty-four changes of course in the 35-mile run down to San Francisco. A 10-foot miss in this impenetrable fog would have put this last of California's stern-wheel freighters on the mud bank, but Skipper Urton did not miss. A submerged pile caught him one day in recent times, and poked a hole in his vessel, but the *Petaluma* was repaired and valiantly plied her course a short while longer. She was finally put out of business by a tow boat–barge substitution, and Jack Urton, one day in 1950, wrote in his log the closing entry "Tied up for good. So end 103 years of sternwheel navigation on San Francisco Bay and tributaries."

But as the fifty-year-old screw-driven *Berkeley* still slides its blunt prow under the Ferry Building apron, debarking overland passengers have the satisfaction of knowing that they are arriving in the seaport city as most arrivals have traditionally done—from the deck of a water-borne carrier.

29

The New Whistle in the Canyons

IT IS TOM WHITE'S turn to take the throttle. The phone rings in his home.

"Tell Tom he's wanted to take a freight over the Hill."

"What kind of an engine is it?" asks Tom's wife eagerly.

"It's a steam hog, Mary. What he's been used to for forty years."

"Just a minute." Silence, while Mary goes to confer with Tom. She returns to the phone. "He isn't feeling very well today. Can you send for him tomorrow?"

Tom White, who has put in a lifetime as a steam locomotive engineer, who not so long ago hated the newfangled diesels with the loathing of an old-time six-horse whip for a world-shaking, snorting diamond-stack, has made the final step in a mental hop-over which has included despising the new contraptions, fearing them as job-destroyers, trying them out, learning their tricks, and loving them. Now Tom would rather play sick than take a steam hog over the Hill—if a diesel can be had by waiting.

It has been a revolution in Tom's thinking, as important as the mechanical and financial revolution caused by the advent of the diesels themselves on America's rails.

But the diesels have won. The argument is over. So are any further SP orders, to the locomotive builders, for prime movers that depend on steam. After nearly ninety years that began with the unloading of the tiny "Governor Stanford" from a river schooner at Sacramento, years during which the SP's steam locomotives grew big and muscular (and ravenous), their proud place on the rails has been usurped by the sleek, purring newcomers.

And the enginemen, once they get over their dislike of something radically different, once they settle the issue of whether the new dingbats should have unnecessary firemen cozily bedded down just to preserve jobs;

once they try the feel of the new equipment and discover how clean, exhilarating, and handy it all is, they too join wholeheartedly in the switch.

Diesels pull heavier loads. They don't need so much help on the grades. They make much longer runs without being serviced. They run three times as far without being due for overhaul. Water tanks along the line have no meaning for them. They are easy on track and passengers and equipment. They operate with less bump and clank behind. And they pile on the speed. As for fuel, a dollar's worth will do what requires perhaps $2.32 with steam. In not too many years, there will not be a steam locomotive left in SP service, except some of the units that were most modern in the early 1950s.

Back in 1869 the iron horse played havoc with the stage horse. Reinsmen and hostlers, horseshoers and innkeepers had to make an adjustment, and soon it was seen that for every job extinguished there were many new ones opened. With the diesels, fewer men are required to move a given amount of traffic. But the railroad believes that it will be able to get and hold more traffic with the diesels and so keep more men at work.

For the shipper of freight the change-over means that there will be continued improvement in the kind of bulk transportation that railroads give. For the passenger, dieselization means comfort to a new degree. So swiftly is change accepted in our modern life that the exciting new trains of any given date become commonplace in a few months.

So from now on it will be the sharp, efficient hoot of the diesels, and not the genial moan of the steam locomotives, that will echo in the canyons of the West and Southwest. The steam whistle's familiar "WoowOOOOOooooo," long and lingering and lonesome and filled with suggestion of far destinations, will die away amid the pines and crags and will not come again.

But that call for eighty years was the voice of man speaking reassuringly to man. Reaching out to the mine on the mountaintop and the ranch house in the valley, it told its listeners of people rushing through darkness and storm, of mail and express hurrying to keep a date, of long strings of perishables winding through sun and heat, of Westerners tripping east and Easterners on their unceasing migration west. It was a voice of civilization in a raw, rich land.

May the air horns of the diesels grow as meaningful.

Something close to "push-button" railroading has made its appearance in recent times. Electric vacuum tubes—marvelously sensitive electric valves and amplifiers capable of instantaneous control of electrical power —are taking their place in the scheme of things in countless ways. Most electronic installations involve large investments. But to the limit of their financial ability, American railroads are going in for electronics, because the electron tubes can be used to accomplish almost any automatic control desired. They enable the railroads to do a better job, and do it easier; ultimately, to do it more cheaply.

Electron tubes make possible radio communication with moving trains and switch engines; communication between head and rear of freight trains; walkie-talkie communication between car checkers in the yards and car clerks in the yardmaster's office.

They multiply the capacity of communication circuits. At present, on some pairs of wires, Southern Pacific has the capacity of carrying four telephone conversations and eighteen teletype or telegraph messages simultaneously. Microwave radio transmission multiplies that by hundreds.

Electron tubes can perform calculations far swifter than the human brain, and without error, such as the complex job of operating punched-card machines to keep track of railroad cars moving along Southern Pacific's 15,000 miles of railroad.

Employing the principles of radar, electron tubes "look" along SP wire communication lines and locate faults many miles away from the testing station, often so accurately that repair crews can be dispatched directly to the point of trouble, saving hours of search.

In SP's testing laboratories tiny traces of foreign matter in a material, such as metal in lubricating oil, may be measured electronically indicating the condition of moving parts in a locomotive. Other instruments probe deep into tools and equipment parts, and with the aid of electronics and other sciences reveal hidden flaws. Thus it is possible to remove faulty items from service before they break down.

There was a fast freight in the blisteringly hot yard at Bakersfield, California, waiting in the sun one summer day for the "highball" to send it on its way after the noon Daylight from Los Angeles had skimmed through. No sooner did Engineer Smith get Conductor Davis's "Everything's on board, let's go" out of the box in the ceiling of his diesel, pick up his hand phone, and reply, "Engineer to conductor, first-806, highball," and make a dozen miles out of town, when the ceiling box squawked again.

"Come in," said Engineer Smith into his phone.

It was the voice of Mechanical Superintendent Levi Franklin—calling, oddly enough, from an automobile on the highway that runs beside the tracks. Franklin happened to be passing the train with its 80 cars of perishables—going the other way, it should be stated in fairness to Smith's sizzling speed—when he'd spotted two hoboes clinging to the Mallet helper locomotive. Franklin had a walkie-talkie in his car.

"Better get rid of those two 'boes before you hit a tunnel," said Franklin, "or they'll be cooked." The long freight stopped, the free riders were pried off, and the freight pounded on again.

With caboose talking to cab, inspectors talking to each other, and superintendents all over the map talking to all and sundry, the step-up in speed and safety is becoming bewildering. As one train passes another, it's becoming a common thing for westbound to say to eastbound, "Give us an inspection, will you?" And the crew of one train, watching closely, is able to respond to the other, "You've got a hot box, but you can make it to the next siding." In the old days, the train with the "smoker" might have had to stop on the spot, put out a flag, and halt traffic while brakemen checked to find the hot box. Perhaps the spot would be one of those mountain points that find the train wound around a curve that is almost three-quarters of a circle. That would have called for five or six brakemen waving newspapers or lanterns on top of cars and up the hillsides to relay signals. Now the brakeman heaves a portable 9½-pound walkie-talkie on his back and hustles up the track. He directs the shunting of the disabled car onto a siding, and soon the rest of the train is rolling again.

The walkie-talkie saves a lot of flagmen the embarrassment of chasing after and losing their trains.

Another bit of radio talking that expedites railroading around the mountain curves is from engineer to engineer on trains moving in the same direction. Warns the engineer ahead, "We've just run into a red block and stopped. Better dog it along." The engineer behind slows to a crawl and before reaching the block is probably notified through his phone, "All clear. Am moving ahead." That reduces the high cost of starting and stopping trains, particularly on grades.

"We have more curves and mountainous territory," says President D. J. Russell, "than any other railroad in the country. This is one of the reasons why electronics is important to us. We have speeded up freight trains until we can get them over the line at fifty miles an hour in the open country, but we still had a bottleneck in the terminals. Electronics has enabled us to cut the terminal time."

At the huge Los Angeles marshaling yard the SP has rebuilt a few miles of track that are returning savings of half a million a year in time once wasted finding the right car and shunting it into the right train. Now, as soon as a train pulls in, a spry young yardman with a walkie-talkie starts down the line, identifying cars and calling their numbers and destinations into his phone.

In the office this report is checked against a list already microphotoed in from the preceding division point. Then the cars roll on to the "hump," a 10-foot hill from which radiates a fan of classification tracks. While inspectors in glassed pits watch the passing wheels and brake beams, the cars are pushed over the hump and sent coasting down to their proper trains, their speed controlled by "retarders" operated from a distant tower with a wide view. The retarders, activated by electropneumatic cylinders alongside the tracks, literally squeeze the wheels to the rails and slow them down with accuracy. The $2,500,000 investment in retarder installation at the Los Angeles marshaling yard is being followed by a $4,500,000 outlay at Roseville.

At headquarters in San Francisco a short-wave radio tower thrusts upward from the roof. By means of it, officials can talk with yardmasters and others of the railroad family all over the bay area. Jim Brannin, who became a wartime radio expert, came back to his railroad job with a new idea, which was to put electronics to work wherever that would speed traffic or expedite maintenance.

For decades the railroad's communications men had thought in terms of telegraph circuits, which failed whenever a wire was broken. Brannin proposed using a new device which he said would shoot radar-type impulses out over broken wires and measure how long it takes them to bounce back from the end of the wire.

The railroad's officers were skeptical, but gave it a try. And it soon proved its worth. Once Brannin was up in Dunsmuir in the Siskiyous when the telegraph line went out of order. He hooked up his radar and within five minutes estimated the trouble to be 72.8 miles up the grade. Repairmen found a pair of wires wrapped together at exactly 73 miles' distance. Brannin demonstrated his gismo again at Sparks, Nevada, when a circuit winked out. He spotted the trouble 120 miles away, and there it was. Now the railroad has radar eyes in eight division centers, with more on order.

He also tested microwave beams which can handle as many as 400 telephone conversations, about 1,000 teletype or telegraph conversations, and a number of photofacsimile transmissions all at one time. And the beams aren't knocked out by falling trees or landslides, for the relay towers are on mountaintops where nothing but the stars can fall on them.

Railroading is changing fast.

30

The Day's Work

SO HERE IS the Southern Pacific, climbing mountain ranges where snow-fall reaches 40 and 50 feet a year; skimming across deserts where its tracks dip below ocean level; staring down into gorges; striding across mesa and prairie.

In its deeds of engineering, of enterprise, and of operation, in its scope, and in its historical position in the American scene it is distinctive. Yet it has been a workaday railroad so long, concerned simply with the details of hauling stuff around, that its own people forget to see anything spectacular or picturesque about it, and the trainman who answered a passenger's query about the name of a peak with "Lady, I can't keep track of all the mountains around here," was just a hard-working railroader with his mind on flags, switches, and torpedoes. The operator in the Sierra snowsheds, who gaped at the hordes of ski enthusiasts that began arriving about twenty years ago, also expressed it when he exclaimed, "How can people see fun in this snow up here? It's something we've been fighting all our lives."

But the magnitude of a modern railroad, and its timelessness, get through at times to the people who run it. An official of the SP's telegraph department one day set out to inspect a portion of the SP de Mexico afoot. In the middle of nowhere he came upon a "tangent," a line of track drawn straight as theodolite could make it for more than a hundred miles.

He trudged and he trudged. Half a week later, he was still striding down the middle of that piece of track and there was still no bend to it, except where it curved up over the horizon behind him and down over the one ahead. He halted and demanded aloud of the telegraph poles and the tarantulas, his only audience, "Does anybody at headquarters really realize what a colossal thing this railroad *is?*"

The SP's total theater of activity, since it runs from Portland on the north to Guadalajara on the south, from San Francisco to Ogden, and from Los Angeles to Tucumcari and New Orleans, occupies an area which, if superimposed upon the eastern part of the United States, would stretch from Maine and New York to Utah and Texas. On a map of Europe, it would throw a loop from London to Moscow to Istanbul to Paris and back to London.

In a sense, it is a railroad that still is looking for a destination—it doesn't yet particularly arrive anywhere. Its lines originate and terminate a lot of freight, but its own terminals at the opposite ends from San Francisco and Los Angeles are pretty much wide places in the road. Portland is famous for roses and Mt. Hood, but it is no Chicago. Ogden isn't famous for much of anything, and it is no Chicago either. Nor is Tucumcari. Nor is Chicago itself on the Atlantic, by a long shot. As for New Orleans— well, everybody loves it. But as a destination for a transcontinental, New Orleans is still far short of the Atlantic seaboard, and the SP knows it and once tried to make up for the fact with connecting steamships.

Still and all, without any tracks of its own reaching beyond the Willamette, the Rockies, and the lower Mississippi, SP is the third largest railroad in the United States in point of operating revenues, its $500,000,-000 a year putting it behind only the New York Central and the Pennsylvania. It is the sixth industrial corporation in the United States in assets, its $1,823,000,000 ranking it behind only American Telephone, Standard Oil of New Jersey, General Motors, United States Steel, and the Pennsylvania.

It has one of the largest debts of any line in America. Even with the reduction since 1939 (it reached a whopping $750,000,000 at the end of that year), it was still $619,000,000 on December 31, 1950. The reduction of long-term debt has amounted to $253,000,000, but the equipment obligations have increased almost $100,000,000. These equipment obligations were required to finance part of the cost of the huge equipment program of the last six years. But it has never missed an interest payment and has gone through all panics without a receivership.

The company's president bosses all this empire between New Orleans and the Pacific Ocean from his simple, functional office on the eighth floor at 65 Market Street in San Francisco. There is nothing in his office but a clock, a plain desk, a 10-foot table, some chairs, and a case of maps. From the windows he cannot even see his railroad, but it is in his head. So are its 83,000 people. A railroad president's job, as he sees it, is to keep close inventory of the human assets of his organization. Two floors down, in an office exactly the same, right down to the map case and the 10-foot table, Vice-president J. W. Corbett looks after "Operations" of the Pacific system, which extends to El Paso. G. L. Buland, at San Francisco, is vice-president and general counsel. East of El Paso, E. A. Craft is executive vice-president of the Texas and New Orleans at Houston. John G. Walsh, in New York, is vice-president in charge of finances.

Over the years, Donald J. Russell was at the bottom of every tough task, helping to lift and pull. When a locomotive capsized in western Oregon, scalding four trainmen to death, it was Don Russell who went in there and lifted the bodies out. When washouts, wrecks, or broken bridges held up the trains, Russell sometimes went sixty hours without sleep until things were running again. The reward for all this, and for his other attributes, was D. J. Russell's election on November 15, 1951, to the presidency of Southern Pacific, to succeed A. T. Mercier, retiring, as of January 1, 1952.

It is men of this stamp who give the railroad its fine, sound character today. They, and the tens of thousands below them who have grown up with watch, flag, and oil can in hand. From bottom to top they are a solidly serious crew, conscious of the public importance of the work they do; vaguely aware of and startled by the rowdy first half century of their embattled outfit's history; more than a little proud of its eighty-year record of outriding crises. They are proud of the probity and honor with which it conducts its affairs. But they are a matter-of-fact lot. They know that the railroad is bigger than any of them; that it was running generations before they came on the scene; and that it will be running when they have handed over to someone else. It will be meeting new crises, fighting new battles. Meanwhile they do the best they can, and that best is good.

Yes, it's a big railroad, originated in rugged times, and operated now by men well attuned to this more sensitive age.

Let old Donald McIntyre, former car foreman at Yuma and past ninety, with descendants in every department of the railroad, speak. Proud of his family tradition, proud of his railroad, Mac, blunt in his opinion of his past bosses, said in 1950 in the hearty language of a railroader, "I never knew a Southern Pacific president or other officer who wasn't a fine gentleman. Even if he was a tough sonofabitch."

Section Foreman Julios Ratti, of the tank-and-siding station of Bango, Nevada, stands in the doorway of his railroad shack and looks about him with satisfaction. The oasis created by his wife, of thorny wild roses brought down from the mountain canyons, and Indian paintbrush, and white-petaled sago lilies, is doing fine in this land of sagebrush and sand. Then he looks off down the rails of his section of Mina branch, Salt Lake Division, his direct responsibility. They shimmer under the rising sun.

"Hot day ahead," mutters Julios. He goes to the shed and throws a wet sack over his tools.

High in the Sierra snowsheds 90 miles distant, Bill Flickinger grins as he hands the interlocking controls over to Bob Duncan, his relief.

"How's the railroad doing?" asks Duncan, picking up the train sheet and studying it.

"Still running, boy," yawns Flickinger, who has put in the night keeping a thousand cars rolling over "the Hill." "Where's Coons?"

"Wetting a trout line. It's warm and clear outside."

"Can I trust this signal interlocking plant to your hands?"

Flickinger, Duncan, and Coons have been with the railroad since 1911, 1913, and 1914, respectively. "You can let me try," grins Duncan.

At Eugene, Oregon, Bill Hannum and his bull voice exhort a crew loading a part of the 350,000 cars of lumber the road is handling this year. At Sacramento, Willis White steps down from his locomotive cab after fifty-two years at the throttle and 2,500,000 kidney-pounding miles. At Apache Hill, Arizona, Jim Beckett of the westbound No. 3 sounds his air horn, cusses, but grinds to a halt. A prospector, waving his hat under a square-armed saguaro cactus, desires a drink of water—and state law says he shall have it.

At Los Angeles, Minna Holt teletypes a shipment of high-style bathing suits onto a seven-copy waybill. Simultaneously, at Dallas, Cornelia Strum whips from her receiving machine the teletyped copy that will be followed, on a fast merchandise train, by the swim suits themselves. Mentally she decides she will have one.

At San Antonio, Sim Higabotham recalls that his outfit uses $51,000,000 worth of fuel a year, and turns off an electric light. At Reno, Bill Milliron, remembering that steam escaping at a hundred pounds pressure through a half-inch opening costs $23.90 a day, picks up a wrench and tightens a radiator valve. At Tepic, Mexico, Pepe Bormejillo, who tamps rock, tries to grasp what his boss has told him—that for every employee of the line, including himself, his company has an investment of $20,000 in tracks, locomotives, cars, yards, shops, signals, and tools. That's about 100,000 pesos. Pepe tamps a little harder.

Oliver Millet, who has retired after thirty-two years as parlor-car porter, looks with pleasure as his familiar lounge-buffet car rolls into Monterey from San Francisco with a new coat of paint and a brand-new name in gold letters. The name? Oliver's heart leaps. In compliment to his years of broom-whisking, his old car has been officially renamed the "Oliver Millet."

And in his office in the eleven-story red brick building in San Francisco, the president of the road arrives early to dictate a message to Julios Ratti, Minna Holt, Pepe Bormejillo, and 83,000 others. The railroad took an unexpected drop in revenue last month, and everybody had better hustle a little harder.

A day's work on the SP has begun.

Appendix A: Relax—You're Safe

IN THE MOUNTAIN TOWN of Dunsmuir, California, a train dispatcher sits in his shirtsleeves at an odd-looking desk. He is deep in concentrated thought. He is following the movements of every train that is running on 80 miles of busy track. C. F. Banish, whose trick it is at this moment, cannot see those trains. But he knows where they are and a lot of other things about them by means of a diagram that operates electrically in front of him. Little lights wink on and wink off as various track sections are occupied and vacated by the trains.

He moves a small lever on the board.

Miles away, around the shoulder of Mt. Shasta, up on the Siskiyou plateau, two trains are roaring toward each other on a single track. One is a freight pulled by a cab-in-front engine, 4174, hauling lumber and pears southward from Rogue River. The other is No. 12, the brilliant streamlined Cascade streaking north for Portland. They are going to meet and pass each other at a selected point without stopping. Their "meet" has been arranged by Charlie Banish, and there are no ifs or buts about it.

The engineer of the varnish string catches his all-clear signal, highballs ahead. The mile-long freight has rolled neatly onto a siding and continues onward. As the passenger train shoots past, the freight glides back onto the main track. Down at Dunsmuir, 18 miles away, Dispatcher Banish notes the winking lights on his panel and moves more levers, presses more buttons. He controls traffic both ways on a long mountain track from Black Butte to Redding over a heavy grade, and there are always more trains, more meets.

Banish is running one of the great pieces of safety apparatus of the modern railroad—automatic electrified Centralized Traffic Control.

There is a 38.3-mile stretch of single track between Sacramento and Stockton (the precise points are Brighton and Akers) where an enormous volume of freight is handled. This stretch was selected in 1930 for the first test of CTC in the Western part of the United States. So successful was it in shoving through the trains that CTC is now also in use from Redding to Black Butte in northern California; Edison to Summit in the Tehachapis; Alhambra to Indio, which includes the Beaumont hill in Southern California; Lucin to Bridge, which includes the bridge over the Great Salt Lake of the Lucin Cutoff; the stretch between Sparks and Massie in Nevada; and over the Santa Lucia Range from Santa Margarita to San Luis Obispo. By means of CTC, dispatchers are running trains as trains never have been run before. They line up siding switches, set signals, arrange for passing points. They have stepped up the capacity of single track as much as 75 per cent. Trains do not have to stop while trainmen throw switches. Written train orders do not have to be handed up to the engineers at way stations, as they are not required. Delays are knocked down to a minimum, and so are mistakes. The engineer operates his train in accordance with the aspects displayed by the wayside signals.

The dispatcher always knows, by a glance at his lights, exactly what portions of the track are in use. The levers on the panel indicate signals displayed and existing switch positions. Below the track chart is a set of levers with colored lights by which the dispatcher controls the siding switches. Indicator lights show that switches at sidings have moved to the desired positions and are mechanically locked in that position before a train can receive a proceed signal to move over the switch. And the indicator lights show that the proper signal lights have been displayed. Signal lights on the panel also warn of landslides or snowslides, of fires in tunnels or on bridges, even of dragging equipment on trains.

The dispatcher also has an automatic train graph on the desk before him. Magnetically operated pens follow the progress of the trains and record the time at which they pass each end of each siding. When the next dispatcher comes on duty, he can read the history of train movements during the preceding trick.

There are roadside telephones over which communication can be had with the dispatcher, and radio telephoning is also coming into vogue. The dispatcher can summon signal maintainers or train crews to the wayside telephones by displaying a small signal light at the ends of sidings. Separate wayside indicators also warn the riders of track cars—roadmasters, signal maintainers, telegraph linemen, water servicemen, section foremen, and track patrolmen—of approaching trains so they can hustle their pop wagons off the tracks.

In the older parts of the nation much traffic flows over double- or four-track lines. But to men like Charlie Banish such railroad work would be sissy stuff. Much of SP is single-track, with trains not only churning after each other in fast progression but roaring at each other, head on. To hold this freight at X, send No. 18 hurtling past, move the freight past Y to Z, have it there without keeping westbound No. 17 waiting—that's railroading. The thing is complicated by way freights, which must pick up cars at various sidings; and by slower paced locals. So, in addition to

Charlie and his kind, there is also the vigilant dispatcher who sits in quiet concentration, noting each train as reported by operators at stations as it passes, observing each unscheduled stop. Before him is a big sheet carrying the data on the train and locomotive crews. Careful check must be maintained to insure that crew members are not continued on duty beyond legal limits.

The news of it all for a layman is this: it is a statistical fact that a person today is safer on a railroad train than in his own home. Safety is close to a precise science with American railroads. Passengers are three times as safe as they were thirty-five years ago and twice as safe as twenty-seven years ago. Today a person has to ride an astronomical 996,000,000 miles on the average to get himself killed. What with the Safety Section of the Association of American Railroads, the Interstate Commerce Commission with its strict requirements and inspections, the modern automatic signal and train-control devices—plus generations of personnel training—the railroads have just about achieved the impossible.

The SP has used plenty of the other fellow's ideas when they have proved good. And it has contributed a number of first-rate ideas itself. Among SP "firsts" in the art of railroading have been:

The first all-steel head end cars (along with some of the first all-steel passenger coaches).

A device which warns of low water level and thus forestalls locomotive boiler explosions.

Derailment safety guides to hold wheels in line with rails when wheels go off the track.

Locomotive-driver-tire retaining clips to hold loosened tires on wheel center until condition can be noted on inspection.

Perfections of safety devices to warn enginemen of possible rock slides, fire damage, high water, or earthquake shock at bridges, or other impairment of track, and the extensive use of track-car indicators.

And more miles of main line equipped with automatic block signals than any other railroad in the country.

An "eastbound"—meaning southbound—Daylight emerged from Tunnel 22 in the Tehachapi Mountains one day in 1944 at a speed slightly under 30 miles per hour, when an inside rail broke. Weight of the train forced the outside rail to turn over. Thirteen cars were flung from the tracks and two partly derailed. Time was when that would have been a major accident, with cars overturned, passengers heaved about, many persons crushed. But in this case no cars turned over. None struck the side of the tunnel. Not a soul was hurt.

The derailed cars had been kept in line and brought safely around the curve by a device invented by SP men, called a derailment safety guide. Suggested by A. D. McDonald when he was president of the company, and worked out by the motive-power department, the device consists of a strong vertical flange extending downward opposite each journal box, parallel to the outside face of the wheel. When a wheel of that Daylight dropped to the ties inside the rail and moved slightly to the side, the flange engaged the outside ball of the rail and prevented further sideslip.

In earlier days boiler explosions were a sort of normal incident of railroading, like tornadoes in Kansas. The public and most railroad men came to think of them as acts of God. SP's George McCormack, who eventually retired as general superintendent of motive power, and Frank E. Russell, Sr., who became chief mechanical engineer, decided to do something about it. They invented a device to release steam into a locomotive firebox when the water in the boiler got too low. A releasing bronze button, activated by a fusible alloy which melted when overhot, did the trick. The temperature in the endangered boiler melted the alloy and blew the button into the firebox, following with a discharge of steam. That made things lively enough in the firebox for the engine crew to become acutely interested, and averted the blowups.

A steam locomotive is a great drinker of water, but likes its water soft. Mud or alkali in the boiling water can do a lot of harm to the engine's innards. So SP set up sixty-three water-softening and purifying plants along its system, besides installing foam meters on many of its locomotives.

The familiar figures in overalls and trainman's cap who goes along crouching under cars and peering into their journal boxes has automatic assistance in his search for hot boxes. On some trains a small metal tube placed in each journal box melts when the temperature reaches 220 degrees, and sends off an offensive smell. Another type of signal is a thermo switch placed in each journal box, that turns on lights inside the car when things get too hot down there among the bearings.

If anybody is in an automobile stalled in front of an oncoming train, it may interest him to know that many SP engines are constructed with pilots, or cowcatchers, of unusually rugged design, constructed to lessen the danger of folding under and derailing the engine when the impact comes. That makes it safer for SP's personnel, if not for the motorist.

Air brakes went into service on the SP sixty-five years ago. Before their introduction, the engineer would whistle "brakes down" for a regular or emergency stop, and brakemen carrying pick handles would scurry along the tops of freight cars or leap through passenger coaches, hurdling portmanteaus and carpetbags, to turn the wheels that operated the hand brakes on each car. Lots of man power was required and the results were never too certain. That situation brought on one of the legendary achievements of American railroading—the air brake.

The first air brakes were "straight air." Braking pressure was applied directly by pumping air through the train line from the engine. If anything happened to the compressor, or the air line broke, Casey Jones and his charges were in for a ride.

In 1885, George Westinghouse sold SP its first automatic air brakes. They worked on an opposite principle. A reduction in air pressure up ahead unbalanced the air pressures in the valve assemblies. That clamped the brakes, impelled by air stored under pressure in tanks under each car.

In 1932 the "AB" pneumatic brake, an improvement over the K–triple valve, was introduced for freight cars. The AB brake was adopted by the American Railway Association in August, 1933, and specifications were adopted by order of the Interstate Commerce Commission in 1934 which virtually require the AB brake to be applied on all freight equipment. Among other details, the specifications require that with an initial reduction of 10 pounds, which would produce a "service application" of the brakes, the total interval in time between the reduction on the first car and on the 150th, if that were the length of the train, should not be more than 20 seconds. In an emergency, the brake on the 150th car must start to apply within 8.2 seconds. That means sending the braking impulse through the train of some 7,500-foot length at a rate of propagation of the braking impulse of about 915 feet per second.

In 1937 the original streamlined SP Coast Daylight introduced one of the first installations of the electromagnetic brake. Its success led to its being placed on other SP streamliners. It is used on passenger trains only. It brings the train to a quick stop without harsh action, by means of the electrical application of the train's air brakes simultaneously throughout the train. The braking action goes on with the train at high speed but automatically eases as the train slows down, and this keeps the wheels from locking and brings everything to a halt that is smooth as silk.

Other safety and comfort devices for controlling the spinning wheels have come along. There is the decelostat, which protects wheels against sliding and developing flat spots. It automatically vents air from the brake cylinder for an instant if the wheel hesitates, and applies the brake pressure again when the wheel is free.

Particularly interesting are the wayside devices which operate the block signals to tell the engineer what lies ahead. Flood detectors are actuated by wooden floats in the areas where floods might occur. When water rises, signals are set against the trains.

Timbered tunnels, snowsheds, trestles, and bridges have been fire hazards from the beginning of railroading. On SP lines, many of these locations are now protected with fusible-joint wires which melt under heat and set signals to stop trains.

On one bridge over the Pajaro River, an earthquake recording device is attached. Should a quake occur, automatic signals are set that stop trains and call for inspection of the structure.

Falling rocks meet automatic guardians as they roll down certain banks or cuts. They hit fences which activate electric circuits and set the signal against trains.

At stations in double-track areas, passengers are protected by "station train indicators," or illuminated signs. These are mounted alongside the track two or three thousand feet in advance of the station. They govern trains on the track nearest the station. If there is no train closely approaching or standing at the station on the opposite track, the indicator shows the word "Clear." If there is a train closely approaching or at the station, the word "Train" shows in red.

The visibility of trains has been heightened with brilliant aluminum paint on the front of each locomotive. For the protection of inattentive motorists, some locomotive headlights are kept burning by daylight, and at night some headlights are double, one a regular beam and the other oscillating in a figure-eight pattern.

On the diesel locomotives another safety feature has been adopted. It is called the "dead man's control." When the engineer becomes incapacitated, his brakes automatically go on.

All SP main-line rail is tested regularly by detector cars. They move along at about 5 miles per hour and write a continuous record of all they find. Flaws invisible to the trackwalker, caused by separations in the molecules of the steel, are noted before the flaw grows to a size to menace the rail.

The trackwalker moves along on foot with his hand-held inspecting device rolling along the rail. He keeps his eye out as well for the condition of bridges, culverts, and roadbed. He is still the faithful, useful symbol whose plodding pace helps to keep fast merchandise and passenger trains speeding.

But the greatest safety device of all, the railroad contends, is the safe man. So the road carries on a never-ending program of written, visual, and verbal instruction that reaches every employee who has anything to do with train operations. The system examiner and his assistants are on continuous tour in an instruction car. Time-tested operating rules for locomotive, car, and train handling, rules that govern procedures for all situations, have been developed and taught to a point where they are practically instinctive. A traveler who "Next time, takes the train," pretty well knows to the dot when he will get to his destination, and practically never thinks of any hazard connected with it at all.

Appendix B: More about Steam

ALMOST AS SOON as the Sierra had been surmounted, bigger and ever bigger locomotives became the railroad's need. When they could not be made much wider or taller, they were made longer and ever longer.

The first locomotive built for Central Pacific freight service was the "Conness," or No. 6. It was of the 4-6-0 type, built by William Mason of Taunton, Massachusetts, in 1865. (A 4-6-0 type would mean a four-wheel leading truck, three pairs of drivers, and no trailing wheels.) The cylinders were 17 inches in diameter by 24-inch stroke and the driving wheels were 48 inches in diameter. The tractive power was 15,350 pounds, length of engine and tender was 52 feet, and total weight with tender, in working order, was about 120,000 pounds. When the "Conness" went on the rails it was the wonder of the age, for with its six driving wheels it could haul 18 small freight cars.

But the ambitious Western railroad had no desire to be dependent upon the locomotive workshops of the East. The Sacramento shops tried their hand and turned out a pioneer 4-4-0 or so-called American-type 52 feet long that weighed 66,000 pounds loaded and had tractive power of 14,480 pounds. The frame of this engine and others of its type built at the Sacramento shops in 1872 and 1873 were made of horseshoe iron, of which Central Pacific had bought a considerable amount. The hand of the old hardware dealers, Huntington and Hopkins, can perhaps be detected here.

The excitement caused by the "Conness" was nothing compared to that occasioned by the news of "El Gobernador," the largest locomotive in the world when it was built in 1884. It was a 4-10-0 and it was designed to handle 14 30-ton cars at 10 miles per hour on an ascending grade of 116 feet to the mile. The day came when the SP's articulated locomotives handled 30 50-ton cars at 14 miles per hour on the same grade—a power output five times that of "El Gobernador"; but in its time "El Gobernador"—last SP locomotive to have a name as well as a number—certainly promised results. It had cylinders of 21-inch diameter and 36-inch stroke, carried 145 pounds of steam; drivers were 4 feet 9 inches in diameter; weight of engine alone was 146,000 pounds, and with tender about 243,000 pounds in working order. The tractive power was 34,300 pounds and length over-all of engine and tender about 65 feet 5 inches.

"El Gobernador" was considered too big to be turned on a turntable for fear it would roll over, and it was not trusted on sidings either; it was kept on the main line. It was built for service over the Tehachapi. The Tehachapi grade had just been relaid with 62-pound rail instead of 50. Governor Stanford, who ordered the locomotive, went to Europe with his family, and while he was away, Charlie Crocker, vice-president of the company, visited the Sacramento shops on a tour of inspection. He came to the skeleton of "El Gobernador."

"What's this?" he demanded.

He was answered by A. J. Stevens, general master mechanic.

"All news to me," howled Crocker, "I want this work stopped at once."

But it was not stopped; it was only suspended. When Stanford returned, his pet was rushed to a finish and ordered into freight service between Caliente and Mojave. But the bridges would not sustain "El Gobernador" on its way south and it had to go in pieces, as freight. It took five cars to carry the parts. And in spite of all, "El Gobernador" ended up a failure. Its boiler was too small and even two firemen could not heat it up.

"All hell," they griped, "couldn't make her steam."

The big fellow was brought back to Sacramento for rebuilding, but never was rebuilt, and in 1894 was broken up.

In 1885 CP was taken over by the SP, and during the next three years different types of locomotives were built at the Sacramento shops from designs prepared by General Master Mechanic A. J. Stevens. All were equipped with the Stevens valve gear, referred to by railroad men as "monkey motion" because of the peculiar antics of the eccentric, which had the appearance, when the locomotive was running, of a monkey hopping along. They were 2-8-os, 4-4-os, and 4-6-os. Ten of the first type, called "monkey hogs" by trainmen, were placed in service by 1888. Cylinders were 19 by 30 inches, diameter of drivers 51 inches, total weight in working order, including tender, 185,000 pounds, tractive power 27,080 pounds, steam pressure 150 pounds. They were the first consolidation 2-8-o-type locomotives used on SP lines. Four of them were put on the Oregon-California run.

Four of the eight-wheeled 4-4-o type were built in 1886 for passenger service. With cylinders 17 by 26 inches, diameter of drivers 69 inches, weight on drivers 52,800 pounds, and tractive power 13,900 pounds, they proved exceptionally speedy with the moderate-sized trains of the time. They could whip along on good track at 75 miles per hour. Twelve more were built in the Sacramento shops in 1888, with cylinders 18 by 28 inches and boilers considerably larger.

The clanging Sacramento shops also turned out 21 locomotives of the ten-wheeled 4-6-0 type in 1886 and 1887. They were wood-burners, with massive balloon stacks. The stacks were 54 inches in diameter at the top and about 7 feet tall. As coal gradually displaced wood as fuel, the balloon stack gave way to the straight vertical stack. But wood-burners were used to a limited extent on some portions of the line into the nineties. The length of engine and tender over-all of the 4-6-0 of this era was about 56 feet, cylinders 18 by 30 inches, diameter of drivers 57 inches, and total weight of engine and tender in working order about 175,000 pounds. Some of them lasted until the year 1916.

Shortly after the turn of the century oil burning was successfully in general use. Although Southern Pacific had tried burning oil in an experimental way in a 4-4-0-type locomotive, the "Young America," in 1879, the first locomotive equipped to burn oil in regular road service on the Southern Pacific was a 4-4-0, converted from a coal-burner in 1895.

Oil was used extensively in 1899 on the Los Angeles division and coal was discontinued on that division in 1901. Locomotives on the Sacramento Division were converted from coal to oil in 1902, and on the Salt Lake Division in 1912.

The first compound locomotive used on SP lines was of the twelve-wheeled, coal-burning 4-8-0 type, which went into freight service on the mountain grades in 1891. The first of this fleet was a Schenectady-built engine of 1887, converted to compound in the SP shops. The rebuilt locomotive had one high-pressure cylinder on the left-hand side to which the high pressure steam was admitted, and thence exhausted into a low-pressure cylinder of considerably larger diameter on the right-hand side. The high- and low-pressure cylinders were so proportioned in regard to diameters as to practically produce equal amounts of power. The cylinders were 20 by 26 inches on the left and 29 inches in diameter by 26-inch stroke on the right.

In the later 1880s, the heavy construction of the valve gear on the SP twelve-wheelers necessitated the addition of an auxiliary water brake in addition to air and hand brakes on some locomotives. These water brakes worked only on the locomotive. But the heavy valve gear necessitated the application of power reverse when the engineer wanted to reverse his engine. This was worked from hot water at boiler pressure taken from the firebox above the mud ring, with the lever to operate it secured to the reverse lever. The La Chatelier brake, which flashed water into wet steam with engine reversed, the pistons acting as air compressors, lasted some twenty years before being discarded and was one feature of the long fight waged by SP against the engineering obstacles of the mountain barriers. The locomotives came from the builders equipped with a number of new devices, such as automatic couplers in place of old link-and-pin couplers, air sanders, automatic air brakes. They were from the works at Paterson, New Jersey, and Schenectady, New York, and were probably the most powerful passenger locomotives of their time, and were used on all the most important and heaviest passenger trains on SP's lines.

Passenger cars had been growing, too; by 1894, 30-ton cars were in use. The 4-6-os that were the pride of the rails at the time were capable of handling 6 30-ton passenger cars at 50 miles per hour over the more severe grades. But they, too, eventually proved too light as requirements marched irresistibly forward, and the last of them was scrapped in 1928.

The era of the 4-6-os also brought in a series of 14 4-8-o heavy coal burning freight locomotives. Built by Schenectady with two single expansion cylinders 22 by 26 inches, boiler steam pressure 180 pounds, and weight on drivers 147,000 pounds, with tractive power 35,650 pounds, the 60-foot-6-inch engines could haul 65 30-ton freight cars at 10 miles per hour over 116-feet-to-the-mile mountain grades. Some of them were later sold to the Southern Pacific of Mexico, but many of the ten-wheelers continued in regular SP service for years on fast freights and local passenger trains where grades were not excessive.

Demand continued for heavier trains and locomotives that could buck grades and snows on schedules that must not fail. Western fruits, vegetables, and other products were gaining an increasing market in the East, and the increasing Western population was drawing ever increasingly on manufactured products from East to West. Locomotives had to keep pace. The SP's locomotive history is one of impressive struggle to meet these insatiable demands.

The road bought from Schenectady in 1898 10 large compound 4-8-os burning coal, for heavy freight service in the mountains. Total weight of locomotive and tender was 292,000 pounds. They were the first locomotives on the SP lines to carry 200 pounds boiler steam pressure. They lasted down the years, though converted to single expansion outfits. When they came from the builders they had all the fancy new improvements of the time, including automatic couplers, air sanders in place of hand-operated sanders, iron tender frames in place of wood, the Sweeney air compressor device to offset possible failure of the air pump, and sectional magnesia lagging for boiler insulation in place of the wood formerly used.

At the turn of the century, 105 2-6-o-type Moguls were delivered by Schenectady and Cooke. Classed as fast freight locomotives for valley service, they stayed in service long enough to be classed among the oldest and smallest locomotives in use on SP main lines, although their total running-order weight of 246,000 pounds, with tender, was some 3,000 pounds in excess of "El Gobernador" of unhappy memory. One step along in the scale of size came the Consolidation, 2-8-0, Schenectady built—12 of them. Coal-burners, they were the first wide-firebox locomotives built for SP.

Locomotives were still growing. Baldwin built 18 ten-wheelers of the 4-6-0 type for SP. They went into service in 1902. They were 72 feet long over-all, and in working order with tender weighed 329,423 pounds. For years these Baldwin Vauclain compounds were used on the through main-line passenger trains of the Coast Line and elsewhere. As the demands of passenger service became heavier, they went to lighter branch-line service. In common with other compounds, they were gradually converted to single expansion locomotives as the compound cylinders and parts wore out.

The year 1902 saw 10 Atlantic 4-4-2-type engines from Baldwin, also of the Vauclain compound type, make their debut on the SP rails. Their 84¼-inch drivers were the largest ever used on SP lines. The great drivers gave them very high sustained speeds. The wide fireboxes were suitable either for coal or oil. Starting as coal-burners, they soon went into oil. They zipped along the valley routes with main-line passenger trains. They were mostly retired from service and broken up in the 1920s, but even then their day was not entirely over. Four other locomotives, to which old Atlantic numbers were given, were rebuilt with 81-inch drivers, and tenders and cabs of two of the high-stepping engines were painted in Daylight colors and assigned in 1946 to Sacramento Daylight trains. Power was not adequate, however, when the trains lengthened out to more than 8 cars.

SP continued to fight the "Sacramento Hill," the Sierra Nevada which rises to above 7,000 feet at Donner Summit. The maximum grade on that so-called "Hill" is about 134 feet to the mile. Not to detail all the types of locomotives built by the company or purchased elsewhere to fight the massive Hill, it may be stated that they were many. Because several Western lines had similar motive-power problems, the Southern Pacific, Union Pacific, Oregon Short Line, Oregon Railroad and Navigation Company, and Chicago and Alton, Harriman lines all, got together in 1902 to standardize the locomotive designs and unify the purchases where possible. The "Associated Lines" continued this practice until 1913. All the locomotives completed from March, 1904, until 1913 were built in accordance with Associated Lines standards.

Between 1904 and 1911, thirty-eight Associated Lines common standard

Pacific locomotives, 4-6-2 type, were built by Schenectady and Baldwin for SP lines. These locomotives, with an over-all length of 74 feet 8 inches, were used on heavy through passenger trains operating in territory where heavy grades were not experienced.

With the steady increase in the length and weight of trains, that grade over the Sacramento Hill continued to demand bigger and more powerful engines. Prior to 1909, the freight trains were handled by consolidation, 2-8-0-type locomotives, generally 4 to a train where the going really got tough. But nothing less than double the tractive power would seem to do. The Mallet locomotive, an articulated type of compound engine, had recently been introduced into the United States, and its advantages on the severe grades and curves of the Sierra seemed obvious.

So two Mallets were built by Baldwin in 1909 for use in this territory. They were built to operate in the conventional manner, with smokestack ahead. But better days were ahead for enginemen. The advisability of providing better visibility and comfort for the engine crew in the numerous snowsheds, tunnels, and curves had at last been recognized. The length and size of these gargantuans emphasized that point. They sent back exhaust steam and gases which made the cabs very uncomfortable places; enginemen were afraid of being overcome by the heat. So the cab was enclosed and placed at the front of the locomotive.

It is believed that the cab-ahead idea originated with George Adams, master mechanic of the old North Pacific Coast Railroad, one of the predecessors of the Northwestern Pacific. In 1902 Adams designed and built a 4-4-0-type locomotive in which the boiler was mounted backward with the cab at the front end over the engine truck and cylinders. It was not satisfactory and was abandoned after only two years of service.

The Southern Pacific cab-ahead design was an improvement over the old Adams design in that the boiler was mounted on the frame in the usual manner, the cab being enclosed and the engine operated with the cab end forward. The fuel-oil tank was kept under 5 pounds' air pressure to force the oil through a pipe from the tender, separated from the firebox by the length of the locomotive boiler.

These SP Mallets were the first 2-8-8-2s built in this country. They were equipped with very large boilers. The firebox was also large. There are limits beyond which the rigid wheelbase of a locomotive cannot be lengthened without causing binding of wheel flanges against the rails in rounding curves. Southern Pacific has not attempted to use more than five pairs of driving wheels under a nonarticulated locomotive, and in such long locomotives a degree of increased flexibility is provided by lateral-motion driving boxes.

However, for efficiency in handling modern trains, the Mallets with boilers longer than could be carried on five pairs of driving wheels employed an articulated design. The driving wheels were divided into two sets, one set installed under one end of the boiler in the usual manner, and the other set with its own pair of cylinders making up a "truck" on which the other end of the boiler rested on a swivel bearing. This double-jointed action enabled them to wriggle gracefully around the curves. Designed to operate on a grade of 116 feet to the mile and to haul on this grade 1,212 tons back of the tender at a speed of 9 miles per hour, they furnished practically twice the performance of the prime movers which had previously been used on this service.

Forty-seven 2-8-8-2s of similar design were built by Baldwin between 1910 and 1913. On a "drag haul," from 6 to 8 miles per hour, these Mallets were extremely powerful and economical in fuel consumption. However, when freight trains of higher speeds entered the picture, one of the Mallets was experimentally converted from compound to single expansion. That produced the desired higher operating speed, and the Mallets thereafter stepped along with their drags at 15 miles per hour. In 1911, the Baldwin works delivered 12 Mallets for passenger work. Changes in wheel arrangement made them into 4-6-6-2s. The Mallet passenger locomotives were capable of handling a train of 10 passenger cars weighing 50 tons each at speeds of 20 miles per hour on an ascending grade of 116 feet to the mile.

Modern cab-aheads are often called Mallets by railroaders as well as nonrailroaders, but not properly so. They are all single expansion engines, and the term Mallet designates the system of compounding the steam cylinders first proposed by A. Mallet of France.

Locomotives of the Pacific class purchased in 1912 were the first to come from the builders equipped with superheaters. The Schmidt super-heater on these engines consisted of a number of loops of pipe through which the saturated steam was passed. These were placed in superheater flues through which hot firebox gases flowed. The saturated steam on its way through the superheater toward the cylinders picked up additional heat. Superheated steam saves fuel and water consumption, reduces cylinder condensation, and increases power.

Three of the Pacifics built in 1913 were transferred to the T&NO, streamlined and painted in colors practically identical to the Daylight locomotives, to power the Sunbeam.

The heavy Pacifics which for about fourteen years hauled passenger trains on the Salt Lake Division were gradually replaced by heavier and more powerful Mikado 2-8-2 locomotives. Later the Mikados have been transferred to freight service in valley territory.

With the entry of the United States into World War I the sudden increase in tonnage to be handled necessitated a freight locomotive capable of handling heavier loads at higher speeds than could the Mikado.

The 2-10-2 type built from 1917 to 1925 was forerunner of the 4-10-2 "Southern Pacific" type to handle trains over mountain section of the Pacific Coast. These were the largest and most powerful nonarticulated (single engine unit) locomotives built up to that time and were the first of the type used by any railroad. The boiler pressure was 225 pounds. Locomotives of this type reached an over-all length of 101 feet 2 inches and a total weight of 736,100 pounds. At speeds of 25 miles per hour, up grades of 116 feet per mile, they had 25 per cent more hauling capacity than any locomotives previously built for the company. Among outstanding features of this locomotive was a third cylinder placed inside the main frames, slightly above and between the two outside cylinders. This middle cylinder was set at an angle from the horizontal and was designed to act on a crank on the second driving axle.

With the 4-10-2-type locomotive, having 96,530 pounds of tractive effort, it was possible to handle as many as 13 cars weighing a total of 950 tons over the Sierra Nevada grades without helpers on the fastest passenger schedules. But even this was not enough. In 1928, because of increased traffic and ever heavier trains, the 4-8-8-2s went into service. Length had extended to 120 feet, total weight to 895,100 pounds.

The day of million-pound locomotives was approaching. These were articulated locomotives, consisting of a frame constructed in two parts joined together with a hinge connection and supplied with steam from one boiler supported by the two engines. Each engine had one pair of cylinders, 24 by 32 inches, each pair of cylinders driving four pairs of 63½-inch drivers. Boiler pressure was 235 pounds. The 4-8-8-2 articulated Consolidation locomotives (the cab-aheads or "ACs" as they are known) soon proved their worth in both freight and passenger service. Largest of them became 125 feet 11 inches long with tender and had a total loaded weight of 1,051,200 pounds, tractive force of 124,300 pounds, and weight on drivers of 514,800 pounds. They developed about 6,000 horsepower at 40 miles per hour. The cab-ahead was a joy to the enginemen.

When the more powerful 4-8-8-2 cab-ahead-type locomotives were put into general use in the Sierra Nevada Mountains the 4-10-2-type three-cylinder locomotives were transferred principally to southern divisions, where they successfully handled fast freight trains.

In 1923 and 1924 came the Mountain-type (4-8-2) locomotives. They were especially designed for fast handling of heavy passenger trains between Los Angeles and El Paso, a distance of 815 miles, without changing engines. They proved their worth on many other passenger runs, some of them longer.

Success of the first 34 Mountain-type locomotives built by the American Locomotive Company for SP in 1923 and 1924 led SP to build 49 of the same type in its own shops in Sacramento. The last 39 had engine beds consisting of one-piece steel castings. The 4-8-2-type locomotives developed 3,413 horsepower at 40 miles per hour. Boiler pressure was 210 pounds.

In 1930 Southern Pacific adopted the 4-8-4 (then called "Golden State" but later named "General Service")-type locomotive. This was a refinement of the 4-8-2 in that the application of the four-wheeled trailing truck permitted an increase in the size of the firebox. Boiler pressure was stepped up to 250 pounds. The General Service locomotives are used in heavy main-line freight and passenger service. In the GS-4s and GS-5s boiler pressure was stepped up to 300 pounds and horsepower raised to 5,500 at 55 miles per hour, the most powerful streamlined steam engines on any rails at the time they were built in 1941 and 1942. Over-all length is 110 feet 2¼ inches. Such engines pull the Daylights.

The SP's steam locomotives were long struggling onward to the million-pound mark, but surprisingly enough not the cab-ahead oil-burners of the Sierra but coal-burning freight locomotives in New Mexico (which later were converted to oil) finally topped the figure when the 12 AC-9s came on the line with their 1,090,600 pounds in 1939. Beside those mighty steel draft horses the "Governor Stanford" and the 43,500-pound "C. P. Huntington" look tiny indeed.

That is probably enough about the story of steam on the SP lines, for the details of which the authors are greatly indebted to D. L. Joslyn of Sacramento, veteran railroader. Enough has been told to indicate that imaginations were not slumbering, and progress, often unseen by the public, was steadfastly being made.

A few years ago one of the authors of this book was in Virginia City, Nevada. He noticed an object on a dump heap down Six-Mile Canyon. The object was made of thin steel and was square and about as big as a doghouse for a medium-sized Saint Bernard. The glass was gone, and the mounting for the kerosene lamp that once may have flared in its interior was missing. But some fancy scrollwork in red and gold and green remained. Badly weathered, it still spelled "C. P. Huntington."

Was this an honest headlight from old No. 3? Or a hoax, or a movie prop? Nobody knew. Did that headlight once wind around the Sierra curves, the whistle behind it moaning hoarsely to the pines, the four 22-ton cars rattling along behind in their valiant conquest of the snow and granite, where the long, long strings of heavy freight cars and the gleaming streamliners flash today?

Appendix C: Under Smoky Roofs

A RAILROAD is many departments, and every true railroad man feels that his department is the most important. He will give you an argument to that effect any time, practically without request.

But the men who work in the general shops at Sacramento *know* that they are the bedrock of the outfit. They either make or repair half the stuff that rolls. In the years since those sprawling, dingy, clanging shops came into existence, the railroad had spawned many more such collections of machinery and men. Other general shops are at Houston, El Paso, and Los Angeles; each division has its big shops also. But the Sacramento general shops are the granddaddy.

They came into being when the railroad did. In fact, their beginnings antedate the Central Pacific. The original machine shop, 36 by 116 feet, that bolted together the CP's first locomotive, was already in business near the junction of the Sacramento and American rivers when Huntington and Hopkins was just a nearby hardware store.

Again, thanks are due to Dave Joslyn for the following:

That machine shop, which was a going concern making anything from mining machinery to mustache curlers, cut its eye teeth on a locomotive axle when the river schooner *Artful Dodger* tied up at the Front Street levee on October 5, 1863, with the first material for the proposed transcontinental railroad in its hold. The crates had arrived at San Francisco on the clipper ship *Herald of the Morning*, after a lengthy voyage around Cape Horn. Included in the river schooner's cargo was a locomotive, CP No. 1, the "Governor Stanford." It was from the works of R. Norris and Sons in Philadelphia and was in semiknocked-down condition, requiring considerable sorting out and assembling.

The brand-new railroad consisted then chiefly of handsomely embellished stocks and bonds. It had no shops and few tools. With plenty of shouting and confusion, the consignment was lifted from the schooner to tracks on the levee. Some blocks northward was that machine shop of Goss and Lambard. It took over the job of assembling the pieces of the

"Governor Stanford" and putting them in running order. Ultimately the workmen of Goss and Lambard's shop at Second and I Streets became the first mechanical employees of the railroad.

But even as early as 1863, the CP was ready to build its own cars, and soon put up a shop 20 by 150 feet to house the work. Benjamin Welch, who had been assistant at the Folsom shops of the Sacramento Valley Rail Road, before that a horsecar builder at San Francisco, took charge.

The Central Pacific crowd fully realized that a Far Western railroad's mechanical and material wants could not be supplied simply by ordering from a manufacturer. Everything that went to make a railroad, except stone and ties, was approximately fifteen thousand sea miles or six months away, with a war racking the nation and a hostile enemy patrolling the water route. Whatever was needed had to be shaped up, if possible, right on the spot. Even though this meant inventing it first, then designing it, then casting or stamping or pressing it from metal or planing it from the original tree.

Often the thing to be made, whether a swinging brass lamp or a pair of drivers, had to wait upon the invention and creation, first of all, of the tool for making it. Fortunately, Sacramento had a supply of artisans who had learned their trade all over the world, and what one man did not know, three others usually did. Or if not, a fifth would step up and invent a method. No phase of the CP-SP story better illustrates the resourcefulness, energy, and initiative of that enterprise than the skill and will of the blacksmiths, carpenters, and machinists who made and fitted the actual bolts while the Stanfords, Huntingtons, and Crockers schemed and dreamed.

A railroad is not a railroad without a roundhouse. The Central Pacific high command ordered work on a roundhouse started in 1867, and what resulted was a house indeed. First, a layer of cobblestones was laid down. Then huge granite stones were set up for the wall foundations, 16 feet wide at the bottom and battered up to a convenient width at the top. Sixteen cranes were required to hoist these foundation stones. On top of this sturdy underpinning rose the brick walls. After a year of work the Sacramento *Union* proudly saluted the edifice: "It is built on a 378-foot diameter, there are 29 openings or stalls for the iron steeds, but only 28 will be used, as the offices for the officials will occupy the south end of the building."

Around and near this, one by one, were built the successive car shops, machine shops, boiler shops, blacksmith shops, forges, foundries, paint shops, planing mills, rolling mill, storehouses, and various other structures and departments which today constitute the 200-and-more-acre plant of one of the greatest railroad general workshops on earth, capable of doing anything from operating on the appendix of a 5,000-horsepower locomotive to plating the dining-car silverware.

The Sacramento Valley Rail Road, Judah's original child and California's first railroad, had discerned even earlier that it was a long way
from the Pacific Coast to the workshops and foundries of the Atlantic
seaboard, and therefore that for repairs and even for fundamental construction it was on its own. At first some car shops on the Sacramento
levee, then shops up the American River at Folsom, had been opened with
iron foundry, space for melting brass, machine shops with one pit, planing
mill, cabinet shop, and car-building shop. In addition to building cars
and keeping up repairs on locomotives and rolling stock, the shops also
turned out cooking utensils, stoves, mine machinery, boilers, and steam
engines.

The shops at Folsom passed to the Central Pacific in 1865 along with
CP's purchase of the Sacramento Valley Rail Road, the Placerville and
Sacramento, the California Central, and the Freeport Railroad. The brick
buildings at Folsom continued to hum until the 1890s, when the last of
their machinery was shipped to Sacramento.

In 1868 the CP took over the entire works of Goss and Lambard, including machine shop, blacksmith shop, and foundry. They became
known as the "Iron Department" of the Central Pacific. One of the buildings, still standing until the middle of this century, was used by the
Stores Department as a place for storing old files and records. It has finally
been torn down.

The general master mechanic, A. J. Stevens, discovered a handy man with
a pencil around the place, and made him a draftsman at $50 a month.
The year 1871 found the industrious draftsman, George Stoddard, whipping up designs for a wheel foundry, as delay in getting wheels from
Eastern works was holding up the repair of rolling stock. A year later
the foundry was in operation, turning out 40 wheels a day. Soon it increased to 100 a day. By 1883 that foundry was outgrown, and a new one
was built. That one is the main iron and wheel foundry of the railroad to
this day. It has produced more than iron and wheels. It has produced four
of the five general foremen who have presided over it, all—except M. A.
Baxter, who came to the railroad from Goss and Lambard—having
learned their trade under that smoky roof.

Along with iron, brasswork had to be turned out on the spot. This
included mountains of cuspidors, without which no transcontinental train
could have rolled a hundred feet. So the railroad soon had a brass foundry
in a corner of the iron foundry. Presently there was shop just for brass,
because the department found itself making all the company's driving-
box journal bearings, passenger and freight-car journal bearings, brass

shoes and wedges, and the large number of ornate brass parts used by the showy passenger cars of the day.

Locomotives had seen punishing service during the CP's construction days, and when the road was completed in 1869 a number of them were brought to the Sacramento shops and, as an old report has it, "set aside in the dead line, awaiting orders." Some were given new fireboxes, some were completely rebuilt. Then, in 1872, the growing shops got the go-ahead to do what they most aspired to do—build some locomotives on their own. The order was for 10 American-type or eight-wheel engines.

The design of these engines from the ground up was drafted by George A. Stoddard at a stand-up desk in a corner of the machine shop. Later, given the title of chief draftsman at $125 a month with two assistants at $60 a month each, and finally a force that had grown to six men, Stoddard designed boilers and engines for ferryboats, steam hammers, punches, shears, cars, rail-curving machines, snowplows, and cable cars. As it was not yet the era of air brakes for trains, Stoddard designed a foot brake for the locomotive, operating through a foot lever on the floor of the cab. It helped the brakemen who had to stop the trains by winding up the hand brakes on each car. When Sacramento needed a pump at its water works, Stoddard designed the pump. There was nothing in the mechanical line that Stoddard as draftsman and A. J. Stevens as general master mechanic would not tackle, and the CP shops would not build.

They were all practical fellows who would try anything not once but ten or a hundred times. Blacksmith Uren got an idea for a huge press which Stoddard promptly designed for him, the function of which was to stamp out links for the chains by which the cars in the trains were coupled together. The two men also designed machines for making rail joints, fishplates, rail bolts, and spikes. Steve Uren was a Cornishman who ruled the blacksmith shop with a temper as hot as a red-hot poker, and who went to church every Sunday complete with long-tailed coat, striped trousers, silk hat, and walking stick.

Iron for the vast miscellany of jobs came from the Pacific Rolling Mill Company at San Francisco and from factories in the East. It was not always on hand when needed, so one day Stevens called Stoddard into his office and said, "Can you design a rolling mill?"

Without batting an eyelash, Stoddard replied, "Yes, I can."

"Then get busy and do it."

Stoddard had never seen a rolling mill, but he soon had one on paper, and soon after the blacksmith shop had it in solid fact. That original mill, frequently added to, ran day and night turning out rounds, flats, and bars made from scrap iron that came in off the road. It lasted from 1876 until 1930, which is pretty good for one improvised practically by ear.

The first locomotive built in the Sacramento shops sprang from its swaddling chains in 1872, as the little eight-wheeler No. 173. She had a 22-foot 1¼-inch wheelbase, a 48-inch wagon-top boiler, 17-by-24-inch cylinders, 56-inch drivers, carried 130 pounds' steam pressure—5 pounds more than any other engine then in service on the line—and weighed 70,070 pounds in working shape. She had a diamond stack and was equipped to burn either coal or wood—or sagebrush, as a matter of fact, for firemen of the period were sometimes glad to use what they could get.

The first cars, both freight and passenger, used wooden brake beams. When the CP started laying heavier rails to replace its original trail of iron, the old 62-pound rails were brought to Sacramento and tossed to a night gang in the rolling mill, who shoved the rails under a steam hammer and whacked them into iron brakebeams. When locomotives began burning coal instead of wood, a yard for firebricks was established down by the river.

Along with boilers for the new locomotives, the shops geared themselves to build boilers also for river steamboats and bay ferries. It was not long before the clanging and general uproar of the Sacramento boiler shops included the ringing cadences of construction of the mammoth boilers for the train ferry *Solano,* for a time to be the biggest ferryboat in the world.

The pride and joy of the car shop was the string of passenger cars it turned out in the seventies and eighties, particularly the private cars for its top officials. The most sumptuous of these, the car "Stanford," was the last possible word in ornate painting and decorating and what passed for comforts. But perhaps more important than all the private cars ever built was the first so-called "Emigrant Sleeper," fashioned by Master Car Builder Ben Welch and Designer Max Eichrodt. For this, and its mates that followed, was the car that populated no small portion of the West, as has been noticed elsewhere in this book.

Back in 1898 a fire broke out in the upper floor of the car machine shop. It touched off the car shop across the alley. The city fire department came racing in the early dawn hours, but was halted by a string of cars at the depot. But a hook-and-ladder hose cart and fire engine from the Young America firehouse smashed their way in through a lumber yard. The shops were poorly lighted, and the firemen could not locate the city fire plug for a time—there was only one in the entire shops. When located, its threading would not fit the hose. By the time the connection was made, the two blazing buildings were beyond saving, and it didn't much matter about the connections anyhow—all that came out of the hose was a stream of mud. Then 12,000 gallons of water sprayed the fire-fighters as the car shop's roof tank tumbled and smashed. It was a lovely day.

And there was the time when a 6,000-gallon tank was being hoisted into place and was high up in the air on a plank supported by a couple of screw jacks when the plank broke, the tank fell with a crash, and at that precise instant a boy was lighting an oil forge heater. It was the custom of those heater fires to catch with a bang, but the youth had not counted on quite *that* bang. Both thunderclaps came simultaneously, and the lad that might have become a master mechanic, a superintendent of motive power, or even president of the railroad—given time—resigned his occupation right there. He lit out, and when last seen, was still running. He never came back for his pay.

The last locomotive built by the Sacramento shops leaped from her gantry cranes in 1937. She was a 0-8-0 switcher. In the sixty-three intervening years that separated her from No. 173, the first locomotive constructed by the big shops, more than two hundred steam locomotives had been turned out complete from driving tires to bell cord. They had been of all sizes, ranging from eight-wheelers, twelve-wheelers, the burly "El Gobernador" that balked ignominiously, giant Mountain types and Consolidations, down to switchers. Today the shops are cleaning up fast, keeping the steam stuff running as long as the stockholders want it so, but spreading the welcome mat for the ever increasing fleet of diesels.

Mileposts

1836 Chicago villagers take out charter for the Galena and Chicago Union (which becomes the Chicago and North Western), Jan. 16.

Texas achieves its independence of Mexico at the battle of San Jacinto, Apr. 21.

The Texas Railroad, Navigation and Banking Company, first railroad chartered by Texas (but not constructed), authorized by the Republic of Texas, Dec. 16.

1837 Houston and Brazos Railroad Company (never constructed) chartered by Republic of Texas, Jan. 26.

1838 Charter granted by Republic of Texas to Brazos and Galveston Railroad (never constructed), May 24.

1840 Houston and Brazos Railroad contracts for 3,000 oak or cedar ties, Feb. 28. Obtains charter from Republic of Texas as the Harrisburg Railroad and Trading Company, Jan. 9, 1841. While never built, this road makes a preliminary survey to the Pacific Ocean via the "pass of the Rio Grande" (El Paso) and San Diego over the route later surveyed by army engineers and ultimately used by the Southern Pacific,

1845 Texas admitted as a state, keeping its public lands. During the ten-year life of the republic three railroads are chartered, but the republic never hears the whistle of a locomotive.

1846 Meeting held in the town of Victoria, Texas, in which a railroad to the Pacific via the route now followed by Southern Pacific is warmly advocated.

1847 Gen. Sidney Sherman of Harrisburg, Texas, and Jonathan F. Barrett, John Angier, and Elisha Allen of Boston form the Harrisburg City Company for the purpose of organizing a railroad, Oct. 31.

This develops into the "Harrisburg Railroad," the Buffalo Bayou, Brazos and Colorado.

1848 Gold discovered in California's American River, Jan. 24.

Galveston and Red River Railway Company, second Texas railroad on which work is actually begun, chartered Mar. 11. Name changed to the Houston and Texas Central Railway Company, Sept. 1, 1856.

Galena and Chicago Union, with 10 miles of track, goes into operation with one locomotive, one passenger car, and one freight car, Oct. 25.

1849 First railroad west of the Mississippi, the so-called "Pacific Railroad" of Missouri, chartered to run from St. Louis to Jefferson City, 125 miles. Grading starts May, 1851. First locomotive operates west of the Mississippi, Nov., 1851.

1850 In this year, nearly every state east of the Mississippi has one or more railroads, and the total mileage in the United States is about 5,000.

The state of Illinois is granted by the Federal government 2,500,000 acres of land to aid the Illinois Central Railroad. The road is quickly built. Other government land in the vicinity of the road becomes salable at $2 per acre and upward.

Gen. James Gadsden is sent by Pres. Franklin Pierce to Mexico City to negotiate for what is now the southern part of New Mexico and Arizona, 29,670 square miles, including Messila Valley and the pass of the Rio Grande—the route used thirty years later by the Southern Pacific. U.S. pays $10,000,000, which is only $5,000,000 less than the U.S. paid Mexico for California, Nevada, Utah, and part of Colorado, Arizona, and New Mexico—total, 529,189 square miles.

Charter of the railroad proposed by Gen. Sidney Sherman is validated as the Buffalo, Bayou, Brazos and Colorado, Feb. 11. This becomes the first actual railroad in Texas and an ultimate link in the Southern Pacific Sunset Route. California admitted as a state, Sept. 9.

Steamer *Kangaroo* in regularly scheduled passenger ferry service between San Francisco and Oakland side of bay.

1851 Grading starts on the BBB&C, first railroad in Texas and second west of the Mississippi, May.

1852 New Orleans citizens subscribe nearly $3,000,000 for railroad to be built west of the Mississippi to the Atchafalaya River.

State-owned lands in Texas worth about 50 cents an acre. Total Texas public domain about 100,000,000 acres. Texas legislature offers 8 sections per mile to railroads which will really build.

Grading begins on the Buffalo, Bayou, Brazos and Colorado. John A. Williams of Boston, chief engineer.

First railroad incorporated in California, the Sacramento, Auburn and Nevada. Never built.

Sacramento Valley Rail Road, first railroad built in California, incorporated. Atlantic and Pacific Railroad Company chartered by the state of New York to build a transcontinental railroad, authorized capital $100,000,000.

The Vicksburg and El Paso Railroad Company, subsequently known as the Texas Western Railway, chartered. Name changed in 1856 to the Southern Pacific Railroad Company. Now extinct. No relationship to present Southern Pacific Company, which started as a California company incorporated in 1865.

1853 Congress orders surveys to determine the most feasible route for a transcontinental railroad.

First railroad service in Texas inaugurated by the BBB&C, 20 miles, Sept. 7. Charles Morgan has three sailings a week from Indianola, Texas. Commodore Vanderbilt sells out his competing line to Panama and Nicaragua to Morgan.

1855 BBB&C reaches east bank of the Brazos, 32 miles from its starting point at Harrisburg, December.

1856 Californians take their first train ride within boundaries of their state, on Judah-built Sacramento Valley Rail Road out of Sacramento, Feb. 22.

BBB&C, which has received total of 887,021 acres of Texas state public domain, reports sales of land averaging 23 cents per acre.

Texas legislature grants charter to The Sabine and Galveston Railroad and Lumber Company to build from the Sabine River in Orange County to tidewater on Galveston Bay, Sept. 1.

1857 San Antonio and San Diego Coach Line, 1,475 miles, established in June and service inaugurated from both ends. Schedule, 30 days.

1859 Cyrus K. Holliday obtains charter in Kansas for the Atchison and Topeka Railroad Company, forerunner of the present-day Santa Fe system—consolidation of over 150 companies.

Legislature of Louisiana addresses resolution to the legislature of Texas informing that it has granted a charter for a railroad from Brashear City to the Sabine River, and also a right-of-way to the Sabine and Galveston Bay Railroad and Lumber Company from Sabine River to New Iberia, authorizing the name changed to "Texas and New Orleans Railroad Company, Louisiana Division," Sept. 1.

Texas legislature, looking with favor on suggestion of Louisiana legislature, changes name of the Galveston Bay Railroad and Lumber Company's Texas operations to "Texas and New Orleans Railroad, Texas Division," Dec. 24.

1860 Judah announces that he has found a feasible route over the Sierra via Dutch Flat, maximum grade 100 feet to the mile, August.

BBB&C, "The Harrisburg Railroad," handles 18,527 tons of freight and performs 53,000 miles of train service.

BBB&C reaches Alleyton on east bank of Colorado River (of Texas), 80 miles from its starting point. Work stops until after Civil War.

1861 Central Pacific Railroad Company incorporated June 28, 1861, under the laws of California, under direction of Leland Stanford, C. P. Huntington, Mark Hopkins, and Charles Crocker, to build eastward from Sacramento to California state line.

Just before suspending business because of Civil War, the Louisiana and Texas divisions, Texas and New Orleans Railroad, advertise passenger service between New Orleans and Houston, 70 hours. Present time by Sunset, 9 hours.

1862 As a military measure President Lincoln signed the Pacific Railroad Act, July 1, authorizing construction of a railroad or railroads between the Missouri River and the Pacific Coast at or near San Francisco "or the navigable waters of the Sacramento River."

Judah's field men complete instrument survey of his route over the Sierra, autumn.

Union Pacific organized at Chicago, Sept. 2.

In 1862, 1864, and 1866, Acts supplementing the Act of 1862 change the meeting points of the Central Pacific and Union Pacific, each change moving the point eastward.

1863 Ground broken for Central Pacific at Sacramento, Jan. 8. Stanford wields silver shovel.

Central Pacific locomotive No. 1, the "Governor Stanford," reaches Sacramento via river steamer. In service Nov. 11.

First rail-ferry service between Oakland and San Francisco by SF&O Railroad Company, Sept. 2.

1864 Central Pacific starts operating trains for public travel, Sacramento to Newcastle, 31 miles; first timetable effective June 6.

Travel inaugurated over San Francisco and San Jose, Jan. 16.

Galena and Chicago Union becomes Chicago and North Western.

1865 California and Oregon Railroad incorporated June 30 to build from Marysville, California, to Portland.

UP holds second ground-breaking ceremonies, Nov. 5.

Southern Pacific Railroad Company incorporated under laws of California to build from San Francisco to San Diego, thence to a junction with a contemplated road from the eastern line of California, to the Mississippi River, Dec. 2.

1866 SP authorized by Congress to build a road to a connection with Atlantic and Pacific at Needles, July 27. The route south of Mojave via San Diego abandoned in favor of the line Mojave to Needles. Congress passes resolution, June 28, 1870, authorizing the SP definitely to build a road over this route.

1867 First Chicago and North Western train steams into Council Bluffs, Feb. 8. First CP diamond-stacker crosses California-Nevada line.

1868 C. P. Huntington, vice-president of the Central Pacific, transmits to Secretary of the Interior the annual report of the Southern Pacific as required by Congress, the report indicating close relationship between Central Pacific and Southern Pacific, Sept. 25.

San Joaquin Valley Rail Road organized to maintain independence of valley. Gathered into Central Pacific, 1870.

Two rival railroad companies in Oregon, both named Oregon Central, break ground at Portland. Ben Holladay joins the faction favoring railroad up east side of Willamette River. Both broke ground in April.

CP opened to Reno, June 19, a townsite laid out by the railroad.

1869 CP forces lay 10 miles of track in a day, Apr. 28, nearing Promontory; Crocker wins wager with UP.

May 10, at Promontory, Territory of Utah, Central Pacific with its completed track meets Union Pacific. The historic "Golden Spike" ceremony.

First regular passenger and freight through service inaugurated on Central Pacific between Sacramento and Chicago, May 15.

First Silver Palace cars arrive at Sacramento from Delaware builder, June 4.

Line completed from Sacramento via Stockton to San Jose, Sept. 15, and to San Francisco Bay at Alameda on Sept. 6 and Oakland on Nov. 8.

Construction of Central Pacific spur up San Joaquin Valley starts Dec. 31.

Los Angeles gets first railroad, 22-mile Los Angeles and San Pedro Railroad, Los Angeles to Wilmington, Oct. 26.

Ben Holladay rebridges Clackamas River in Oregon, gets a locomotive across, and qualifies for government aid with only hours to go, Dec. 23.

1870 The properties of the BBB&C, having been sold to satisfy a judgment, are purchased by Thomas W. Peirce of Boston, and associates.

Texas legislature authorizes BBB&C name change to the Galveston, Harrisburg and San Antonio, and the new owners decide to extend to San Antonio.

Central Pacific acquires the California and Oregon with right to build north to California border.

Public hears rumors that CP and SP are to be merged. Stanford and associates deny it.

June 23 and Aug. 22, proceedings to consolidate other companies with the Central Pacific, and Oct. 12, proceedings for the absorption of other companies by Southern Pacific Railroad Company, mark fusion in fact of the two roads. On Oct. 12, ownership and control of the Central Pacific and Southern Pacific by the same men, Leland Stanford, Charles Crocker, C. P. Huntington, and Mark Hopkins, and their associates, made matter of official record. From that date to this the properties have been under a common control.

Southern Pacific becomes the owner of a line, San Francisco to San Jose, built in 1864, and also of a company which was to build the 20 miles from Gilroy to Tres Pinos.

Southward-building California and Oregon reaches Salem Sept. 29 in time for state fair. Locomotive the big attraction.

1871 Congress passes the Texas and Pacific Act authorizing Southern Pacific Railroad Company to build south from Tehachapi Pass via Los Angeles to a connection with the Texas and Pacific at or near the Colorado River, Mar. 3. Thus is given the right to build to Yuma as well as to Needles, under the same conditions that govern construction to Needles. This line was built from the Goshen (San Joaquin Valley) terminal of the Central Pacific.

O&C opened to Eugene, Oregon, Oct. 15.

1872 Holladay bankrupt in Oregon, Henry Villard takes over the Oregon and California.

Huntington and Hopkins, like Crocker, are eager to sell out. Too much personal liability surrounds railroad stock—nobody will buy.

CP inaugurates rail service to Merced, Jan. 15; to Fresno, May 28; both town-sites staked out by CP.

July 25, the first Southern Pacific unit in the San Joaquin Valley completed and leased to the Central Pacific for operation. Thereafter as each additional unit is ready for operation it is similarly taken over by the Central Pacific so that all of the mileage of the Southern Pacific comes under operation by the Central Pacific, under the name of Central Pacific and leased lines, except the 100 miles between San Francisco and Tres Pinos, via San Jose and Gilroy, which is operated under the immediate direction of Leland Stanford and his associates, the same interests that control the Central Pacific. This continues until 1885.

Single-track bridge across Missouri River completed.

Line completed to Redding, California, Sept. 1, terminus for 12 years.

1873 Huntington tries to sell SP to Tom Scott. Refuses $15,000,000, asks $17,-000,000. Deal falls through, Jan. 5.

SP Coast Line to Los Angeles reaches Soledad, Aug. 12; terminus for 13 years. Panic in New York, September. Money troubles drive Huntington almost to despair.

The Texas and Pacific, building west, reaches Dallas. Work halts until 1876.

1874 SP reaches Sumner (now East Bakersfield), Nov. 8.

Atlantic and Pacific bankrupt. Subsequently reorganizes as St. Louis and San Francisco ("Frisco"). Santa Fe ultimately buys half interest, deriving right to build to Colorado River opposite Needles.

1876 Special "lightning express" makes run from Jersey City to Oakland, and thence ferry to San Francisco, in 84 hours, 17 minutes. June 1–4.

Aug. 27, Black Friday. Mining stocks collapse in San Francisco. Panic. Huntington soon able to snatch Cajon Pass from J. P. Jones.

Hood's loops conquer the Tehachapi Pass.

San Francisco and Los Angeles linked on Sept. 5; "Last Spike" at Los Angeles.

1877 SP rails cross Colorado Desert, reach the river in May and plunge across when the U.S. Cavalry at Fort Yuma is not looking.

San Antonio reached by the Galveston, Harrisburg and San Antonio Railway (successor to the BBB&C), Feb. 5.

Oct. 9, Huntington gets executive order from President Hayes authorizing operation of trains across Yuma Reservation. Scott whipped. Now to beat Gould, who succeeds Scott in control of T&P.

1878 Mark Hopkins dies Mar. 29.

Julius Kruttschnitt gains his training in railroading while extending SP lines westward in Louisiana.

Congress passes Thurman Act, requiring CP and UP to set up sinking fund for ultimate payment of their borrowings from the government.

1879 SP tries burning oil in locomotive "Young America." Oil comes into general use on SP lines after turn of century.

1880 Tucson greets first SP train, Mar. 20.

C. P. Huntington, who has been contemplating a juncture of the eastward-pushing Southern Pacific with the westward-building Texas Pacific, enters into negotiations with Thomas W. Peirce in joining SP and GH&SA. The plans eventually materialize and the SP follows the more southern route via San Antonio.

1881 SP reaches El Paso, May 19; Sierra Blanco, Nov. 25.

The Southern Development Company, which is owned by the SP, contracts on July 15 to build the GH&SA westward from San Antonio. Construction begins at El Paso eastward and at San Antonio westward in June and July. Railroad reaches Del Rio in early winter.

1882 Roy Bean opens saloon in the vicinity of site of Pecos high bridge. Administers rough-and-ready "law west of the Pecos." Judge Bean's siding, called Langtry, was named for a construction foreman of that name, and not for Lily Langtry, noted actress, for whom Bean is said to have nursed a secret yearning.

1883 Jan. 12, construction forces from west and east meet on the west bank of the Pecos, 227 miles west of San Antonio, where the rails join that complete the transcontinental line. Sunset Route of the SP becomes an accomplished fact. First train from New Orleans reaches San Antonio Feb. 6; first train from San Francisco reaches San Antonio Feb. 7. The through service thus inaugurated continues without interruption or change of ownership from that time to this.

Huntington acquires the Morgan's Louisiana and Texas Railroad and Steamship Company, giving him access to New Orleans. Later the Morgan Line of steamships, under the SP house flag, carry Sunset Route rail passengers to Atlantic ports by sea. This service of "100 golden hours at sea" continues until World War II.

July 1, SP line finished to Needles, met by Atlantic and Pacific Aug. 9. Henry Villard completes the Northern Pacific into Portland.

1884 Oregon and California built to Ashland, work halts while California and
Oregon builds northward. Villard regime collapses.

Union Pacific gains entry into Portland via Oregon Railroad and Navigation Company.

Santa Fe trains move over Mohave Desert from Needles westward, September. Attains transcontinental stature with train out of San Diego, November,
1885.

Southern Pacific Company incorporated Mar. 17 under laws of Kentucky.

1885 Feb. 17, Central Pacific Railroad Company executes lease to Southern
. Pacific Company, Leland Stanford signing it as president of the Central
Pacific and next day being elected president of the Southern Pacific Com-
pany. The lease is for 99 years from April 1, 1885. (Other leases to Southern
Pacific Company, of various SP railroads and affiliates, effective Mar. 1.)

Apr. 1, Southern Pacific takes over for operation all companies of common
ownership, including Central Pacific, The Southern Pacific Railroad Company of California, Southern Pacific Railroad of Arizona, Southern Pacific
Railroad of New Mexico, the two companies organized in Texas, and the
two in Louisiana.

SP buys its first Westinghouse air brakes.

1886 Feb. 6, Lease of Central Pacific Railroad to Southern Pacific Company is
submitted by President of the United States to House of Representatives in
response to House resolution of Jan. 27 asking for contracts and leases filed
with the Secretary of the Interior by railroads which had received land grants
or other aid from the U.S.

1887 Mar. 3, President Cleveland appoints three commissioners to investigate
affairs of railroads receiving aid from the government, having in mind particularly the financial obligations yet outstanding to the government.

Mar. 6, Santa Fe and Southern Pacific in rate war slash fare from Missouri
River to Los Angeles to as low as $1 a head. Los Angeles receives 120,000
persons in single year, San Diego 50,000.

First SP train into Santa Barbara, via San Joaquin Valley line, Aug. 19.

Big Four take over Oregon and California by lease following Villard's
financial collapse.

California and Oregon reaches Hornbrook near California line in May.
Siskiyous ahead. Ashland finally reached, Dec. 17, and rails become continuous between Portland and all points on SP system.

Dec. 1, Federal commission reports on debt of Central Pacific to the government and the leasing of the lines of that company to the SP in 1885, and
states that in its judgment the value of Central Pacific property taken by
itself and without the auxiliary aid to be derived from connecting lines
would not be sufficient to pay the debt due the United States, but states that
the SP has not diverted any traffic from the CP.

1888 GH&SA shops removed from Harrisburg to Houston and consolidated with
those of the T&NO. Subsequently employing up to 5,000 men, they became
and are the largest railroad shops in the Southwest.

Charles Crocker dies, Aug. 14.

1890 Feb. 17, United States Senate Committee, after considering the report of the
railway commission appointed by President Cleveland, reports back to the
Senate mentioning plans for the adjustment of indebtedness of Central
Pacific to the United States. Recommends that all the associated lines form-
ing the Southern Pacific Company become parties to the obligation for the
refunding of the debt. The report shows that the statement of the affairs
of the Southern Pacific Company with accumulated surplus would indicate
the SP to be in condition to guarantee the debt.

July 2, Sherman Antitrust Law goes into effect. SP later points out the fact
that it is passed five years after the lease of Central Pacific to Southern Pacific
and twenty years after Oct. 12, 1870, when public records showed that the
lines had come under the common control of Stanford and his associates.

1891 SP builds a new crossing of the Pecos, a bridge 2,180 feet long and 321 feet
above low water, and at the time one of the three highest bridges in the
world. Cost, $250,000; time of steel erection, 87 days; of construction includ-
ing masonry piers, 103 days.

1893 Leland Stanford dies, June 21.

Union Pacific goes into receivership.

1897 Harriman gains control of Union Pacific.

1898 July 7, bill passed and signed by the President appointing the Secretaries
of Treasury and Interior and the Attorney General as a commission acting
under the President, to settle the debt of the Central Pacific Railroad on
payment of full amount in twenty semiannual payments.

1899 Feb. 16, agreement executed between the government committee and the
Central Pacific approved by President of the United States under which the
SP guarantees payment of the Central Pacific debt. Negotiations carried
on by Huntington with both the commission and the President, in association with the Speyer banking interests concerned. SP guarantees uncon-
ditionally the payment of principal and interest of two issues of bonds of
CP (aggregating $125,000,000), by purchase of $12,000,000 of the preferred
stock with obligation to purchase $8,000,000 more when needed by the CP.
Common stock also purchased by SP, issuing in payment its own common
stock at par plus $25 in bonds of the SP Company.

1900 Collis P. Huntington dies, Aug. 13.

1901 Harriman becomes chairman of SP's executive committee, April; by summer has control of over 45 per cent of SP stock; in September assumes presidency.

SP establishes "colonist fares" from Chicago to Coast, $33; Missouri River points to Coast, $25. Between 1901 and 1916 SP brings 794,824 persons west on colonist fares.

Coast Line opened Mar. 31 to Santa Barbara, trains using Santa Paula and San Joaquin Valley routes to reach Los Angeles.

1902 An SP master mechanic tries out the cab-ahead idea.

1903 Lucin Cutoff completed across Salt Lake; opened to traffic Mar. 8, 1904.

1904 Harriman starts spending $1,000,000 a mile on a 9-mile stretch of tunnels and fill out of San Francisco.

Final link in Coast Line completed south of Santa Barbara through Oxnard and Santa Susana tunnels to Los Angeles, Mar. 20.

1905 Colorado River bursts its bounds in July with the first of a long series of floods that almost wash Imperial Valley out of existence. SP takes on the fight to return the river to its channel. Railroad moves its rails many times as Salton Sink becomes an inland sea.

1906 Apr. 18–19, San Francisco earthquake and fire. SP evacuates 224,000 persons.

Harriman starts double-tracking the SP over the Sierra.

Pres. Theodore Roosevelt appeals to Harriman in November to close the Colorado River break-through, which is in Mexican territory. SP accepts President Roosevelt's plea. Traffic disrupted for 1,200 miles while trainloads of rock are rushed.

Pacific Fruit Express Company incorporated by SP–UP, Dec. 7.

1907 Engineers along Colorado River report the break finally sealed, Feb. 11. Cost to SP estimated at $4,000,000.

Northwestern Pacific Railroad Company, a consolidation of seven short steam and electric lines serving the California north coast counties formed under joint SP–Santa Fe ownership, Jan. 8.

1908 Feb. 1, suit of the United States to force the Union Pacific to sell its interests in SP is begun.

1909 Harriman dies, Sept. 9.

Feb. 1, the last of the Central Pacific's debt to the government, plus interest, is paid off—the total amounting to $58,813,000. Other debts of the Central Pacific also satisfied.

First Mallet engines go on SP rails.

1910 Because of increased weight of trains, SP strengthens Pecos Bridge, doubling its weight of steel. Cost, $400,000.

1911 William Sproule becomes president of SP, Sept. 25.

1913 Kruttschnitt becomes chairman of the Executive Committee of the Southern Pacific Company, Jan. 13. Holds post until May 31, 1925. Dies fifteen days later.

June 30, Decree entered under Supreme Court decision obliging Union Pacific to sell all its SP stock.

1914 Feb. 11, government begins suit against SP to oblige it to sell all its stock in Central Pacific Railway Company.

1915 Northwestern Pacific opens to traffic, San Francisco to Eureka, the 106-mile unit through Eel River Canyon. July 1.

1917 Mar. 9, U.S. District Court decides dismemberment suit (severance from Central Pacific) in favor of SP, and government appeals to Supreme Court. This court ultimately decides in favor of dismemberment. Congress then acts to relieve impossible situation that would create transportation chaos.

1917 American railroads, including SP, discover the pleasures and pains of government control; learn much about the mass handling of troops and military supplies. Federal control from Dec. 28, 1917, to Mar. 1, 1920.

SP's new General Office, 65 Market St., San Francisco, occupied during September, 1917.

1922 U.S. Supreme Court decides the SP–Central Pacific dismemberment suit against Southern Pacific and decrees that it shall sell its stock, the subject going back to District Court to determine necessary procedure.

Forerunner of present-day Daylights receives trial on San Francisco–Los Angeles run.

"Prosperity Special" of 20 SP new locomotives crosses continent in June heralding upswing in nation's economy.

1923 Feb. 6, Interstate Commerce Commission finally decides the momentous question raised by the government in 1914—whether SP should continue in control of Central Pacific, or the two intermeshed systems should be dismembered. In accordance with a new Act of Congress, ICC decides the common ownership, control and management to be in the public interest.

1924 Acquisition of El Paso and Southwestern system, Nov. 1.

1925 Double-tracking of Sierra completed.

1926 Cascade Line, 270 miles, opened Sept. 1 to freight and local passenger trains; to all traffic Apr. 17, 1927.

Second main line in Arizona opened through Phoenix, Nov. 14.

1927 SP de Mexico line opened to Guadalajara, Apr. 17.

1929 Paul Shoup succeeds William Sproule as president, Jan. 1.

Decade sees the completion of many miles of track in southeastern Oregon, northeastern California, and Nevada. Era of high net income.

SP acquires full ownership of the 515-mile Northwestern Pacific and its ferryboats. Ownership previously shared with Santa Fe.

1930 Establishment of coordinated train-truck overnight merchandise freight service.

Completion of $10,000,000 double-track bridge across Suisun Bay, 35 miles from San Francisco. End of the famous Benicia–Port Costa train ferries.

Government settles with SP for sealing the Colorado River break-through in 1906. Check is for $1,012,700.

First Centralized Traffic Control, 40 miles, between Stockton-Sacramento, installed in April.

1931 Installation of automatic block signals completed on all SP primary main lines.

1932 Revenue ton-miles drop to half of 1929's.

A. D. McDonald becomes president, Aug. 1.

SP adds the Cotton Belt Line to its system, Apr. 14.

1934 Twelve corporations comprising SP's lines in Texas and Louisiana are placed under the name Texas and New Orleans, June 30.

1935 The fast Overnights (merchandise trains for expediting freight at passenger-train speed) introduced; waybills teletyped. San Jose gets a $3,250,000 line change. Trains into New Orleans operate over new public-built bridge across Mississippi.

1936 Business turns upward. Large-scale buying of rolling stock. West's first streamlined train, City of San Francisco, on Ogden Route. Diesel-electric locomotive.

Bridges across San Francisco Bay spell doom of most of the ferries, which had carried 40,000,000 passengers a year.

1937 The modern Daylights, streamliners, placed on Los Angeles–San Francisco run. A new era of color, comfort, and profitableness.

Sunbeams (streamliners) placed in operation between Houston and Dallas. Electromagnetic brake introduced, on Coast Daylights.

Sacramento general shops build their last steam locomotive. More than 200 turned out in previous 63 years.

1938 Roadbed moved to make way for Shasta Dam and Lake, a $15,000,000 removal. Work completed in 1942.

Streamliner City of San Francisco becomes a grown-up 17-car train. Twin added in 1941.

1939 Last commuter SP ferry run on Bay, Jan. 14.

Official headquarters moved from New York to San Francisco. Board of directors reorganized with all-Western executive committee. Board chairmanship abolished and its duties transferred to president, July 13.

Los Angeles opens its new $11,000,000 Union Passenger Terminal, May 7.

1940 Huge bulge in freight due to national defense program. In August, as test, U.S. sends 119 special trains of troops over SP's Pacific and T&NO lines.

New Lark goes on the San Francisco–Los Angeles run.

1941 Interurban train service of SP over Bay Bridge ended July 26.

Nov. 15, death takes President A. D. McDonald; succeeded by A. T. Mercier, Dec. 11.

Dec. 7, Pearl Harbor. President Mercier confers with Gen. John L. De Witt, pledges full support of railroad, a pledge magnificently redeemed in spite of man-power shortage; 19,980 SP men and women eventually join the armed forces.

1942 Promontory, Utah, ceases to be on railroad map as last rails are removed from historic site.

1944 Record year for freight and passenger traffic. Last steam locomotive placed in service.

1947 First SP diesel-electric freight locomotives take the rails.

Corporate residence of Southern Pacific Company moved from Kentucky to Delaware, Sept. 30.

1948 The Golden State, fast modern streamliner. Chicago to Tucson, 33¾ hours; Phoenix, 36¼ hours; Los Angeles, 45 hours.

1949 Shasta Daylights, superb coach streamliners, placed in operation between Oakland and Portland.

1950 All-streamlined Cascade overnight train placed in operation between San Francisco–Oakland and Portland, 16½ hours.

New Sunset Limited, loveliest train on wheels, goes into service between New Orleans and Los Angeles. The 42-hour schedule clips 5 hours from the old Sunset run.

1951 Giant strides taken to put West Coast and Gulf Coast into postures of defense.

A. T. Mercier retires as president as 1951 closes; succeeded by D. J. Russell, former executive vice-president.

Bibliography

BANCROFT, H. H., *History of California*. San Francisco: The History Company, 1888.

—— *Chronicles of the Builders of the Commonwealth*. San Francisco: The History Company, 1891.

CAMPBELL, LINDSAY, AND HEATH, ERLE, *Trail to Rail*. San Francisco: The Southern Pacific Company, 1930.

CASEY, ROBERT J., AND W. A. S. DOUGLAS, *Pioneer Railroad: The Story of the Chicago and North Western System*. New York: McGraw-Hill Book Company, Inc., 1948.

CROFUTT, GEORGE A., *New Overland Tourist and Pacific Coast Guide*. Omaha: The Overland Publishing Company, 1880.

DAGGETT, STUART, *Chapters on the History of the Southern Pacific*. New York: The Ronald Press Company, 1922.

GALLOWAY, JOHN DEBO, *The First Transcontinental Railroad . . . Central Pacific, Union Pacific*. New York: Simmons-Boardman Publishing Corporation, 1950.

GLASSCOCK, C. G., *Bandits and the S.P.* New York: F. A. Stokes Co., 1929.

HEATH, ERLE, *Seventy-Five Years of Progress*. San Francisco: The Southern Pacific Company, 1944.

INGRAM, KARL C., *Winning Your Way with People*. New York: McGraw-Hill Book Company, Inc., 1949.

Interstate Commerce Commission Reports, Vol. 76, "Control of Central Pacific by Southern Pacific."

KNEISS, GILBERT H., *Bonanza Railroads*. Stanford: Stanford University Press, 1941.

LEWIS, OSCAR, *The Big Four*. New York: Alfred A. Knopf, 1938.

MACMULLEN, JERRY, *Paddle-Wheel Days in California*. Stanford: Stanford University Press, 1944.

MARSHALL, JAMES W., *Santa Fe, the Railroad That Built an Empire*. New York: Random House, 1949.

NEWMARK, HARRIS, *Sixty Years in Southern California*, 1853–1913. Boston: Houghton Mifflin Company, 1930.

PACIFIC RAILWAY COMMISSION, Testimony Taken by the Commission. Washington: Government Printing Office, 1887.

REED, S. G., *A History of the Texas Railroads.* Houston: The St. Clair Publishing Co., 1941.

WILSON, NEILL C., *Treasure Express.* New York: The Macmillan Company, 1936.
———— *Silver Stampede.* New York: The Macmillan Company, 1937.

Manuscript by D. L. Joslyn on CP–SP locomotives and Sacramento General Shops.

Manuscript reminiscences of various officials in Houston and San Francisco archives of the Southern Pacific Company.

Letters of Collis P. Huntington in Huntington Library, San Marino.

Files of the following newspapers and periodicals:
  Leslie's Weekly
  San Francisco *Daily Alta California*
  San Francisco *Bulletin*
  Sacramento *Union, Record-Union, Bee*
  Southern Pacific Bulletin, San Francisco. Emmett Fitzpatrick, editor
  Southern Pacific Bulletin, Houston. J. C. Carter, editor
  Bakersfield *Californian*
  Santa Monica *Outlook*
  Virginia City *Territorial Enterprise*
  San Bernardino *Argus, Guardian*

Index

A

"AC" locomotives, 224
Adams, George, 222
Ahern, Tom, 149, 150
Alameda (ferry), 194
Arizona and Southeastern Railroad Company, The, 81
Artful Dodger (schooner), 226
"Associated Lines," 221, 222
Association of American Railroads, AB brake adopted, 215
   Safety Section, 213
Atchison and Topeka Railroad, the "Santa Fe," chartered, 84
Atlantic locomotives, 221
Atlantic and Pacific Railroad, 50
Averill, W. C., 70

B

Bailey, James W., 9, 16
Baltimore and Ohio Railroad, 110, 171
Baxter, M. A., 228
Bayley, G. W. B., 3, 67
Bean, Roy, 77
Beatty, J. H., 140
Berkeley (ferry), 194, 195, 200
"Big Four," 11, 12, 48, 51, 61, 63, 89–101, 103, 104, 106
"Big Four and a half," 52
"Black Goose" (locomotive), 19–20
Brannin, Jim, 205
Brenna, Jack, 137, 138
Briscoe, Andrew, 71
Broderick, David C., 52
Brown, Arthur, 23

Buffalo Bayou, Brazos and Colorado Railroad, 4, 7, 71, 73, 171
   bogged down by Civil War, 72
   reached San Antonio, 73
Buland, G. L., 208
Butterfield stage route, 75

C

"C. P. Huntington" (locomotive), 15, 225
Cab-ahead locomotives, 222, 224
California Central Railroad, 8, 228
California Development Company, 140
California and Oregon Railroad, 89
California, Oregon and Eastern Railroad, 113
California Pacific Railroad, 47
California Steam Navigation Company, 193
California Street Hill, 100
California (train), 164
"Cape Horn," 18, 19
Carson, Kit, 1
Carson and Colorado Railroad, 159
Cascade (train), 166
Cascade Line opened, 112, 114, 115
Central Pacific Railroad, 13
   acquires California Pacific, 47
   becomes part of SP system, 103
   capital stock, 42
   changes name at Goshen Junction, 52
   completed, 30
   control by SP challenged in court, 121
   control by SP upheld, 122
   cost to build, 42

Central Pacific Railroad, debt paid to
     government, 106
  early offices, 44
  earnings, 101
  earnings of 1873, 57
  first locomotive into Nevada from
     California, 24
  first roundhouse, 227
  first 31 miles, 17
  first train, 15
  passenger fares, 86
  rumors of merger with SP, 50
  starts spur up San Joaquin, 49
  takes over ferries, 192
Centralized traffic control, 211–213
Ceres (steamboat), 68
Challenger (train), 164
Chesapeake and Ohio Railroad, 51, 99
Chicago and Alton, 110
Chicago and North Western Railroad,
     28, 163
Chinese laborers, 20, 26, 29
Chorpenning, George, 22
Chrysopolis (river boat), 193
City of San Francisco (streamliner), 38,
     163
  wrecked, 178, 179
Clark, Sen. William A., 88
Clay, Henry, 2
Coast Line, construction of, 126–128
Colton, David Douty, 51, 61
Columbia (steamer), 68
Comanche (steamer), 69
"Conness" (locomotive), 217
Constitution (steamer), 69
Contra Costa (first ferry of name), 193,
     196
Contract and Finance Company, 50, 89,
     96
Converse, James, 78
Cooke, Jay, and Company, 56
Corbett, J. W., 207
Cory, H. T., 143–146
"Cotton Belt" Line, 133
Craft, E. A., 133, 208
Crawford, James U., 61

"Crazy Judah," 8
Credit Mobilier of America, 28, 64
Crocker, Charles, 9
  announces "mile of track a day," 29
  builds mansion, 52
  chief contractor, 15
  decides to drop out, 51
  describes achievements, 21
  dies, 104
  drives "last spike" on Shasta Route,
     92
  drives "last spike" at Tucson, 76
  early career, 11
  exhorts workers, 17
  returns to "Big Four," 57, 64
  undertakes 10 miles in one day, 29
Crocker, Charles Frederick, 148
Crocker, E. B., 51
"Crocker's Pets," 18

                    D

Dalton brothers, bandits, 183–187
Davis, "Big Jack," bandit, 180, 181
Daylight (train), 88, 162, 215
De Autrement brothers, bandits, 187–
     190
Denver and Rio Grande Railroad, 84
Depression, 161
DeWitt, Gen. John L., 157
Diesel electric locomotives, 161, 162, 231
Dodge, Gen. G. M., 29, 108
"Dollar Days," 161
Donahue, Peter, 48
Donner party tragedy, 22
Donner Summit, 20–23, 134, 135, 153,
     154, 157,
Douglas, Sen. Stephen A., 2, 4
Durant, T. C., 13, 27
Dyer, Joe, 178

                    E

Earthquake and fire, San Francisco, 137
Edinger, F. S., 142
Eichrodt, Max, 230

El Capitan (ferry), 193
"El Gobernador" (locomotive), 217, 218
"Emigrant Sleepers," 230
Encinal (ferry), 195
Eureka (ferry), 198
Evans, Chris, bandit, 182–187

F

Fair, Jim, 193, 194
Farnum, Henry, 13
Ferries, end of, on San Francisco Bay, 198, 199
Fish, Stuyvesant, 107
Fisk and Hatch, brokers, 55, 56
Fort Sutter, 22
Fouratt, Capt. John R., 192
Freeport Railroad, 228
Frémont, John C., 1, 50
Fresno (ferry), 197

G

Galena and Chicago Union Railroad, 28
Galveston, Harrisburg and San Antonio Railroad, 73, 75, 77–79
Galveston, Houston and Henderson, 171
Galveston and Red River Railway, 71
Garden City (ferry), 195
"General Service" locomotives, 225
Gentry, A. M., 70
Gibbs, James E., 3, 67
Gillis, John H., 19
Gloss, Antone, 199
Golden Palace car, 33, 35, 37
"Golden spike" ceremony, 30
Golden State (train), 88, 141
Golden State Route, 81, 164
Goodman, F. H., 194
Goss and Lambard, 226, 227, 228
Gould, Jay, 65, 66, 77, 107
    meets with Huntington, 74, 75
    races Huntington and Peirce with rails across Texas, 75

Gray, George E., 24, 50
Great Northern, 114, 115
Greeley, Horace, 98
Green, Duff, 27
Green, E. H. R. ("Ned"), 80
Green, Hetty, 79
"Governor Stanford" (locomotive), 15, 201, 225
    arrives by sea, 15, 226

H

Hack, W. L., 153, 154
Hale, W. W., 169–171
Harriman, Edward Henry, 106–115
    battle with Colorado River, 145
    "community of interest" policy, 110
    in control of Illinois Central, Oregon Railway and Navigation, Oregon Short Line, Salt Lake line, 109–110
    death, 110
    obtains Southern Pacific control, 109
    obtains Union Pacific control, 107–109
    rail outlets for San Francisco, 112
    tours with Kruttschnitt, 109
    unfinished plans, 112
"Harrisburg Railroad," 71
Harrisburg Railroad and Trading Company, 4, 71
Haswell, C. C., 183
Heber, H., 140
Hector (ferry), 192
Heinrichs, E. O., 190
Hepburn Act, 109, 119
Herald of the Morning (clipper ship), 226
Hewes, David, 30
Hill, Jim, 109
"Hill," The, 26, 221
Hind, Tom, 143–145
Holladay, Ben, 90–92
Hood, William, 50
    builds longest curve and tangent, 76
    builds over Tehachapi, 58

Hopkins, L. P., 31
Hopkins, Mark, 9
  builds mansion, 52, 100
  dies, 103, 104
  disposition of estate, 104
  early life, 11
  inspects San Joaquin Valley, 49
  "loses the books," 43
Hopkins, Timothy, 104
Houston Tap and Brazoria, 171
Houston and Texas Central Railroad,
    71, 171
"Hundred golden hours at sea," 105
Huntington, Archer M., 93
Huntington, Collis Potter, 9
  acquires BBB&C, 73
  acquisition of Mexican International,
    124
  agrees to place Los Angeles on main
    line, 63
  aligns with Peirce to fight Gould, 75
  blank letters of credit, 13
  chats with Horace Greeley, 98
  chides about lost trunk, 97
  dies, 106
  early life, 11
  final row with Stanford, 105
  financial panic, 55
  funeral attended by Harriman, 109
  hard times correspondence, 53–58
  implacably in harness, 104
  lets Santa Fe into California at
    Needles, 85, 86
  letter about Stewart, 46
  meets with Jay Gould, 74, 75
  not well, 53
  his opinion of Stanford, 96
  plots to take Pacific Mail into camp,
    97
  querulous to Mark Hopkins and
    others, 45
  race against Tom Scott, 64–66
  reminiscences, 41
  scolds Hopkins, 101
  his SP stock held by Union Pacific
    ordered sold, 115

Huntington, Collis Potter, urges Hop-
    kins to rest, 99
  his vast interests, 104, 105
  wants to retire, 99
  wants to sell Southern Pacific, 94
  wants trestles watched, 38
  "we have drawn the elephant," 10
  "we may fail," 14
  wonders at unpopularity, 99
  writes of train lamps, 34
Huntington, Henry E., 106
Huntington and Hopkins Company,
    44, 57, 93, 96, 97
Hustler (train), 162, 163

                     I

Illinois Central, 4, 108
International Railroad Company (Mex-
    ico), 124
Interstate Commerce Act, 118
Interstate Commerce Commission, 119
  safety requirements, 213, 215
  upholds CP control by SP, 121, 122
Interurban Electric Railway Company,
    198
Iowa Central Railroad, 108
"Irish terriers," 29

                     J

"J. B. Stephens" (locomotive), 90
Jackson and Sharp, car builders, 33
Johnson, Grove L., 119
Johnson, Hiram W., 119, 120
Jones, Sen. J. P., 61
Jones, T. R., 35
Joslyn, David L., 225, 226
Judah, Theodore Dehone, 6–10, 16, 30,
    228
Judah Ridge, 16
"Judah's Wisp," 8
"Jupiter" (locomotive), at Golden Spike
    ceremony, 30

K

Kangaroo (ferry), 192
Kelly, J. R., 182
Key Route, 196
Kirkbride, W. H., 16, 69, 70, 131, 179
Kitchen, Pete, 76
Kruttschnitt, Julius, 69, 70
    battles Hetty Green, 80, 81
    chairman, executive committee, 155
    refuses help to Salton Sink, 142
    tours with Harriman, 109
Kuhn, Loeb and Company, 107

L

La Chatelier brake, 219
Lark (train), 88, 163
Larue, James B., 192
Leach, John, 199
League of Progress, 118
"Lightning Express," 37
Lincoln, President Abraham, signs Pacific Railroad Act, of 1862, 12
    of 1864, 17
Los Angeles and Independence Railroad, 61
Los Angeles and San Pedro Railroad, 63
Lucin Cutoff, 31, 103
    construction, 110–113

M

McComb, Henry S., 28
McCormick, George, 214
McDonald, A. D., 213
    death, 156
    president, 155
    at wreck, 178
McDonald, L. B., 178
McIntyre, Donald, 208
McKenzie, H. J., 129, 133
Mallet locomotives, 222, 223
Maw, Herb, 31
Merchants' Shipping Association, 119

Mercier, A. T., 133, 146–147, 157
Mikado locomotives, 223
Millet, Oliver, 209
Mills, D. O., 51, 54, 95, 159
Minturn, Charles, 102, 193
"Missouri Bill," 20
Monroe, W. H., 78
Montague, S. S., 18, 19, 49, 59, 148
Morgan, Charles, 68, 69
Morgan, J. Pierpont, 109
Morgan's Louisiana and Texas Railroad and Steamship Company, 69
Mountain-type locomotives, 224
Mussel Slough, Battle of, 116, 117

N

National Railways of Mexico, 124
Natron Cutoff, 112–115
New Orleans, Opelousas and Great Western Railroad, 3
New York Central, 171, 207
Newark (ferry), 194
Newport News Shipbuilding Company, 51, 98
Nob Hill, 52
Norris, Frank, 117
North American Navigation Company, 119
North Pacific Coast Railroad, 333
Northern Pacific, 114
Northwestern Pacific Railroad, 158, 172, 192, 197, 198, 222
Norton, Lott D., 49

O

Oakes, Ames, 28
Oakland (ferry), 193, 195
Occidental and Oriental Steamship Company, 44, 118
O'Connell, Dan, 189
Octopus, The (novel), 117
Ogden Route, 122
Oil-burning locomotives, 219

Olcott, N. R., 70, 79
"Opelousas," 3, 5, 7, 67, 69
Oregon Central Railroad Company, 90
Oregon Eastern Railroad, 112
Oregon Railway and Navigation Company, 110
Oregon Short Line, 110
Oregon Trunk, 114
Overland Route, 123
    double-tracked, 129–130
Overnight (train), 173–176
Owl (train), 163

P

"Pacific" (locomotive), 15
Pacific Electric Motor Transport Company, 175
Pacific Electric Railway, 175
Pacific Fruit Express, 170, 172, 173
Pacific locomotives, 223
Pacific Mail Steamship Company, 44, 105, 118
Pacific Motor Transport Company, 175
Pacific Motor Trucking Company, 172, 175
Pacific Railroad Act of 1862, 10, 12, 13, 14, 15, 17, 40
Pacific Railroad Act of 1864, 41, 42
Pacific Rolling Mill Company, 229
Parker, G. M., 37
Pecos high bridge, 78, 79
Peirce, Thomas W., 69, 72, 73
    builds west from San Antonio to beat Gould, 75, 77–79
    drives "last spike" for Sunset Route, 78
Pennsylvania Fiscal Agency, 27
Pennsylvania Railroad, 171, 207
Petaluma (river boat), 199–200
Peterson, Claude, 166
Piedmont (ferry), 195, 197
Pollok, Allan, 164
Populism, 118
Port Chicago explosion, 136
Princess (ferry), 199

Promontory, Utah, 30, 31, 111
Pullman, Albert B., 36
Pullman, George, 33
"Push-button" railroading, 203

R

Railroad Commission, California, 118
Ralston, William, 51, 54
Randolph, Epes, 124
    takes charge of Colorado breakthrough, 142, 144–146
Red Jacket (ferry), 192
Reed, S. G., 71
Reed, W. V., 184
Roberts, George D., 185–186
Rock Island Line, 166
Rockwood, C. R., 140
Roosevelt, President Theodore, 109
    battle with Colorado River, 145
    looks into UP–SP fusion, 115
    "malefactors of great wealth," 119
Ruef, Abe, 119
Russell, D. J., 204
    president, 208
    railroad career, 208
Russell, Frank E., Sr., 214

S

Sabine and Galveston Bay Railroad and Lumber Company, 70
Sacramento (ferry), 199
Sacramento, Auburn and Nevada Railroad, 6
Sacramento Valley Rail Road, 6, 228
St. Louis and San Francisco Railroad, 84
Salt Lake line, 110
San Francisco and Oakland Railroad Company, 193
San Francisco and San Joaquin Valley Railway, 118, 119
San Francisco and San Jose Railroad, 47
    affiliate of early Southern Pacific, 48
Santa Clara (ferry), 194, 197

Santa Fe Railroad, 84, 85, 110
Schiff, Jacob, 108
Scott, Thomas A., 53, 54, 55, 63, 64, 65
    gives UP over to Gould, 74
Searles, Edward T., 104
Seger, A. S., 68
Sharon, William, 54, 159
Shasta Daylight (train), 165
Shasta Route, 89–92, 123
Sherman, Gen. William T., 65
Sherman Antitrust Law, 120
Shoup, Paul, 155
Silver Palace cars, 32–38
Small, J. A., 125
Snowsheds, 23, 24, 148, 149
Solano (train ferry), 196, 230
Sonora Railway, 85, 124
Sontag, John, bandit, 182–187
Sophie McLean (ferry), 192
South Pacific Coast Railroad, 193,
    194
Southern, May, reminiscences, 150–152
Southern Pacific Company, battle with
    Santa Fe opens, 84
    debt, 207
    headquarters to San Francisco, 156
    huge Kentucky taxes, 103
    a Kentucky corporation, 102
    "kicked out of politics," 119
    largest railroad in Texas, 71
    leases Central Pacific, 102
    medalion, origin of, 70
    no Federal cash, 48
    passes to Harriman control, 110
    rate war with Santa Fe, 86, 87
    showdown row with UP, 120–122
    succeeds Southern Pacific Railroad
        Company, 102
    sued to release CP, 120–122
    sued by Texas and Pacific Railroad,
        78
Southern Pacific Railroad Company, a
    paper enterprise, 48
Southern Pacific Railroad Company of
    California, 44
    rumors of merger with CP, 50

Southern Pacific of Mexico, 123–125
Southern Pacific Railroad Company of
    Texas, an independent enterprise,
    71
"Snowshoe" Thompson, 22
Spreckels, Claus, 118
Sproule, William, 155
Stanford, Jane Lathrop, 105
Stanford, Leland, 9
    dies, 105
    early career, 11
    founds university, 104
    ground-breaking for CP, 13
    inspects San Joaquin Valley, 49
    mansion, 100
    obtains beneficial legislation, 40
    row with Huntington, 105
    sets low commuter fares, 194–195
    stops work on Coast Line, 126
Stanford, Philip, 41
Stanford University, 104
    almost closes, 105
Starlight (train), 163
Stevens, A. J., 218, 228, 229
Stewart, Sen. William M., 46
Stoddard, George, 228, 229
Strahorn, Robert E., 113, 114
Strobridge, J. H., 29
    builds GH&SA, 77
Strong, Daniel W., 8
Stubbs, J. C., 103
Sunbeam (train), 162, 163, 164
Sunset Limited, 81, 82
Sunset Route, 120, 123
Sutter, John A., 7

T

"T. J. Judah" (locomotive), 15
Tamalpais (ferry), 198
Tangney, John, 139–141, 143, 146
Terry, Judge David, 52
Tevis, Lloyd, 48, 54, 95
Texas Central Railroad, 80
Texas and New Orleans Railroad Com-
    pany, 66

Texas and New Orleans Railroad Company, embraces twelve corporations, 155
Texas and Pacific Railroad, 63, 75–79
Texas Pacific Railroad, 63
Texas Western, 71
Thompson, John ("Snowshoe"), 22
Thoroughfare (ferry), 199
Thurman Act, 101
Towne, A. N., 36, 50, 103, 194
Trans-Continental, train newspaper, 36
Transcontinental Association of Railroads, 118
Transportation Act of 1920, 121

U

Ukiah (ferry), 195
Union Pacific Railroad, 12, 13, 20, 21, 74, 81, 84, 102, 163, 166
  construction, 27–29
  interests Harriman, 107–109
  projects under Harriman, 112
  sued to dissolve union with SP, 115
Uren, Steve, 229
Urton, Capt. Jack, 199, 200

V

"Valley Railroad," 199
Vicksburg and El Paso Railroad, 71
Villard, Henry, 91, 92

W

Webster, Daniel, 1, 2
Welch, Benjamin, 227, 230
Wells Fargo Express, 90
Western Pacific (first of name), 46, 57
Western Pacific (modern), 115
Westinghouse, George, 215
Williams, John A., 4
Wilson, Charles L., 6, 7
Witham, G. T., 35
Woods, Miss, 134

Y

"Young America" (locomotive), 219

Z

Zulu trains, 81–87

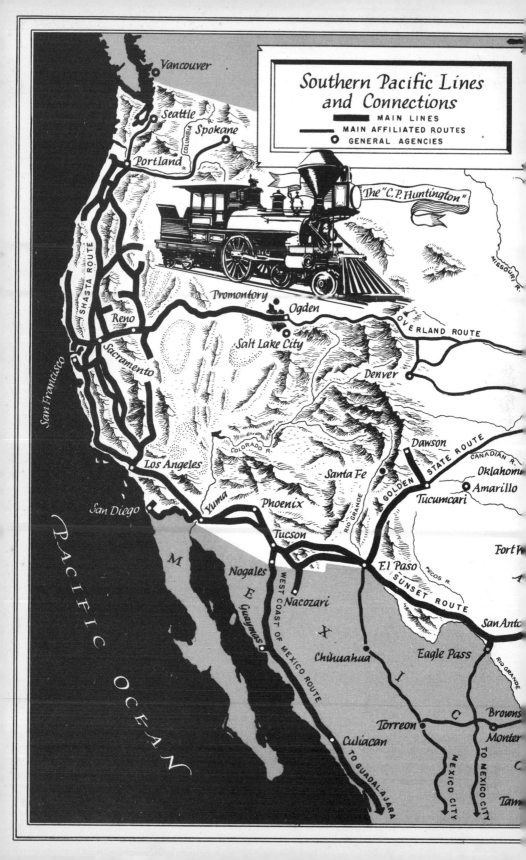